SUBWAY CITY

SUBWAY CITY

CITY

RIDING THE TRAINS, READING NEW YORK

MICHAEL W. BROOKS

RUTGERS UNIVERSITY PRESS

NEW BRUNSWICK, NEW JERSEY, AND LONDON

Publication of this book was supported, in part, by a grant from Furthermore, the publication program of the J. M. Kaplan Fund.

Library of Congress Cataloging-in-Publication Data

Brooks, Michael W., 1936–
    Subway city : riding the trains; reading New York / Michael W.
  Brooks.
      p.   cm.
    Includes bibliographical references (p.   ) and index.
    ISBN 0-8135-2396-6 (alk. paper)
    1. Subways—New York (State)—New York. 2. New York (N.Y.)—
  History. 3. Technology—Social aspects—New York (State)—New
  York. I. Title.
  TF847.N5B77   1997
  388.4′28′097471—dc21   96-39309
                                                  CIP

British Cataloging-in-Publication information available

Manufactured in the United States of America

For Lois
who took three subways and a bus
to get to high school

CONTENTS

ILLUSTRATIONS

ACKNOWLEDGMENTS

L I K E most American scholars who have worked on long, complicated projects I am endebted to the National Endowment for the Humanities. It allowed me to participate in Thomas Bender's seminar on Cities, Biographies, and Texts. I am grateful to the seminar participants for the stimulation they offered. Theodore Eakins, especially, gave me valuable guidance on interpretations of the city in American art. Later a Travel-to-Collections grant allowed me to consult the morgue for the *New York American* and the *New York Evening Journal* at the Harry K. Ransom Humanities Research Center at the University of Texas in Austin.

I am also grateful to the J. M. Kaplan Fund for a grant toward publication.

This book would never have been written without Leslie Mitchner's interest, criticisms, and encouragement. I am also grateful to William Kelly of the City University of New York Graduate School and University Center for penetrating criticisms of an earlier version of the manuscript.

I have incurred many debts while researching this material and I regret that I cannot name all the librarians and curators who took considerable trouble to answer queries or direct me to out-of-the-way pieces of information. This book could never have been written without the Library of Congress and the research collections of the New York Public Library. Among the librarians and curators I can name are M. Darcie Alexander of the Williams College Museum of Art, Terry Ariano of the Museum of the City of New York, Ken Craven of the Harry K. Ransom Humanities Research Center at the University of Texas, Holliday T. Day of the Indianapolis Museum of Art, Ashley W. Dunn of the Albany Museum of Art, Kathleen A. Erwin of the Detroit Institute of Arts, Ilene Susan Fort of the Los

Angeles County Museum of Art, Domenic J. Iacono of the Syracuse University Art Collection, Stephen B. Jareckie of the Worcester Art Museum, Gabriela A. Magnuson and Amy S. Young of the Edwin A. Ulrich Museum of Art at Wichita State University, Lina Muehlig of the Smith College Museum of Art, Michael H. Schreiber of the Shore Line Trolley Museum, Eveline S. Overmiller of the Library of Congress, David D. J. Rau of the Cranbrook Academy of Art Museum, and Nancy Rich of the Smith College Museum of Art. I am grateful to Susan Teller of the Susan Teller Gallery for guidance through the art of the thirties. Alvin Tresselt recommended the article on elevateds in *St. Nicholas*. John Gruen directed me to the Keith Haring Foundation.

Among those who helped me with information about the New York City subway system I would like to thank Daniel Scannell, Ronay Menschell, Frederick A. Kramer, Sally Charnow, George Horn, Gail Dawson, and the staffs of the New York City Transit Museum and the Transit Archives.

I am grateful to Jennie Skerl for assistance with NEH grants and to West Chester University for a College of Arts and Sciences Support and Development Award. Erminio Braidotti and Silvana Aurilia helped me with Fortunato Depero. Patricia Pflieger and Patricia Johnson kept a sharp eye out for subway references. I would like to express special gratitude to the Inter-Library Loan office of West Chester University.

Portions of Chapter One appeared first in *Nineteenth Century*. Portions of Chapter Nine appeared first in *Scholars*. I am grateful to the editors of those publications for permission to republish material from their pages. The lines from "Subway Vespers" are from *Original Love: Poems by Molly Peacock*. They are copyright © 1995 by Molly Peacock and are reprinted by permission of W. W. Norton & Company, Inc. The excerpt from "The Subway" is from Allen Tate, *The Collected Poems, 1919–1976*. Copyright © 1977 by Allen Tate. Reprinted by permission of Farrar, Straus & Giroux, Inc. The lines from *The Bridge* are from *Complete Poems of Hart Crane*, Marc Simon, editor. Copyright © 1933, renewed 1958, 1966 by Liveright Publishing Corporation. Copyright © 1986 by Marc Simon. Reprinted by permission of Liveright Publishing Corporation.

I would like to thank Stuart Mitchner for his careful reading of the manuscript and Karolina Harris for her design of the book.

Finally, I would like to thank my wife, Lois, for years of firm support and months of ruthless editing.

SUBWAY CITY

INTRODUCTION

O N the day I began to write this book I decided to ride the subway for an hour or so, not to reach any particular destination but simply to pay attention to something that New Yorkers often take for granted. Riding the subway is a common experience and I wanted to start with its commonness. Thinking about the subway as a cultural artifact would come in the evening. For the morning I would be simply an eye, transparently recording experience.

All of semiotic theory cries out against this dream of objective perception, warning instead that our most seemingly innocent observations are already shaped, constituted, inhabited by ghostly hordes of earlier meanings. On this morning, at least, the theory was right. As I approached the newsstand by the stairs leading down from the sidewalk I saw that both the *Daily News* and *Newsday* had the same headline: "SUBWAY HELL!"

The experience that the news columns described was bad enough: power had failed in a rush-hour train, forcing conductors to lead passengers single file through the dark tunnel to safety. Still, reading about the ordeal hours after it was safely over, I had the luxury of looking past the drama of the event to consider the literary strategy of the headline.

The subway as Hell is a metaphor that some, including many who have never visited New York or ridden its trains, are likely to think all too appropriate. But the identification of the subway with the infernal realm long predates the wave of graffiti and the rise in crime that seem to justify it. It was a fixture of popular speech even before the first trains began running.[1] The system had not been open a year when the *New York World* published a cartoon showing Dante gazing sternly at suffering riders. During the next nine decades the metaphor would appear in films, in poems, in paintings, and in the jokes of standup comics. After a prolonged contact with the metaphorical subway, it is an anticlimax to walk through the turnstiles and ride the relatively clean, reasonably efficient trains that carry millions of New Yorkers without incident each day.

My experience with the headline had reminded me of two important lessons: first, that the subway is never experienced apart from our cultural preconceptions and, second, that the most common images of the New York City subway system are astonishingly negative. This book is an effort to explain why this should be so.

The explanation begins with our need for simplifying images of our vast, bewildering cities. O. Henry, always one of the most perceptive students of New York life, wrote a story entitled "The Making of a New Yorker" which can serve as a parable for urban theorists. It tells the story of one Raggles, a tramp who is also a traveler, an artist, and a philosopher. Knowing that each city has its own distinct soul, Raggles delights in summing up each one he visits in a choice image. Chicago is the contrast between Mrs. Partington, all plumes and patchouli, and the depressing aura of potato salad and fish. Pittsburgh is *Othello* performed in the Russian language in a railroad station by Dockstader's minstrels.

But what was New York? Raggles had read other cities as easily as a primer but New York leaves him defeated, puzzled, discomfited, frightened. He shrivels in what the author calls "the bleak embrace of the undecipherable."[2] O. Henry quickly provides a happy ending but not before he has taught us two important truths: We must construct poetic images of our cities in order to live in them and we are subject to a peculiar, soul-destroying anxiety when we cannot do this.

New York's readability has always been in doubt. It is too vast, too diverse for easy comprehension. Alan Trachtenberg points out that nineteenth-century New Yorkers constantly imagined their city as a mystery—"a swarming mass of signals, dense, obscure, undecipherable."[3] "New York," said a guidebook in 1868, "is a great secret, not only to those who have never seen it, but to the majority of its own citizens."[4] "In truth," said another in 1894, "no one man can fully know New York by personal observation. He would find the city constantly growing beyond his reach, getting ahead of his studies."[5] Henry James, contemplating the new skyline ten years later, worried that "the monstrous phenomena themselves" had "got the start, got ahead of, in proper parlance, any possibility of poetic, of dramatic capture."[6] Steven Marcus has argued that the most salient characteristic of the city in modern literature is precisely its illegibility.[7]

The human imagination rises to this challenge by seeking coherent images of its surroundings. One strategy for creating them to is seize on some aspect of the built environment and employ it as what rhetoricians call a synecdoche—the part that stands for the whole. Thus Wall Street, a relatively tiny geographical location, represents the power of capitalist finance. The tenement, a specialized housing type, embodies the destructive force of a slum environment. The streets, coextensive with the built-up city, become a still more complex symbol. Sometimes, as in sentimental songs about the sidewalks of New York, they reduce the city to a big, friendly neighborhood. At other times, as in every mother's warning to her children not to hang around the streets, they represent the lawlessness and moral temptations of metropolitan life.

The subway is a vital part of the physical city which can easily be made to represent the urban whole. New York is not the only city where this has happened. The eleven-year-old heroine of Raymond Queneau's *Zazie dans le métro* speaks for thousands of tourists when, on arriving in Paris, she demands to be taken at once to the Métro, "ce moyen de transport éminemment parisien."[8] But in New York this tendency has gone further than elsewhere. In 1930 a journalist comparing the transit systems of the world concluded that New York's subways were more an expression of itself than any in Europe. "In no European city," he said, "would the subway be chosen as a symbol of urban life."[9] The subway represents New York City as surely as the freeway represents Los Angeles.

Even more than the streets, the subways are a protean symbol. It may surprise modern New Yorkers to learn that they once represented a civic miracle. They have functioned equally well as a symbol of the ordinary and the quotidian. They have, at different times and in different contexts, represented both racial harmony and racial conflict. Within very recent memory they have both provoked fear and inspired visions of a renewed, habitable city.

The meanings of the subway start with an archetypal image. When underground travel was first proposed in the eighteen-sixties, New Yorkers at once thought of the subterranean journeys of Odysseus and Aeneas. In 1900, when construction was just beginning, chief engineer William Barclay Parsons complained that "underground railways have always been associated in the public mind with dark, damp, dank, smoke-laden tunnels—veritable approaches to the lower regions."[10]

But the archetypal image does not explain why it is the New York subway in particular that carries such a burden. Some variant of the headline SUBWAY HELL has no doubt appeared from time to time in London, Paris, or any of the other more than sixty cities that now have subways but it seems more inevitable in New York than elsewhere. It has certainly been more frequent. To understand why we have to turn from archetypes to history.

Four decades before it was actually built the subway was essential to a dawning awareness of a new kind of city. If, as historians tell us, modern urbanism is born in the transition from a compact city in which work and home were spatially close to a much vaster one in which they are separated by long daily journeys, then it follows that rapid transit would do more than just serve the city. It would arrange its spaces, structure its movement, and define its textures.

New York's nineteenth-century debate over rapid transit was really an educational forum in which New Yorkers used their as yet unbuilt subways to discover and define a new kind of metropolis. Optimists easily repressed the ancient implications of underground journeys to focus instead on the promise of a better future. The subway would end traffic jams. It would empty the slums by opening up undeveloped land for inexpensive housing. Because it was underground, it would even bring relief from the extremes of winter cold and summer heat. To the most ardent enthusiasts it promised not simply a bigger city but a utopian one in which political corruption would have been banished and civility between citizens restored.

Yet the most important thing about the evolution of the subway as a symbol is that it starts by expressing faith in the city's future and, once built, quickly becomes a handy rhetorical tool for expressing discontent with its present.

To understand this reversal we must turn to city politics and subway economics. Within a year of its opening the subway was uncomfortably crowded. This should have been relieved by the rapid expansion of the system. Expansion, however, was blocked by a series of angry debates. Should the new lines be financed and controlled by private companies or should they be owned and operated by the city? Should they serve the West Side or the East Side? How deeply should they penetrate into Brooklyn or the still sparsely populated borough of Queens? Should the fare remain at five cents forever or should it rise as expenses did in the post-World War I inflation?

These were just the questions that would inevitably arise in the creation of a vast transit system. They should have been vigorously debated and then, as the trains became more and more crowded, as the pressure for new lines grew more intense, they should have been settled by a series of workable compromises. That is what happened with the first subway. It happened again with the expansion of the system but it happened much too slowly. Crowding worsened and morning and evening journeys became a twice-daily ordeal in a rattling sweatbox.

The reasons for the delay in expanding the subway are complex but one of the most important has a direct bearing on the way in which New Yorkers were learning to use their subway to think about their city. William Randolph Hearst, the city's most ambitious politician and most powerful publisher, seized on the transit issue as a foundation for his dual careers. His interest was always in advancing a personal agenda, never in building a city and never in compromise. He demonized his opponents. He invented a mythical Traction Trust and showed the city writhing in its grip. He transformed the subway into a symbol of a city in which the suffering many were constantly swindled by the powerful few.

When it opened in 1904 the subway had offered visible proof that all New Yorkers could unite to accomplish a great civic good. By 1924 it represented a city in stalemate. Oppressive, crowded, and filled with strangers standing in uncomfortably close proximity to one another, the subway became the natural symbol of a city gone wrong. Influenced by the forceful polemics of Lewis Mumford, city planners looked at the jammed trains and concluded that they were the inevitable result of a kind of centralized city that should never have been built.

That was the situation when writers and artists began interpreting the subway in the mid-twenties. It is a common phenomenon that a new social fact does not enter immediately into literature and art. The subway gathered a certain semantic weight and emotional complexity for several decades before finally making its appearance in novels and paintings. That is why this book deals with real estate promotions, political speeches, and newspaper crusades in its first half and poems, plays, novels, and paintings in its second. This division is an inevitable consequence of the way in which the subway evolved as a symbol.

The particular case of the els, which will be explored in part of Chapter One and in Chapter Two, reveals the pattern that we will find in the larger case of the subway. Their promise of a better future was conveyed first in pamphlets and speeches. Once the els had become a hectic presence in daily life, they became a natural subject for the press. Journalists naturally covered them as a subject—along with street openings, police activities, and municipal elections. Much more important, however, they were used to explore the new city in frequent human interest articles. Journalists had already established the el as the symbol of urban life when William Dean Howells introduced it into *A Hazard of New Fortunes* (1890) and when members of the Ash Can school began putting it on canvas.

The same thing happens with the subway but over a longer time line. An underground transit system was first seriously proposed in 1864 and opened in 1904. Although it was a perennial subject for journalists, it didn't attract artists and writers until the mid-twenties, when Elmer Rice, John Dos Passos, Hart Crane, and Reginald Marsh seemed to discover it almost simultaneously. Having adopted a symbol that had already been established in the newspapers, and without sacrificing any of its public meaning, they extended it to express a new range of private fears and anxieties.

A remarkable number of writers and artists turned to the subway in the following decades, among them Ann Petry, Louis Lozowick, Elmer Rice, John Dos Passos, Hart Crane, Saul Bellow, Ralph Ellison, Betty Smith, Walker Evans, Minna Citron, Paul Cadmus, James Baldwin, Isabel Bishop, Sol Yurick, LeRoi Jones, Tom Wolfe, Keith Haring, and Donna Dennis. They do not invariably use the subway to dramatize civic and emotional failure but they do, without exception, employ it as a testing ground. Their shared assumption is that any optimism about the city or any respect for its citizens that can survive exposure to the subway must be rock-solid.

It must be said, however, that the tendency to treat the subway as a negative symbol dominates. For every optimistic Isabel Bishop there is an angry LeRoi Jones and a mocking Tom Wolfe. The Bernhard Goetz case was not an inexplicable eruption. It was a culmination: the public acting-out of a revenge narrative that had been taking shape in newspaper, in film, and in popular narratives over the past decade.

By the late eighties the reputation of the subway seemed to have become permanently unmoored from the institution that gave it birth. As the system steadily improved, its symbolism remained disastrous. It is only very recently that the city has realized that changing the symbolism of the subway is as important as improving the stations and ensuring on-time performance.

This book traces a rise and fall and rise again. The first three chapters are about optimism and achievement as the subway is built. The next two are about a failure as the subway is left crowded and underfunded, with the Subway City only partially realized. In Chapters Six, Seven, and Eight optimism alternates with despair as New York writers and artists ask what the subway reveals of the booming capitalist city of the twenties, the Depression City of the thirties, and the postwar New York of the forties and fifties. Despair seems to triumph in Chapter Nine when the subway becomes the official logo for the urban crisis.

In Chapter Ten, however, hope begins to reemerge. Graffiti is scrubbed and on-time performance improves. Just as significantly, the Metropolitan Transit Authority recognizes that it has an obligation not only to improve the physical functioning of the system but also to address the symbolic meanings with an ambitious program of station renewal and art patronage.

I hope this study will be something more than an agnostic survey of a complex piece of urban semiotics. I had better declare at the onset that I love New York and even its subway. I certainly do not think either one a hell—or at least I only think that very occasionally in moments of high frustration. Nevertheless, New York is a difficult city, filled with large problems and small inconveniences, and the subway became an emblem of its difficulties long before the fiscal crisis of the seventies and eighties. Today both the city and its subway have crossed a border from despair to renewal. They can only be reborn together. The ultimate purpose of this book is to reassert the centrality of the subway to the New York imagination.

CHAPTER ONE

IMAGINING A SUBWAY

Q. WOULD THERE BE ANY DIFFICULTY IN VENTILATING A TUNNEL FROM THE
   BATTERY TO UNION SQUARE?
A. THE ENGINEER IS ACCUSTOMED TO SAY THAT NOTHING IS IMPOSSIBLE.

*—Testimony during the New York State Senate Railroad Committee
hearings on the Arcade Railroad Bill, 1868.*[1]

NEW YORK'S rapid transit debate took place within the context of its transition from a Walking to a Riding city. By 1864, when the first serious proposal for a subway was advanced, every New Yorker understood that the distance between offices, factories, and shopping in the southern portions of Manhattan Island and the residential neighborhoods in the north would continue to expand. A new technology was needed.

But the debate was not merely technical. New Yorkers used their discussions of alternate plans for subways and els to visualize a city that they hoped to create. They started by asking what route the tracks should follow and quickly extended their discussions into such areas as the cost of political corruption, the relations of men and women in public places, and the ability of the poor to escape their crowded tenements. Seemingly dry questions of engineering led to utopian visions of a reborn city.

A DILEMMA AND A SOLUTION

Much of New York's traffic problem grew out of a mismatch between its transit patterns and its geographic form. In theory, cities ought to develop in a circle. Had New York been able to do so in the early nineteenth century, it could have accommodated a large amount of growth within a radius of about a mile from City Hall and remained a place where it was possible to walk from one end to the other without serious strain. But Manhattan is a long, narrow island. Where a circular city could have spread one mile in all directions, New York stretched to the north.

This problem was exacerbated by the commissioners' plan of 1811, which divided Manhattan into its gridiron street plan. At a time when development scarcely reached Greenwich Village, the commissioners laid the groundwork for the future megalopolis. But while they saw that New York would be huge, they didn't accurately foresee that it would organize itself on a north-south basis. In 1811 it was still reasonable to assume that most economic activity would take place along the rivers. Accordingly, the commissioners provided many streets running east-west from the East River to the Hudson but few north-south avenues along the length of Manhattan Island. Indeed, they proposed eliminating the diagonal Broadway, and the present Madison Avenue was not part of their plan.

As the city grew, it discovered that its street plan didn't match its traffic patterns. In 1860 the *New York Times* complained that "while the commercial centre was creeping toward Union Square, the residential quarters were striding by the half-mile toward Central Park."[2] New York, the paper realized in 1865, had become a city where "the entire population is turned daily into Broadway and four avenues—Third, Fourth, Sixth and Eighth—and [is] thrown like shuttles from one end to the other."[3]

The daily crush on the omnibuses and horsecars became a defining experience in the new city. New York's journalists competed to see who could describe it most vividly.

"Modern martyrdom may be succinctly defined as riding in a New York omnibus," said the *Herald*.[4] The horsecars were just as bad. "At starting there is a general rush and scramble for admission," said the *Times*. "Women and children stand no chance whatever in the *melee*."[5] A rider usually had to push past a group of cigar smokers on the rear platform and then through passengers standing "in rows, down the middle, where they hang on by the straps, like smoked hams in a corner grocery."[6]

If lucky enough to find a seat on a musty cushion, "upon which millions of passengers have sat, and which [is] saturated with their maleficent emanations,"[7] the rider soon had a headache from the "foul, close, heated air." Packed with a mass of humanity, "like sardines in a box, with perspiration for oil," a well-dressed citizen was an easy prey for pickpockets. "Handkerchiefs, pocketbooks, watches, and breastpins disappear most mysteriously."[8] Attempting to leave, the rider had to shove "through a dense mass of persons, and may think himself well off if he alights on his feet, with sound limbs and untrod garments."[9]

Most New Yorkers saw that while horsecar crowding started with traffic patterns, it was exacerbated by machine politics. Much of the *New York Times*'s famous 1871 exposé of Boss Tweed centered on his corrupt relations with the horsecar companies. In 1871 a conductor told the *New York Herald* that when he complained to the police about four ruffians on his car he was "advised to let it drop, for they were in with Alderman Rough and Common Councilman Jack Scavenger, and would surely get 'square' with me sooner or later." [10]

Women, who were supposed to be protected in public by an elaborate system of good manners, were among the worst sufferers from horse car crowding. The *New York Illustrated News* reported in 1864 that they were "thrust about, taken hold of by the shoulder, by brutal conductors, and compelled to stand during a ride of several miles, until they are ready to faint from exhaustion." Their only relief, if no gentleman offered a seat, was "a short strap, hung so high, that no woman of ordinary size can reach it without straining her body and limbs to a degree that is not only painful but positively injurious." [11] A *Harper's Illustrated Weekly* engraving of 1871 shows two middle-class angels temporarily out of their house confronting the semi-bestial conductor of a car labeled "Pickpocket's Paradise" while male thugs leer from the windows. The front of the car repeats the warning that Dante saw inscribed over the gates of Hell: "All Hope Abandon Ye Who Enter Here" (Ill. 1).

If horsecar conditions sullied New York's present, they also threatened its future. Merchants warned that the city faced an economic crisis as the cost of moving goods through congested streets forced businesses to depart. The tax base would shrink and rents would soar in congested residential quarters. New Yorkers began to experience the recurring nightmare that their city would become, as the *New York Times* predicted in 1873, "a city of the very rich and very poor, of those who can afford to stay and those who cannot leave." [12]

1 ▪ "Beauties of Street Car Travel in New York."
Harper's Illustrated Weekly, 1871. Courtesy: Library of Congress.

The solution was obvious to all. "We want to live uptown," said the *Tribune* in 1871, "or in the adjacent county of Westchester; and we want facilities for getting quickly, cheaply, comfortably, from our homes to our work and back again."[13] This could be accomplished, said the *World* the same year, "by a system of rapid transit, established so that men can reside on the upper portion of the island and do business downtown."[14]

Nineteenth-century New Yorkers saw rapid transit as a form of social deliverance. In *The Machine and the Garden*, one of the classics of American cultural studies, Leo Marx shows that many Americans regarded the railroad's technological incursion into the countryside as a wound. This sense of technology as intrusion is wholly lacking in New York City. Trains, whether above the street or below it, would restore civility, empty the slums, reclaim waste lands, and bring prosperity to all. Rapid transit was the savior. "A golden harvest awaits the corporation that shall enter upon the work," said the *Daily Graphic*. "There is no such opportunity for enterprise and profit elsewhere in the land."[15]

RAILS ABOVE THE STREETS

The first proposals for elevated railroads began appearing in the eighteen-forties. In 1854 the editors of the *Scientific American* complained that "it is difficult for us to remember all the plans which have been presented to us for elevated railroads on Broadway during the past eight years."[16] The first carefully developed plan for a subway dates from 1864. By 1867 the legislature was trying to choose between three proposals for subways and more than forty plans for elevateds.[17] By 1873 Simeon Church, a crusader for rapid transit, proclaimed that "all manner of schemes, underground, overground, three-tier, viaduct, depressed, arcade, marginal, tube, tunnel, and what not have been pressed with all manner of pictures, plates, models, drawings, and designs endorsed by imposing certificates, bearing imposing and illustrious names" but he had to add in frustration that "we stand today with absolutely nothing done."[18]

The proposals for subways and els that are spread through the pages of *Frank Leslie's Illustrated Newspaper*, *Harper's Illustrated Weekly*, and, especially, the *Scientific American* are much more than quaint technological fossils. They show New Yorkers not only debating alternate technologies for mass transit but also trying to imagine the experience it would afford and the city it would create.

The Engineer and Speculator and Promoter (the three roles were often combined in the same person) had to resolve several difficult issues. First he had to decide whether his line would go above or below the street. Then he had to decide whether it would go through Broadway and face the wrath of the merchants who feared the loss of business during construction or through the center of residential blocks and arouse the opposition of home owners. If the line was to be on Broadway, should it go over the sidewalks or down the middle of the street? How would a passenger get from the sidewalk to the platform? Once on the platform, how would he or she get on the train? Could the transit be truly rapid if the train had to make frequent stops? Finally, there was the all important question of motive power—should it be horses, or steam, or was there some other possibility?

Some of the answers to these questions now seem obvious but that is entirely a matter of hindsight. Questions that seem quite settled for us were very much at issue in the middle decades of the nineteenth century.

For most promoters the choice between an elevated and a surface route was comparatively easy. Occasionally someone tried to combine both possibilities. In 1867 the legislature debated a three-tier road—a multilevel structure consisting of elevated trains up in the air, horsecars on the street, and subway tracks for freight deliveries below.[19] Such a system, it was claimed, would have carried the greatest volume of traffic in the most compact possible space. Most promoters, however, preferred to go either above the ground or below it and proposals for elevateds far outnumbered those for subways.

Many engineers thought of the transitway as simply a doubling of the street. This was especially true when the street was Broadway. An 1854 proposal for an elevated includes a sidewalk with pedestrians strolling next to the horse-drawn cars (Ill. 2). This attempt to treat the elevated road as a second street makes more sense than might appear at first glance. The opportunity to stroll and window-shop was what drew citizens to Broadway in the first place. What was more natural than to double the opportunity for promenading?

2 ▪ Proposed Elevated Railroad Terrace for Broadway.

Gleason's Drawing Room Companion, April 1, 1854. From the Collections of The Henry Ford Museum and Greenfield Village.

3 ▪ Speer's Endless Railway Train.

Frank Leslie's Illustrated Newspaper, March 21, 1874. Author's collection.

That might calm the merchants by giving them, in effect, an entirely new area for shop windows.

In 1874 Alfred Speer proposed what was by all odds the most remarkable effort to treat the elevated structure as a street. He proposed eliminating the railroad from his elevated structure altogether. Instead, he would build a city-long platform, carried on friction wheels powered by below-ground engines, that moved up and down Broadway at ten or twelve

miles an hour (Ill. 3). This giant conveyance would preserve all the qualities of fashionable Broadway. Pedestrians could stroll and show off their clothes. A gentleman could ride in a smoking compartment. Ladies could repair to toilet rooms provided with female attendants. Or they could all stand at the rail, watching the city move past. New Yorkers in a hurry could walk. Their legs and the moving platform would reach a combined speed of sixteen miles an hour.

One of the most farseeing proposals to build over the sidewalks was offered by John Randel in 1846. Randel had done the surveying for the 1811 commissioners' street plan and he had thought long and hard about streets and transportation patterns. He proposed to build six miles of track—three miles over each of the Broadway sidewalks. He hoped to mollify the merchants by proposing a structure that would actually increase Broadway's charm as a show street. He would build a "colonnade promenade" of cast iron and glass. The glass would have been ground to opaqueness on its upper surface, so that passengers on the elevated line could not peer down on the heads of pedestrians, but molded into prisms on the lower surface so that as much light as possible would have been transmitted to the street below. The iron pillars would have been painted white to cast reflected light into store windows. The structure would have protected promenades from the rain and enhanced the charms of Broadway.

Those who proposed going down the middle of the street tried to offer a structure that was as light, airy, and ornamental as possible. This was to answer critics who loudly insisted that an elevated structure would leave the street in deep night (Ill. 4). Rufus Gilbert offered to build graceful, open Gothic arches in cast iron (Ill. 5). The Gilbert el, however, sacrificed the chief advantage of the middle of the street which was that the broader space available permitted the construction of a three-track railway.

Three—or, better, four—tracks would make possible the express-local system. This was a brilliant solution to a major dilemma of New York rapid transit in that it reconciled the need for speed over long distances (which required few stops) and convenient entrances and exits (which required many). The express-local system emerged slowly in nineteenth-century debates over rapid transit and in 1904 became (and still remains) a unique feature of the New York subway.

In 1866 William Hemstreet proposed an early version of the express-local system for the

4 ▪ "What We Are Coming To. Good Bye Amity Street."

Parsons Collection, Science, Industry and Business Library, The New York Public Library, Astor, Lenox and Tilden Foundations.

three tracks of his Elliptic Iron-Arch Arcade (Ill. 6). His outside tracks were for locals but the middle one was reserved for express cars running downtown in the morning rush hour and uptown in the evening. They would have made the trip from South Ferry to Union Square (with stops at Wall Street, City Hall Park, and Canal Street) in only twelve minutes. But of course Hemstreet gained his three tracks at the cost of darkening the street. He tried to compensate by arguing that his structure would give the street a roof, catching the rain and snow and letting it run off through downspouts in his iron pillars.

Once the engineer had designed his elevated structure, he had to find a way to get his passenger up to it from the street. Some, such as William Hemstreet, proposed stairways inside adjoining buildings so that passengers would walk on a second floor landing to the elevated platform. This would have increased trade in the adjoining store and amply repaid the cooperating merchant. John Randel would have had his passengers ascend (since the safety elevator had not yet been invented) "by a screw shaft, containing a sofa, on which they ride from pavement to the promenade."[20]

The next task was to get the passenger onto the train or moving platform. Speed of transit would be lost if it came to a halt frequently. One solution was to keep it moving and provide an intermediary vehicle. In John Randel's proposal, passengers boarded a tender car at a stationary platform. It then started to pick up speed until it moved as rapidly as a second car which never stopped at all. When that happened the passenger could transfer from the

FRANK LESLIE'S ILLUSTRATED NEWSPAPER

Entered according to the Act of Congress, in the year 1871, by Frank Leslie, in the office of the Librarian of Congress, at Washington.

No. 807—Vol. XXXII.]   NEW YORK, MARCH 18, 1871.   [Price 10 Cents. $4.00 Yearly. 13 Weeks, $1.00.

COAL.

How can the maxim "All's fair in love" may apply to politics is a grave question. Partisan editors, however, seem to think that any advantage, fair or unfair, that may be taken of an opponent, is legitimate and moral. For example, we have here two classes of men, differing, we presume, in good faith, on a purely economic question, styled respectively Protectionists and Free Traders. One insists on adjusting duties on imports so as to stimulate American industry; the other maintains that all duties are in the form of direct drafts on the pockets of consumers, and both aver that their respective policies are best for the country.

Of late we have had a dearth of coal, owing to complications at the mines not necessary to enumerate, since everybody is familiar with them. As a consequence, the price of coal is nearly doubled, causing considerable distress among the poor. Whereupon a Free Trade newspaper before us exclaims in agonizing capitals, interspersed with italics, "See what Protection has done! It has trebled the price of coal!" And a Solon of our immaculate Legislature introduces resolutions demanding the immediate repeal of the duty on coal.

Now, what is the truth of the matter? Nine-tenths of all the coal used in New York is anthracite; this is the only kind that has advanced in price. And on this kind there is no duty whatever! The rise has therefore no more to do with Protection or duties than it has with the perturbations of the planets.

There is, however, a kind of coal known as the bituminous, used almost exclusively for steamers and manufacturers, which is "protected" from British competition by a duty of

NEW YORK CITY.—IMPROVED PROJECT OF A COVERED ATMOSPHERIC ELEVATED RAILWAY FOR CITY TRANSIT. BY DR. R. H. GILBERT.—SEE PAGE 7.

5 ■ Dr. Rufus H. Gilbert's Covered Atmospheric Railway.

Frank Leslie's Illustrated Newspaper, March 18, 1871. Courtesy: Library of Congress.

BROADWAY RAILROAD—THE GRAND ELEVATION OF THE GROUND RAILROAD.—Designed and Patented by William Hemstreet, Proprietor.

6 ▪ William Hemstreet's Elliptic Iron Arch Arcade.

Frank Leslie's Illustrated Newspaper, March 6, 1866. Courtesy: Library of Congress.

tender to the regular car. At the end of the journey he or she would then transfer back to the tender for an eventual exit. Speer's Endless Railway used a similar plan, with a small, covered transfer car bringing the passenger up to the rate of the endlessly moving platform. The express-local system avoided this clumsy contrivance but, of course, at the cost of darkening the street with a heavy structure.

Finally, the engineer who had negotiated all these dilemmas had to solve what was, after all, the main problem: what would power his trains? The easy answer was a steam engine. This, however, raised fears of an explosion in the built-up area of the city. The 1854 *Gleason's Pictorial* proposal featured single cars drawn by horses. Horses, however, sacrificed speed. John Randel promised to draw his cars on an "endless rope" or cable. Gilbert would have sent his cars through pneumatic tubes.

In 1866 A. H. Caryle submitted a plan to use compressed air. Previous proposals for compressed air, he explained, had required enough new air to be taken in at each station to drive the train to the next one. This required an immense pressure of compressed air, which was as dangerous as steam. Caryle hoped to avoid this problem by with a continuous wrought iron tube which would carry compressed air for refueling but never reach sufficient concentration of pressure to cause an immense explosion.[21]

In 1868 Robert A. Chesebrough offered a safer technology using gravity—the trains would be raised, then sent down an inclined plane for half a mile or so, then raised again in order to begin a new downward journey. This, however, would have been slow and cumbersome. An increasing number of engineers said that the city would have to drop its ban on steam engines.

Even if the intractable engineering problems could be solved, promoters faced an incredibly complicated selling job. It was usually necessary to build a scale model and prepare a colored lithograph. It was also desirable to publish an illustrated pamphlet. This required substantial capital. John Randel was said to have worked for two and a half years on his working model, and to have spent between four and five thousand dollars.

Next, it was essential to secure as many favorable references as possible in popular newspapers and magazines. We cannot be sure how many of these stories were purchased but many look more like puff pieces than journalism. Backed by a group of expansion-minded Democrats with heavy investments in many rapid transit schemes (including August Belmont, father of the man who would finance the subway in 1900), the *World* gave favorable publicity to many proposals. Horace Greeley was among the backers of the Viaduct Railway and the *Tribune*'s reporting on the proposal is extraordinarily complimentary. When three fictional crooks named Sam Slykes, J. Coolie Planning, and Lyman Risk set out to make their fortunes with an elevated railway in the Rev. John McDowell Leavitt's polemical novel *Kings of Capital and Knights of Labor* (1885), their first move is to buy a newspaper to publicize their scheme.

It was also necessary to engage in a certain amount of visual sleight-of-hand. The elaborate lithographs issued for the public and the engravings published in such periodicals as *Harper's Weekly* and *Frank Leslie's Illustrated Newspaper* were often startlingly mendacious. Artists invariably made elevated structures appear much lighter than they really were. Few artists ever showed one casting a shadow. The train in the engraving of Gilbert's Gothic-arched railway is smaller than the sash window in the adjoining building—it would have been a train for Munchkins. Alfred Speer's engraving makes Broadway, which, in spite of its name, is not an especially broad street, look as though it is at least a hundred yards across.

Once the drawings had been prepared and publicized, it was necessary to hire agents who knew how to transform the general demand for mass transit into excited public meetings with bands and banners to support their projects. Promoters also employed the simpler method of offering free shares to the town's most influential politicians. José Navarro, a prominent real estate man, would testify under oath that he and his fellow organizers of the Metropolitan Elevated put aside $650,000 in a special "corruption fund."[22]

HUGH WILLSON'S METROPOLITAN RAILWAY

Although most promoters wanted to go over Broadway, the true visionaries wanted to build under it. The major subway proposals advanced in the eighteen-sixties and early seventies were the Metropolitan Railway, the Pneumatic Tunnel, and the Arcade Railway.

Hugh Willson, the Michigan railroad man who promoted the Metropolitan, had been present at the opening of London's three-and-three-quarter-mile Metropolitan Railway on January 9, 1863. Although it was the world's first subway, London's Metropolitan was not quite a model for New York. For one thing, it ran around the northern edge of the city connecting railway terminals, while the New York route would have to go straight through a built-up area. For another, only about half the London underground ran beneath buildings and streets, with the other half left open to provide ventilation for the system's steam engines. But the stations (some of them, such as King's Cross, still in use) were impressively roomy and the cars, with heavy carpets, upholstered seats, and polished hardwood paneling, were inviting.

Willson urged New York to build twelve miles of an entirely covered subway. The engineering problems were formidable but so was the potential market. The *New York Illustrated News* declared in 1864 that "an underground railroad may not be accomplished this year or next, but it is as certain of being in operation at the end of five years, as that New York will continue to grow and prosper."[23]

Willson and his engineer Asa P. Robinson proposed a two-track road that would start at the Battery, proceed under Broadway to 23rd Street, then go north under Fifth Avenue until it divided into separate branches around Central Park. Each two-car train would be pulled by a diminutive engine. Each passenger car would be divided into eight crosswise compartments as in English railways (Ill. 7).

Since Willson proposed to use steam engines, he had to deal with public anxiety about ventilation. The London Metropolitan, in spite of its open cut sections, was plagued by noxious fumes. His solution was to use pipes carrying air from track level through the roof of the tunnel. They would release air through hollow cast-iron lampposts installed at 100-foot intervals along the street.

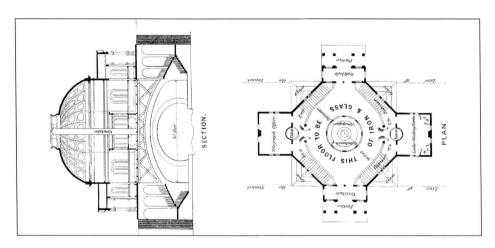

7 ▪ Plan of Metropolitan Railway Station.
Parsons Collection, Science, Industry and Business Library, The New York Public Library, Astor, Lenox and Tilden Foundations.

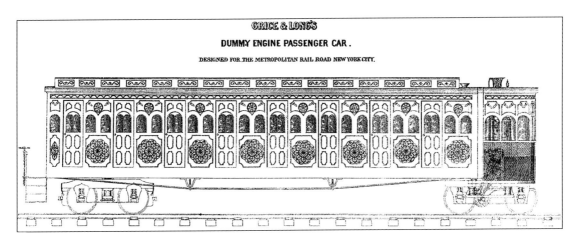

8 ▪ Metropolitan Railway Car.

Parsons Collection, Science, Industry and Business Library, The New York Public Library, Astor, Lenox and Tilden Foundations.

Several of the stations would have been located in city parks (Ill. 8). These would have been domed, neo-classical structures with a ticket booth, a newspaper stand, and a ladies' waiting room at street level. A glass floor would have admitted light onto the stairway leading down to the platform.

These trains were to move through the system in an intricate mechanical ballet. To avert collisions, Robinson wanted no more than one train moving between any two stations at any given time. Therefore he proposed to equip the entire system with electric clocks running on the same circuit. At a given signal all the trains would start to move simultaneously. Proceeding at a uniform speed over the half-mile between stations, all would stop at their destinations at the same time and wait for the signal to start again.

A pamphlet describing the Metropolitan concluded with an enticing vision of a way of traveling utterly different from anything New Yorkers had yet experienced:

> There would be no dust. There would be no mud. Passengers would not be obliged to go into the middle of the street to take a car. They have simply to enter a station from the sidewalk and pass down a spacious and well lighted staircase to a dry and roomy platform. The temperature would be cool in summer and warm in winter. There would be no delays from snow or ice. The cars would not be obliged to wait for a lazy or obstinate truckman. The passenger would be sure of a luxurious seat in a well lighted car, and would be carried to his destination in one-third the time he could be carried by any other conveyance. These would be the advantages to those who ride, and for the other great public in the streets where would be no collisions, no broken wheels or fractured axles, no frightened horses or run-over pedestrians. Everything would be out of sight and hearing, and nothing would indicate the great thoroughfare below. [24]

This is an impressive vision. Why was it not realized? In retrospect we can see that it had important disadvantages. It failed to take advantage of the express-local system. Worse, its two-car trains would never have accommodated the volume of city traffic. New Yorkers saw that their city was growing rapidly but they still didn't imagine the congestion to come. But no one offered these criticisms at the time.

Instead, Willson's plan was delayed by unexpected opposition from an important source. The pipes bringing New York water from the Croton Aqueduct were under Broadway. In 1865 Asa Robinson had been careful to secure an opinion from Alfred Craven, the engineer of the aqueduct, that the underground railway could be constructed without damaging the water pipes. In 1866, however, Craven reversed himself and declared that while the work was in progress the inhabitants of side streets would be cut off from water entirely and those in lower Manhattan, already complaining of an insufficient head of water, would find the pressure further diminished. Robinson immediately reassured the public but Willson had lost momentum. The Metropolitan Railway soon faced fierce competition from two other subway proposals.

ALFRED ELY BEACH'S PNEUMATIC TUBES

Any successful rapid transit promotion required an inventive engineer and a brilliant publicist. Alfred Ely Beach was both. His father, Moses Beach, had helped Benjamin Day found New York's first penny paper, the *Sun*. The elder Beach bought the paper in 1838 and involved his two children, Moses Jr. and Alfred Ely, in running it. Alfred Ely Beach thus grew up learning the techniques of mass communication.

In 1846, he purchased a small magazine called the *People's Journal*, renamed it the *Scientific American*, and made it the country's foremost periodical of popular science and engineering. In connection with the magazine, Beach founded a bureau to represent inventors in patent applications. He also pursued his own career as an inventor. In 1853, for example, he won a gold medal at the Crystal Palace Exposition for his typewriter for the blind. Rapid transit was a challenge that quickly became a passion. He used the *Scientific American* to publicize not only his own plans but also many others that looked ingenious.

Like Willson, Beach was attracted by an English precedent. In 1861 a pneumatic tube for packages had been exhibited in Battersea Fields and in 1864 a large pneumatic tube for passenger traffic was built at the Crystal Palace in Sydenham. Beach hoped a city nervous about steam power would embrace travel through pneumatic tubes.

He did not at once reveal his plans. He proposed only to construct a miniature pneumatic railway for packages like that in use at the London Post Office. In 1866 he organized the Pneumatic Dispatch Company to move the mails. Ironically, both Hugh B. Willson and Asa P. Robinson were among his directors.[25]

The next year Beach revealed that his real ambition was to transport people. He presented his plan in an 1867 exhibition held in Armory Hall on 14th Street (Ill. 9). While the exhibit was still on he published a pamphlet describing how pneumatic tubes might run under or even over New York streets (Ill. 10). The basic elements were simple: a tube, a car, and two fans which would create air pressure behind the car and a vacuum in front.

Beach claimed that a passenger leaving a City Hall station could reach Madison Square

Fig. 7.—The Pneumatic Passenger Railway, as Erected at the American Institute, Fourteenth Street, New-York, 1867.

9 ■ The Pneumatic Passenger Railway.
Alfred Ely Beach, *The Pneumatic Dispatch.* Parsons Collection,
Science, Industry and Business Library, The New York Public
Library, Astor, Lenox and Tilden Foundations.

in five minutes, Harlem in fourteen, and Washington Heights in twenty. Skeptical readers were invited to visit the exhibition at the Armory, climb the stairs to his demonstration tube, and sail comfortably over the exhibits below.

Unfortunately for Beach, the legislature had only authorized a limited "pneumatic dispatch" for packages. He decided to take the city by surprise. He announced that he was building two small tubes, each fifty-four inches in diameter, but what he actually constructed was a tunnel nine feet in diameter and 312 feet long.

The work had to be done in secret. Beach began digging in the basement of a store at the corner of Broadway and Murray Street. His workmen went deep enough to be below the level of the Croton water pipes, then tunneled out toward the center of Broadway and south toward the post office in Nassau Street.

They worked with a tunneling shield that Beach himself had invented. Pushed forward by eighteen powerful hydraulic rams, it made a bore the size of its own diameter through the sand. The loosened sand was carried back to an elevator at Warren Street and, to avoid attracting attention, carted away at night. By February 1870 the workmen had built 312 feet of tunnel. It was enough for a demonstration. Beach issued a triumphant broadside headed with the words FAIT ACCOMPLI! and opened for business.

Beach understood that New Yorkers needed to be reassured in the unfamiliar environment of underground travel. Passengers entered through Devlin's "large and splendid marble edifice," went past a ticket office, and paused to examine the fifty-ton aelor or blowing engine. They then entered a waiting room that, according to Beach's pamphlet, had the familiar ambiance of a middle-class parlor: "The walls are handsomely finished and adorned with interesting pictures, while comfortable settees, looking-glasses, fountains, saloons for ladies and gentlemen, render the place at once cheerful and attractive."[26]

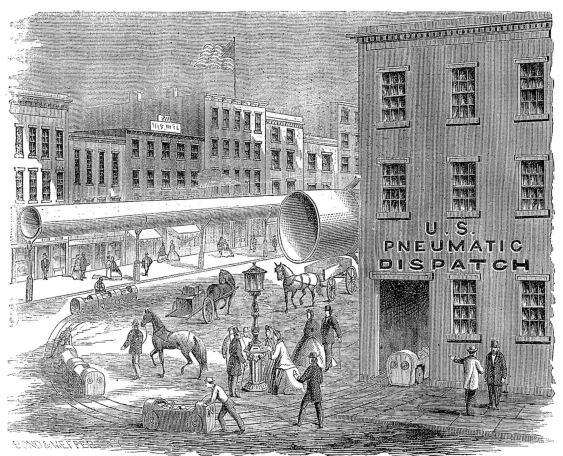

Fig. 10.—The Pneumatic Elevated Railway. (Designed by A. E. Beach.)

10 ▪ The Pneumatic Elevated Railway—Tubes Overhead.

Alfred Ely Beach, *The Pneumatic Dispatch*. Parsons Collection, Science, Industry and Business Library, The New York Public Library, Astor, Lenox and Tilden Foundations.

Engravings in the *Scientific American* show three gentlemen inspecting the tunnel while another relaxes in a setting clearly intended to recall a Victorian parlor (Ill. 11). The passenger car featured richly upholstered seats for twenty-two persons and light closely resembling daylight provided by new oxygen or zirconia lamps.

Beach's promotional pamphlet quotes a rider saying that the only way to tell that the car was being moved by atmospheric pressure was to hold a hand against the ventilator over the doors. "I need hardly say," this testimonial continues, "that the ventilation of the pneumatic car is very perfect and agreeable, presenting a strong contrast to the foul atmosphere of the ordinary city [i.e., horse-] cars."[27] On leaving visitors were asked to sign a memorial to the state legislature demanding the pneumatic railway.

To reassure those who worried that it would undermine the heavy commercial palazzos on Broadway, Beach offered statements of support for such leading architects as James Renwick, Richard Morris Hunt, Russell Sturgis, H. H. Richardson, H. Hudson Holley,

Henry Fernbach, and George B. Post. Both the East Side Civic Association and the West Side Civic Associations endorsed his plan. Alfred Craven declared that the Croton water pipes were safe.[28]

Beach also organized public meetings. The first was held on March 25, 1871, at Harmony Hall at 119th Street and Third Avenue. Its organizers drew a crowd with blazing tar barrels in the street and a band playing "Walking Down Broadway." The second was held on March 28, 1871, at Irving Hall near Union Square.

The speeches at these meetings are fascinating because they display such a mixture of selfless idealism and shrewd self-interest. They express three intersecting ideas. One is the capitalist folk wisdom that time is money and that a long commute was a waste of both. At Harmony Hall Colonel George Webster exclaimed:

> I want every hour of my own time saved. I cannot afford to lose two hours a day; I cannot afford to lose seventy days of ten hours each per year. I want a different arrangement made, so that I can come and go from my business in ten minutes instead of an hour and a quarter, and I do not like to hang on the outside of a street-car, like a bundle of old clothes. I do not like to be packed in with scarlet fever, which I have had, or with small pox, which I have not had. I want to save my hundred dollars a year that I lose.

In a more idealistic vein, the Rev. M. Steele argued that the pneumatic railway would be the salvation of the hard-working artisan:

> Down in the narrow thoroughfares of the city and the over-crowded tenement-houses the poor are packed and crowded until they are forced to overflow into the suburbs to find homes. This should be the home to which they should turn—this Harlem. . . . The people have a right to quick transit, and they demand it, they insist upon their right. The proposed tunnel road is one which will attain this end. It is the poor man's road; the poor man claims it, and the poor man must be heard. (Applause)

But this vision, since it depended on selling homes to the struggling workman, easily merged with the hope that rapid transit would create higher land values. At least some of the vigorous clapping that greeted Rev. Steele's speech came from men and women who had their eyes fixed on a pot of gold. John Foley told the crowd: "You have no idea of the happiness, comfort, and prosperity which quick transit will bring you here in Harlem. Your vacant lots will be built upon, your vacant houses filled, your business doubled and trebled, your property vastly enhanced in value, if this can be secured." Both rallies embraced the slogan: "From New-York to Harlem in Fifteen Minutes."[29]

Not surprisingly, the meetings rang with denunciations of the downtown merchants who opposed construction in Broadway. Alexander T. Stewart, the man who first developed a department store in New York City and the leader of the merchants who fought any possible disruption of their business, was a particular target. John Foley reported that "some three months ago I met Mr. Stewart riding down in a Madison Avenue car, and in reference to this pneumatic tunnel bill he said excitedly, 'Foley, I will spend ten millions of dollars to beat it.'" Such men as Stewart, Foley insisted, were "a curse to the community": "These men desire to protect their property, but they are not willing that we shall improve ours."[30]

But contemporaries agreed that it was not the merchants who defeated Beach. It was the city's political boss William M. Tweed. Beach courted Tweed's support and for a short time he seemed to have it. On March 18, 1870, the *New York Times* reported that Tweed had "taken the contract" to put a bill granting all of underground New York to the Beach Pneumatic Transit Company.[31]

But Tweed soon abandoned Beach. He seized instead on a plan that had been proposed independently by architect Leopold Eidlitz and engineer John J. Serrell for a stone viaduct that would have avoided Broadway altogether. Starting just northeast of City Hall, an area expected to become even more of a traffic hub now that the Brooklyn Bridge had been authorized, Serrell and Eidlitz's four-track line would have gone right through the city's residential blocks on a massive stone structure.

Eidlitz was a master at adapting medieval styles to nineteenth-century uses. His downtown terminal (Ill. 12) would have juxtaposed a powerful medieval castle to the eighteenth-century delicacy of City Hall and his viaduct (Ill. 13) would have brought a Gothic archway to each of 340 different street crossings. The *Tribune* thought that it would add to New York streets that artistic element "which travelers so much admire in European cities."[32]

For a short time it seemed as if Boss Tweed could not possibly fail. Even Beach's *Scien-*

11 ▪ Pneumatic Tunnels and Cars.
Scientific American, March 5, 1870. Courtesy:
Library of Congress.

tific American conceded that "the men who back this scheme are men who cannot be played with."[33] Since they were not ripping up Broadway, A. T. Stewart agreed to serve on the board of directors. So did John Jacob Astor, August Belmont, and real estate developer José Navarro. Sensitive to public opinion, Tweed and Sweeny enlisted James G. Bennett of the *Herald*, Horace Greeley of the *Tribune*, Charles A. Dana of the *Sun*, and Manton Marble of the *World*. Though the fares could have been as high as twenty cents from King's Bridge to Chambers Street, the Viaduct directors bid for popularity by proposing two special workingmen's cars a day for five cents.

But opposition to the project, and to the immense opportunities for graft that it offered, mounted. By the time Tweed endorsed the Viaduct Railway the *New York Times* was already preparing the sensational exposé that would result in Tweed's downfall and imprisonment. On March 10, 1871, it warned its readers that the Viaduct "would furnish one of the fattest jobs the Ring has had for a long time, besides providing a permanent field for official thievery and corruption."[34] Tweed's collapse began before the year was out and, with the Boss out of the way, the Viaduct disappeared from view.

Meanwhile, Beach kept trying to line up support. Simeon Church, a transit reformer, said that he distributed stock to influential politicians.[35] Beach got his bill through the

12 ▪ The Viaduct Railway Bridge Over Broadway.
New York Tribune, June 7, 1871. Courtesy: Library of Congress.

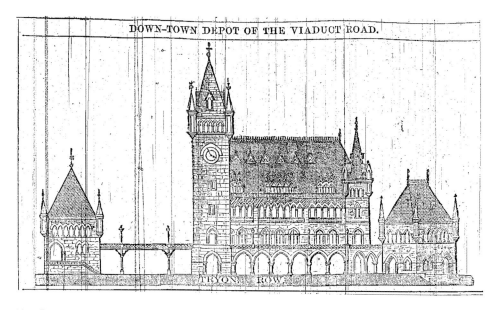

13 ▪ Downtown Depot of the Viaduct Road.
New York Tribune, June 8, 1871. Courtesy: Library of Congress.

legislature twice and twice faced the governor's veto. He finally obtained the governor's signature on a bill authorizing construction in 1873 but the depression that began in September of that year made it impossible to raise capital.

Beach's tunnel was used as a shooting gallery for a time, then forgotten. Astonished workmen came across it when they were building the BMT Broadway line. The idea of the forgotten subway entered the city's folklore. In *Ghostbusters II* Dan Aykroyd discovers ectoplasmic slime flowing through an underground tunnel labeled Pneumatic Transit system. "I can't believe it!" the ghostbuster exclaims. "It's still here!"

MELVILLE SMITH'S BROADWAY BENEATH BROADWAY

The most visionary plan for a subway was proposed by Melville C. Smith in 1866. He proposed nothing less than a new street underground.

Like other promoters, Smith displayed a model and issued a handsome colored lithograph as well as a black-and-white version for the press and a pamphlet (Ill. 14). The print shows a dignified Broadway above with a brand-new Broadway below. The subterranean street has shop windows, strollers on wide sidewalks, and natural illumination coming through lightwells in the street above. The middle of the arcade contains four tracks for express and local trains drawn by steam locomotives (in an early version the local cars would have been drawn by horses).

Not only did Melville Smith promise New York a new street but he offered to reconstruct its underground water, gas, and sewage pipes in the process. The hollow cast-iron pipes which would henceforth support the upper surface of Broadway were to funnel rainwater from the surface to the sewage system below. There was even room for a pneumatic package delivery system beneath the track bed.

This was a bold scheme and its promoters challenged New Yorkers to become city builders. Two 1870 magazine articles, both of them obviously publicity pieces for the Arcade, reveal the kind of vision that New Yorkers were asked to embrace.

The first appeared in the monthly magazine *Galaxy*. Titled "The Future of New York," it made a detailed comparison of growth patterns of London and New York. London, it pointed out, was a much broader city than New York. Its east-west traffic from London Bridge to Hyde Park was somewhat greater than its north-south traffic from Euston Square to Clapham Common. Its tangled streets offered its citizens a multiplicity of possible routes between any two points. In New York, by contrast, there were only a few avenues and "it is, and it obviously will be a question of 'uptown' and 'down-town,' and no more."[36]

Moreover London was not so crowded as New York. The traffic "flows over London Bridge smoothly and rapidly as the river that runs beneath; while the traffic along Broadway is like the struggle of a muddy, turbulent steam against the obstruction of incessant snags, and bars, and sand-banks."[37] The London Metropolitan was a mere convenience. A railroad under Broadway was a desperate necessity.

The advantage of the Arcade over all other possible schemes was that it would extend Broadway's historic functions as a street of travel, shopping, and fashionable strolling. It

PROPOSED ARCADE RAILWAY.
UNDER BROADWAY.
VIEW NEAR WALL STREET.

14 ▪ Proposed Arcade Railway.
Harper's Weekly, March 19, 1884. Courtesy: Library of Congress.

would create "a lower Broadway of steady and regular work, a channel along which the city's daily and monotonous immigration and emigration may float uninterrupted, while the upper and brighter Broadway remains the lounge of the *flâneur*, the Rialto of the merchant, the promenade of the *belle*, the wonder of the stranger, the picturesque, vivid, characteristic illustration of the many-colored life of New York."[38]

The second article appeared in the March 27, 1870, issue of the *World*. It is a utopian dream vision in which a scientific genius, one Dr. Bremmer, gives the narrator a special liquid to circumvent the limitations of time and space. The narrator falls asleep on July 3, 1870, and awakens on July 3, 1900, to find a transformed New York. One of the most startling transformations is beneath his feet. Hearing a clatter of feet and a whirl of vehicles, he steps to a grating and peers through it. Astonishingly, there is a second Broadway beneath his feet. "Broadway is a two-story street now [Dr. Bremmer explains]—has been so for twenty years or more. So are all the avenues of thoroughfare running northward. Surface railroads were always a nuisance, to be abated by scientific engineering. 1885 saw the last of them." Dr. Bremmer explains that after tunnels had been found wanting and pneumatics had been discovered to be wind indeed, engineers had adopted the arcading system. Most of the major north-south avenues are, like Broadway, two-story streets. Some crosstown streets, like 14th and 23rd, have also been arcaded, connected to New Jersey and Brooklyn by viaducts.

New York is now a commuter city. Everybody works at one end of Broadway but lives at the other: "Three millions of people swarm into the city at nine in the morning, attend to business six hours, and swarm out of the city again in the afternoon; and, at night, New York is a vast necropolis of mausolea, with a few policemen stalking up and down like so many sextons." But if Manhattan Island has been divided in two, it has also become the center of what we now call a metropolitan region. Connected with Long Island and New Jersey by a network of rapid transit, viaducts, bridges, and tunnels, it is now "the heart of a vast city, fifty miles in diameter and inhabited by eight millions of people; a vast city symmetrically adapted in all its details to answer the beating of its central heart."

These changes in the physical shape of the city have been accompanied by a moral transformation. The Tweed gang has repented—though not, apparently, refunded. Rapid transit has given the poor an escape route from the tenements that corrupted them:

"Why sir [Dr. Bremmer explains], the crowds that congested the tenement wards were hardly to be blamed for criminal doings. The conditions under which they existed were really generative of larceny and prostitution and murder and vicious instincts as a dead body is generative of worms. . . . Thirty years since," continued the doctor, indignantly, "New York City was nothing more nor less than an illustration on a grand scale of the Malthusian system of political economy—a leprosy spot on the civilization of the century. Its tenement dens were nests of physical and moral typhoid."

By means of the arcading system, the "commercial and popular circulation had been brought into *rapport* with the civilization of the century." The spokesman for the future (though here he is beginning to pass beyond the simple narrator's comprehension) sees the age of positivism and materialism giving way to a new era of freedom. "'Thus,' concluded the doctor grandiloquently, 'have the limitations been circumvented. Thus the world moves. Thus Hegelianism begins to enter practically into the solution of the problem of man.'"[39]

This is a startling conclusion to a publicity piece for a subway. What began as a solution to a traffic blockage becomes first the indispensable condition for the city's economic development, then the key to the moral regeneration of its poor, and finally the means of realizing the absolute idea in history.

But for all the eloquent support he received, Melville Smith did not fare any better than Willson or Beach. He campaigned for two frustrating decades. He displayed a model and issued a colored lithograph that now hangs in the Museum of the City of New York. He planted engraved versions of his lithograph in such periodicals as *Harper's Illustrated Weekly* and the *Real Estate Record and Builder's Guide*. He published frequent pamphlets, one of them consisting of seventy-three pages of favorable newspaper editorials. He sold stock to such influential citizens as ex-President Chester Arthur and ex-Vice President Levi P. Morton as well as a secretary of the Treasury, the president of the Chamber of Commerce, and several generals. He spent $500,000 on surveys and engineering studies.

Though bills authorizing construction were vetoed by New York governors in 1870, 1881, 1884, and 1885, Smith maintained his optimism. In 1882 Smith promised a reporter that he would soon be able to travel underground from the Battery to 42nd Street in only twelve minutes.[40] In 1884 he told reporters that the first section of the road "would probably be commenced within a few weeks."[41] "Of all the numerous schemes of rapid transit that have been organized, flourished for a season, and eventually made shipwreck upon the rugged reefs of the law," said the *New York Times* in its long obituary article on Smith's dream, "the New York Arcade Railway came the nearest to practical fruition and enjoyed the greatest share of public favor and confidence."[42]

The company was finally defeated by a property owners' suit. New Yorkers had long been accustomed to extend their cellars out under the sidewalks. A new Broadway beneath Broadway would have eliminated these convenient storage places. The homeowners sued to block construction. Smith was in a vulnerable position. Unable to gain approval in Albany, he had purchased the franchise of the Beach Pneumatic Tube Company and wanted to use its legal authority for construction. But in 1889 the State Supreme Court declared that the Beach franchise applied only to pneumatic tubes that would not exceed fifty-four inches in internal diameter. The Arcade Railroad was finally dead. The *New York Times* noted that some promoters had devoted the best part of their lives to an effort to build a street and railroad under Broadway.[43]

By the depression year of 1873 the city was in despair. "Rapid-transit roads—on paper—burrow under us and hang over us everywhere," said the *New York Times*. "We have the great pneumatic bore under Broadway, which has become a bore indeed. There is the celebrated Gilbert Elevated, which some people thought, in the beginning, was chimerical, and which has become in fact a chimera. There was the famous Ring Viaduct, which was to be more enduring than the brass of Tammany, but it still exists only in the imaginations of the men who thought to build it at the public expense and then pocket all its receipts. There are numberless other rapid-transit charters for schemes which live only in the memory of those who lobbied them through the Legislature."[44]

After so many grand dreams, the actual elevateds started on a very small scale. If a newspaper reader following the ambitions of Hugh Willson, Alfred Ely Beach, and Melville Smith saw anything about these lines, it was probably a small notice about receivership or bankruptcy.

Charles T. Harvey's West Side and Yonkers Patent Railway must have looked like an especially pitiful venture. It followed the east side of Greenwich Street over the sidewalk and then the west side of Ninth Avenue to the passenger station of the Hudson River Railroad at 29th Street. Since it had only a single track, an uptown car had to turn out onto a special siding to allow a downtown car to pass. The cable mechanism which pulled the cars was so noisy that the railroad was known as the rattletrap line. When the cable snapped all passengers had to wait until a team of horses came to the rescue.

By November of 1870 Harvey's line was bankrupt. The entire company, including elevated tracks, three complete passenger cars, and four vaults containing the steam engines to run the cables were sold at sheriff's auction for $960. The most important asset the purchaser acquired was the company's 999-year franchise. A new company abandoned cable for steam engines concealed within small locomotives that were designed to look like passenger cars. It, too, failed to meet its obligations.

Meanwhile Rufus Gilbert was struggling to begin construction of the Sixth Avenue elevated. A medical man who devoted the later part of his career to mass transit, he promised to create a more healthy city by enabling the poor to escape their crowded downtown tenements. But by November 1, 1873, the *New York Times* could describe the Gilbert Elevated Road as a railroad on paper: "The company has an office on Broadway, but scarcely anything else."[45]

When the 1873 business crisis made it clear to all that subways were far in the future, wealthy capitalists turned to the els. The faltering lines were rapidly completed. Harvey's road became the New York Elevated going up Third and Ninth Avenues. Gilbert's became the Metropolitan Elevated serving Second and Sixth Avenues. The simple device of concealing the steam engine in small dummy cars apparently convinced New Yorkers that there was no danger of explosion. By 1879 few residents of Manhattan were more than a ten-minute walk from rapid transit.

In that year the popular children's magazine *St. Nicholas* published a story by Charles Barnard titled "The Railroad in the Air." It marks a distinct comedown after the 1871 *World* vision of a utopian New York but it gives a clearer image of how typical New Yorkers thought about their city.

The story presents young Master George Timson and his brother, Walter, who live with their parents in an apartment near the Bowery. The four members of the Timson family find themselves crammed into only three rooms—a little kitchen with only one window, a sitting room with only two, and a bedroom with none at all. Even worse for George and Walter, the nearest playground is four miles off in Central Park. Mr. Timson explains to his children that he is obliged to be at his work early in the morning, and that to ride up and down in the horsecars from the uptown neighborhoods would take more time than he could possibly spare.

But one day when the two boys are wandering on the crowded Bowery in a vain search for fun, they find some unusual and very fascinating construction going on, with horses hauling heavy pieces of cast iron and men digging great holes in the sidewalk. Full of these wonders, they rush home to tell their mother about the new elevated railroad:

> Walter suggested that if there was a good railroad, one that would go real fast, so that father could move up-town, perhaps they would live in some place where they could play.
>
> "I'm quite out of practice with my ball, and as to playing any kind of a game, it's no use to try it, that is if you have to run about; and who wants to play sittin'-down games all the time? So I do hope the railroad will be built. It would be such a comfort to have a place where you can stretch your legs without upsetting something." [46]

Sure enough, on the day the elevated opens the Timson family ascends its stairs for a ride to their new uptown home. "It is in this way," the article concludes, "[that] the people of New York hope to live in comfort in their crowded city. The stores are to be at one end of the town, the homes at another, and the elevated railroads are to join the two." [47]

The new city in which young Master George and his brother were to grow up was not a utopia but neither was it the same New York that their parents had been born into. It was now a longer city, dominated by morning and evening "tides" of traffic. It was a noisier city. It was, if possible, more crowded. The new New York was not an incomprehensible chaos, exactly, but it was a land not yet conquered by the imagination. Not surprisingly, the elevated structure that had helped bring it into being also offered the most convenient available path for its exploration.

CHAPTER TWO

AN UNHEAVENLY CITY

BY 1880 the els were complete. For six decades the streets of Manhattan were dominated by four noisy, reverberating metal structures—they could be seen if you took a walk, they could be heard if you sat at home reading. The Sixth Avenue el was torn down in 1939. The Ninth Avenue and Second Avenue lines followed in 1940 and 1942. The Manhattan portion of the Third Avenue el was finally demolished, amid much civic fanfare, in 1955. But until then the els were a natural focus for journalists, novelists, and painters who portrayed New York.

What kind of city did the els symbolize? If imagining the subway encouraged utopian visions of a city that had solved its problems, scrutinizing the els revealed a New York so filled with contradiction that it was difficult even to apprehend. No traditional frame of reference seemed to contain it. The journalists, artists, and writers who portrayed the New York of the late nineteenth century were all searching for a way to represent a noisy, bustling, smelly, jarring chaos.

Certain formulas suggested themselves. Everyone knew that the city of the els was transitional. Just as elevateds were only a stopgap solution in a city that really needed a subway, so the ten-to-fourteen-story buildings they served were only a step on the way to the Wonder City of the twenties. Everyone knew as well that the city of the els was dynamic. Journalists portrayed it as a rushing spectacle. After a few years artists and writers discovered that both the el structures and the city around them became, when seen from the right point of view, unexpectedly picturesque. That is how they appear in William Dean Howells's great portrait of urban life *A Hazard of New Fortunes* (1890). The meaning of the els changed as the city grew taller. In the twentieth century they ceased to represent modernity. John Sloan painted them with the growing sense that they dominated streets that progress was rushing past. By the fifties the stations of the Third Avenue el were ornate antiques that had no place between curtain walls of glass and they inspired considerable nostalgia.

THE NEW CITY OF THE ELEVATEDS

In 1888 a city official told the *New York Times* that the elevated railroad and the elevator were transforming metropolitan life. The els had greatly extended the area available for residences and, at the same time, had enabled large numbers to crowd into the downtown business district. Elevators had made it possible to fill that district with buildings ten, eleven, even twelve stories high. The official offered two predictions: first, the population would fill every available foot of space on Manhattan Island and, second, of all the buildings erected during the past twenty years, not one in a hundred would remain ten years hence.[1]

The city that New Yorkers saw emerging all around them was not the one they had expected a decade earlier. They had been told during the eighteen-seventies that rapid transit would move merchants, artisans, and the poor out of the crowded downtown streets into areas of small cottages and detached villas. Frederick Law Olmsted, writing in 1879 on the "The Future of New York," had observed that Boston was now composed of healthy, charming neighborhoods around an urban core. He expected that New York, with its new elevated railroads, would develop in the same direction.

But New York did not follow Boston's lead. Instead, the areas within reach of the elevated lines were soon given over to apartment buildings of five or more stories with two or more families on each floor. This development took everyone by surprise. The *Real Estate Record and Builder's Guide* looked on with astonishment as middle-class New Yorkers rushed to live in buildings with such faux-dignified names as the Stuyvesant, the Albany, the Knickerbocker, and the Chelsea. "It is," the magazine observed, "a little remarkable that, at the very time of the development of our railroad system, which would naturally tend to diffuse the population in large cities, these apartment house should come into vogue."[2]

Rem Koolhaas has described New York's physical plan as a blueprint for a Culture of Congestion. In a nation that still glamorized the Eden of the family farm and the moral virtues of a detached house with a garden, New Yorkers were practicing concentration rather than dispersal. The *Real Estate Record and Builder's Guide* pointed out that "our women crave companionship other than that of their own families."[3] *Appleton's Journal* warned that "men having social and intellectual wants" could never be satisfied with "a metropolis that simply multiplied the space and conditions of a village." It observed that the virtues of concentrated cities included not only the opera, the art gallery, and the promenade, but also "the inspiring contact of crowds."[4] The *Real Estate Record and Builder's Guide* agreed that New Yorkers "like to live in a crowd—to see their fellows daily and hourly."[5]

Some New Yorkers even imagined the future as a still more glorious concentration of population. Architect George DaCunha foresaw a day when five million people would live in Manhattan.[6] A visionary real estate broker foresaw "twenty-story steel buildings covering entire blocks with parks in the centre, streets on the roof, elevators in every corner, moving sidewalks all around, each floor and the building generally containing in itself all the elements of a city."[7]

The els, along with the streetcars, provided a necessary underpinning to the new urban lifestyle. From 1884 to 1893 travel by rapid transit in New York increased 250 percent.[8] Perhaps more important, the growing number of rides came not only from the expanding population but also from the fact that each year a typical New Yorker took an increasing number of trips for business, shopping, and entertainment. This dependence on transit helped set New York apart from the great European capitals. The number of per capita rides on public transit for 1890 was 74 in London and 91 in Berlin but 233 in New York.[9]

Like the new city itself, the elevated system was a genuinely complex and contradictory phenomenon. It was, to begin with, an undeniable utilitarian intrusion into a city that valued Victorian ornateness. As the 1874 report of the American Society of Civil Engineers declared: "No structure for rapid transit can be made ornamental in the purely artistic sense of that word. Its long straight lines will not admit of much architectural effect."[10]

At the same time, however, the els provided a certain visual richness to the city streets. Their horizontal lines made a striking contrasts to the increasingly vertical emphasis of the new architecture. Their stations were ornamented with finials, wooden panels, stained glass windows, and even little pot-bellied stoves that were decorated, according to *Frank Leslie's*, "in an artistic manner, so as to mar as little as possible the appearance of the place."[11]

The impact of the els on the streets was similarly complex. They made walking in the city even more of a challenge. In 1893 the *Scientific American* reported that "chunks of coal, bolts of iron, hot and cold water, fiery coals . . . are only a part of the droppings that fall from the rattling trains." Doctors discovered that the elevated trains were producing a new class of eye troubles because at each station stop small iron particles were ground off each train's brake shoes. Experimenters passed a magnet along only six feet near an el station and collected more iron filings than along an entire block on Broadway: "Viewed under the microscope, their dangerous character becomes apparent. The greater part were bordered by a jagged fringe with very fine points, compared with which the point of a cambric needle appeared dull."[12]

Moreover, the els were extraordinarily noisy. Classes at Cooper Union had to be shifted to the side of the building furthest away from the Third Avenue el. A property owner who lived near the Sixth Avenue line complained piteously: "I only obtain sleep between the hours of 12:30 at night and 5 o'clock in the morning. It is impossible to get any rest before midnight. You can only get relief by jerks—a minute and a half of sleep being obtained between each jerk."[13]

Yet all agreed that the els had increased the pace and variety of city life.[14] In the twentieth century they were regarded as a drag on real estate but this was not true in the nineteenth. *Frank Leslie's* noted in 1878 that "with steamcars, rattling above, the horse-cars tumbling below, the dashing of ordinary vehicles, the surging and crowding of the greatly increased *habitués* of the avenue, the glare of hundreds of lamps and flaming devices of business houses, [Sixth Avenue] bids fair to attain even more of the characteristics of Vanity Fair than does the Bowery now possess."[15]

The great department stores on Sixth Avenue near 23rd Street and later the huge Gimbel's and Macy's stores at Herald Square were built to be near the els. The *Scientific American* pointed out in 1892 that many valuable buildings were erected next to them and that these were "tenanted by families who, strange as it may seem, appear to take pleasure in the din and dust raised by the steam trains close under their windows."[16]

THE SPECTACLE AND THE PICTURESQUE

It was precisely because the els were both appalling and charming that they were such an effective symbol of New York. Journalists used them to show how rapidly the city had progressed, to portray the behavior of its crowds, and show that even the most brutal aspects of urban life could be unexpectedly picturesque.

A typical use of the els to exemplify progress appears in an engraving in the September 23, 1882, issue of *Harper's Weekly*. At the top it portrays the city of A.D. 1682 with an orderly group of Dutch burghers standing in quiet attention as a town crier reads off the latest proclamation. At the bottom an equivalent scene two hundred years later shows a crowd pausing to buy newspapers before dashing up the el stairs. Authors constantly stressed that this riding city of the newsstand, the rushing crowd, and the elevated had sprung up within the experience of a single generation. "There are persons still living," a writer in *Scribner's* marveled, "who have heard it said that the proper place for a tradesman to live was over his shop."[17]

But the contrast with the older city was frequently only a prelude to an amazed description of the astonishing sights of the new one. Writers in the daily papers emphasized the city's spectacle and they often found their best example in the el.

"Nobody has seen New York thoroughly," the *New York Times* remarked in 1880, "who has not made the 'grand tour' of the elevated roads."[18] Journalists filled the papers with such articles as "Travelling Up in the Air,"[19] "A Ride on the Elevated,"[20] "Fast Time up in the Air,"[21] "Life on the Elevated Road,"[22] "In a Commission Train,"[23] and "The Many Woes of the Guard."[24] What was remarkable about these articles was that they presented something the reader had already experienced—was quite possibly experiencing at the moment of reading. By showing the city as a spectacle, they encouraged the reader to see the zestful drama of what had previously seemed a daily grind.

When the els were new passengers were struck by the sheer novelty of traveling over the wagons and pedestrians below. *Harper's Weekly* reported that on the Bowery "the tracks run along at the dizzy height of thirty feet from the street, so that the passengers will be nearly forty feet from the pavement as they are whirled along up or downtown."[25] The *New York Times* reported that "the train appears to be moving in midair upon nothing" and added that "it requires some little nerve to sit at the car window and look steadily down upon the street."[26]

The opportunity to peer into second- and third-story windows proved endlessly fascinating. It was possible to catch successive glimpses of a gold-beater with his mallet raised, a brush-maker with his bristles, and a bookbinder in white apron and square paper cap. The elevateds provided a direct view into the housing of the poor. "You soon pass the old-fashioned, low houses of Division-street," said a *Times* reporter, "whose owners are no doubt worrying because they cannot pack more than four or five families into one house, when there is that new building, on the same size lot, that takes in fifty. Here is a tremendous building, five or six stories high, with an almost countless number of windows in front, and a light in every window. Look in through any of the windows, which are all open, and you see . . . a supper table spread and the family seated around it. You will generally see a bed in the same room, for there is no space to spare."[27]

But the greatest fascination of el travel was always the el crowd itself. "The surprising fact to me," said Superintendent Onderdonk of the New York Elevated in 1879, "is how all these persons travelled before the elevated road was built. The street-cars seem to have now as many as they can comfortably carry, and we have thousands more."[28]

New York journalists sought even more inventive ways to show the crowd-in-a-hurry. The *World* urged aficionados of mass behavior to take up a position near the steps of the Houston Street station:

> Go and look at it on a stormy evening after ten thousands of umbrellas have sprung up like mushrooms on the most prolific beds. Watch men, women and children slip and stagger through the boggy, greasy mud, cross the car-tracks under the very noses of horses, while truckmen and drivers swear and yell at them or ogle and throw kisses to the pretty girls— for there are, as in every crowd of New Yorkers, innumerable pretty girls, dressed in cheap stuffs with a taste that a Parisienne might envy.
> And after you have seen the tide surge across the street, watch it rise up those stairs. And don't fail to observe the crowd of loungers who block the sidewalk between the stairway and the house next to it, who jeer and elbow people, and hurl slang at each other until a rare policeman comes along and orders them to "move on."[29]

A similarly astonishing sight was available on station platforms. The *Tribune* described the rush hour scene: "Pushing, swaying, leaning forward to peer down the track, crowding past one another with the intention of getting to the points which they calculate will be opposite the car platforms when the train stops, they run the risk of being pushed upon the track at every moment."[30]

Many writers focused on the station guards and platform attendants who occupied the uncomfortable interface between the impersonal needs of the system and the passions of the crowd. The station employees were usually presented as hardened to their roles. "You ought not to slam the gate spitefully in a man's face, as if you would like to wrench his nose off," a philosophical brakeman told the *Tribune* in 1882. "Some men do that, but I don't. You ought not to strike a man with your fist, if he tries to force his way in. You should keep him firmly off the car, and not go out of your way to injure his feelings. But you know it is a hard thing to be excessively polite under the circumstances."[31]

Journalists who emphasized the daily rush of the crowd presented it as a spectacle. Those who portrayed the el in quieter moods showed that it was picturesque. Where the spectacle grows out of the city's hectic uproar, the picturesque depends on a frame of reference imposed by the beholder. If enjoyment of the spectacle encourages exaggeration, the picturesque requires the artistic eye to prune the scene until it becomes visually appealing. While the spectacle is a permanent fact of city life, the urban picturesque belongs to a relatively narrow historic period. It was extremely important in the eighties and the nineties. It helped tame the disorder of the city and make it acceptable to cultivated temperaments.

As an aesthetic category, the picturesque had been elaborated at the end of the eighteenth century to describe objects which were neither beautiful nor sublime but which were nonetheless attractive to artists because they were rough in texture and irregular in outline. Although first defined in terms of landscape, the concept easily migrated to urban scenes where it was applied to ragged street urchins and crumbling buildings.

M. G. Van Rensselaer's article "Picturesque New York" in the December 1892 issue of the *Century Illustrated Monthly Magazine* is a reliable guide to late-nineteenth-century thinking on the subject. Miss Van Rensselaer offers the picturesque as a reconciling vision. It starts with scenes that ordinary people never notice and makes them speak to the aesthetic sense. New York, she says, has become especially amenable to the picturesque vision. Young artists "do not say that New York is beautiful, but they do say that it is 'most amusing'"— and this, she tells us, "is the current studio synonym for picturesque." [32]

Of course not all subjects are suitable. The picturesque is above all a selective vision. "[If] when we walk through our streets we want to appreciate all the picturesqueness they contain, we must cultivate the artistic faculty of seeing only just as much at a time as we ought to see." We must first select our subjects, then suppress those aspects which are inappropriate. If we do this, however, the city is filled with riches and Van Rensselaer takes us on a walk through the streets to point them out. Immigrants are picturesque. Jefferson Market is *very* picturesque.

The els were a special challenge. They represented the most brutal aspects of the city but, with the proper distance, they were surprisingly easy to subdue. Van Rensselaer asserts that they "delight our eyes with striking effects never seen until they were built" whenever a sudden puff of steam from the engine cuts into the azure sky or when, at night, their long rows of lighted windows sparkle at the end of a vista.

Picturesque views of the city were a staple of such popular magazines as *Frank Leslie's* and *Harper's Illustrated Weekly*. Full-page steel engravings were accompanied by evocative prose descriptions. "No part of New York is more picturesque than the Bowery," we learn in the essay that accompanies a drawing by Henry Muhrman, "with its fruit-stands lighted by flaring lamps, its beer-gardens, its multitudinous drinking shops, its small hotels with big signs, its pawn shops, and street vendors of all kinds." [33]

W. P. Snyder's "A Bitter Night at an Elevated Railroad Station," we are told, presents its scene in "very picturesque circumstances" (Ill. 15). It contrasts the well-dressed riders in the foreground with the boy in the newsstand who, in spite of the bitter cold, preserves "the unagitated and normal appearance from which it is known that newsboys almost never relax." [34]

By bringing the els under the formulas of the spectacular and the picturesque, the daily press and the weekly magazines developed conventions by which the new city could be represented. They also offered traps to the writers and artists who would enlarge on their work—a too easy acceptance of surface drama, a patronizing delight in the purely aesthetic

A BITTER NIGHT AT AN ELEVATED RAILROAD STATION.—DRAWN BY W. P. SNYDER FROM A SKETCH BY F. RAY.—[SEE PAGE 99.]

15 ▪ W. P. Snyder. *A Bitter Night at an Elevated Railroad Station.*
Harper's Illustrated Weekly, February 5, 1887. Author's collection.

aspects of the complex urban scene. Both William Dean Howells and John Sloan explored the conventions that the newspapers and magazines created but also exposed and undermined them.

WILLIAM DEAN HOWELLS'S NEW YORK

Critics have rightly praised Howells's *A Hazard of New Fortunes* as a pioneering example of American literary realism without ever quite appreciating its insight into New York City. Some complain that Howells allows his chief characters, Basil and Isabel Marsh, to spend entirely too long searching for an apartment. Others, more perceptive, recognize that an apartment hunt is a brilliant way to explore the city but are too stingy in recognizing Howells's insight into the relation between its physical geography and its psychological climate.

Mario Maffi, in an article which says many sensible things about the ways in which Basil and Isabel interpret their new city, asserts that they never penetrate beyond a *façaderie*.[35] This seems to me wrong. Basil and Isabel quickly become experts in the causal relation between New York's street plan and the layout of its apartments. In addition, they display a shrewd sense of the ways in which the framework of seeing reshapes what is seen. Basil, in particular, first understands how the artistic formula of the picturesque can tame the city's spectacle and then comes to realize the inadequacies of the picturesque.

A Hazard of New Fortunes is organized around the launching of a new illustrated magazine. The Marches are Bostonians who take their move to New York as an imaginative challenge. They don't want to just survive in their new city. They want to live in it and that means that they must find a way to make it comprehensible. First, they compare their new city to the Boston they loved. Then they begin exploring New York on its elevated trains. Finally, Basil decides to use his el journeys as the basis for a series of journalistic sketches.

The comparison of Boston and New York was one of the established *topoi* of nineteenth-century American culture. Boston was genteel and literary; New York was obsessed with self-promotion and wealth. Boston was provincial; New York, as the publisher of *Every Other Week* proclaims, belongs to the nation.

In Boston the Marches had lived on Nankeen Square. There never was an actual Nankeen Square but it corresponds to Chester and Wooster Squares in the South End. Both are small, elongated parks, not square at all, lined with gracious homes. The Marches were content there because these intimate spaces encouraged a life of cultured domesticity.

The Marches are sure that such harmony of personality and architectural space would be impossible in a New York flat. "I could never have any inner quiet in New York," Isabel complains; "I couldn't live in the spirit there."[36]

Much of the presumed harshness of New York life was the result of its gridiron street plan and its habit of flat living. Frederick Law Olmsted drew a direct connection between the two. He pointed out that the 1811 commissioners' plan had not only laid out the city's streets but had also divided it into blocks of uniform size and then subdivided each block into uniform 25′ by 100′ lots.

By the eighteen-eighties the price of land forced builders to fill nearly the whole of each lot with a multistory building. The only convenient way to arrange rooms in these narrow structures was in a row. This produced what was often called a railroad flat. The trouble with this arrangement was that only the front and back received direct light. "In the middle parts of all these deep, narrow cubes [Olmsted complained], there must be a large amount of ill-ventilated space, which can only be imperfectly lighted through distant skylights, or by an unwholesome combustion of gas."[37]

In 1879, when New York's elevated system had been completed, Olmsted wrote in the *Tribune* that Yorkville and Harlem, five or six miles from the downtown center, were being filled with "new houses of the ridiculous jammed-up pattern, as dark and noisome in their middle parts and as inconvenient throughout as if they were parts of a besieged fortress." This was true of all the flats that such people as Basil and Isabel March might consider. "What are advertised as apartment houses for people in New-York of more moderate means," Olmsted charged, "such as must be looked to by teachers, artists, artisans, writers, and nearly all the rank and file of the superior life of a metropolis, are as yet only a more decent sort of tenement-house, nearly half of their rooms being without direct light and ventilation. The same classes that are compelled to live in them in New-York would regard them as intolerable in Philadelphia, or in London, Paris, or Vienna."[38]

Or, we might add, in Boston. Nevertheless, Basil and Isabel search for a flat that will meet their needs. There must be an elevator. There must be steam heat. There must be a bedroom for Basil, another for Isabel, and a bedroom each for the girls. Basil must have a study; Isabel must have a parlor. There must be a sunny kitchen and a dining room. All the rooms must have outside light. There must be hall-boys to do errands and a pleasant janitor. The rent must not exceed $800 a year.

Not surprisingly, this apartment is impossible to locate. Throughout their search Basil and Isabel make two criticisms that might be expected from any Bostonian searching for a New York home.

First, they regard the flat as hostile to domesticity. None, Basil realizes, have that important innovation of late-nineteenth-century house architecture, the living room: "They have drawing rooms to foster social pretense, and they have dining-rooms and bed-rooms; but they have no room where the family can all come together and feel the sweetness of being a family" (67). Flats are for social show, not for domestic tranquillity. "No," Basil finally pronounces, "the Anglo-Saxon home, as we know it in the Anglo-Saxon house, is simply impossible in the Franco-American flat" (68).

Second, the Marches echo Olmsted's complaint that New York flats are invariably laid out to have light at either end but darkness in the middle. Although she specifies at the beginning that "the rooms must *all* have outside light" (45), Isabel finally concludes that while two or three of the rooms in a New York flat might have glimpses of the day through small windows, the rest were in perpetual twilight.

As they walk the streets in a vain search for the perfect flat, the Marches inevitably encounter the four elevated structures which dominated Second, Third, Sixth, and Ninth Avenues. Not surprisingly, they are at first appalled. Their Boston had contained nothing similar. (The elevated tracks which ran down the South End's Washington Avenue were not constructed until 1899.)

Before long, New York's elevateds and its flats merge into a single monster. After days of riding the trains and inspecting apartments, Isabel has a nightmare which combines the sequence of rooms in a flat with the cars of an el train. In her dream she finds herself pursued by "a hideous thing with two square eyes and a series of sections growing darker and then lighter, till the tail of the monstrous articulate was quite luminous again" (62).

But Isabel's nightmare is a turning point. Once it is past the Marches begin to enjoy their new city. When Isabel returns to her Boston home on a visit late in the novel, she finds herself longing to get back to "the immense, friendly homelessness of New York" (308).

One sign of Basil and Isabel's changed attitude is their new appreciation of the els. The els "kill the streets and avenues," Basil concedes, "but at least they partially hide them, and that is some comfort." He chooses the bends in the el just below the Cooper Institute as emblematic of the city (Ill. 16). "They're the gayest things in the world. Perfectly atrocious, of course, but incomparably picturesque!" (62).

Basil soon decides that this extraordinary city will provide the basis for a series of sketches, each one to be illustrated by a staff artist, in the new magazine he is to edit. He

1859 by Peter Cooper 8th St. Junction
eighteen 1904 by William H. Rau

16 ■ El tracks below Cooper Union.
Courtesy: Library of Congress.

embraces the urban picturesque which was so common in *Harper's Illustrated Weekly* and other late-nineteenth-century periodicals.

Recognizing the similarity between Basil's perceptions and those of contemporary journalism, Kenneth Lynn complains that he simply echoes "the outmoded and sterile aesthetic formulas of the 1870s."[39] This is misleading on two counts. First, Basil is aware of how much both the city and the art which reveals it have changed since the seventies. Second, Basil both adopts the standard of the picturesque and explores its inadequacies.

Basil and Isabel had in fact visited the city in 1870. Their experience was described in Howells's first novel, *Their Wedding Journey* (1871). When they compare the Broadway of the eighties to the street they had encountered on their honeymoon, their memories closely resemble Sol Eytinge's 1870 engraving in *Harper's Weekly* (Ill. 17): "You do not now take your life in your hand when you attempt to cross it; the Broadway policeman who supported the elbow of timorous beauty in the hollow of his cotton-gloved palm and guided its little fearful boots over the crossing, while he arrested the billowing omnibuses on either side with an imperious glance, is gone" (53). The disorderly traffic of the omnibus has been replaced by the tracks of the horsecars: "The grind of their wheels and the clash of their harsh bells imperfectly fills the silence that the omnibuses have left, and the eye misses the tumultuous perspective of former times" (54).

As the city had changed by the eighteen-eighties, so had the *Harper's Weekly* representation of it. Its artists gave less attention to little human dramas and more to purely visual qualities—to contrasts of natural light with the new artificial illumination and to moments when unexpectedly harmonious compositions emerged out of the seeming disorder of the city.

When Basil and Isabel pause on the bridge over the tracks at the 42nd Street station and gaze up and down the rails over Third Avenue, they are fascinated by precisely the same visual effects that *Harper's* artists loved to capture: "The track that found and lost itself a thousand times in the flare and tremor of the innumerable lights; the moony sheen of the electrics mixing with the reddish points and blots of gas far and near; the architectural shapes of houses and churches and towers, rescued by the obscurity from all that was ignoble in them, and the coming and going of the trains marking the stations with vivid or fainter plumes of flame-shot steam" (76–77). Such a city is a fairyland and living in it is an adventure.

The virtue of the picturesque is that it tames the visual uproar of the city and makes it

17 ▪ Sol Ettynge. *Crossing Broadway.*
Harper's Weekly, March 12, 1870. Courtesy: Library of Congress.

enjoyable. Its fault is that it substitutes an aesthetic for a moral response and averts its eyes from the social injustice that the city contains.

Howells conducts two lengthy explorations of the picturesque—one in Chapter XI of Part Two when Basil rides the Third Avenue el to visit the anarchist Lindau and another in Chapters II and III of Part Four when Basil's explorations take him from the Upper West Side to the southern tip of the island. In these expeditions, Basil encounters the turbulence of the physical city: its jumble of architectural styles, the intrusion of its four elevated structures, and the notorious clutter of its streets. He also sees the architectural forms which the elevator made possible: "the new apartment-houses, breaking the old skyline with their towering stories" (299) and, in the downtown business district, the "heights and masses of many-storied brickwork for which architecture has yet no proper form and aesthetics no name" (303). The function of the picturesque in Basil's wanderings is to make these alien forms acceptable.

It plays a similar role in shaping Basil's attitude toward the city's immigrant population. His wanderings provide an atlas of the city's ethnic geography. The uptown sections, he discovers, are the "American region." The crowds on Madison Avenue include "American Hebrews"—that is, German Jews established in New York before the immigration from eastern Europe began. The Sixth Avenue el carries "American husbands" and "American wives." On the East Side, however, and especially downtown, Basil encounters Russians, Poles, Czechs, Germans, Scandinavians, and, above all, Italians.

A Hazard of New Fortunes was written during a period of growing alarm at the volume of new immigrants in general and at those from eastern and southern Europe in particular. Hostility focused on the Italians and the allegedly unsanitary conditions of their lives. "Laborers who live in tiers of bunks in a shed and upon spoiled pork," said the *New York Times*, "who wear their clothes until they drop off, and who combine in clubs of nine or ten to maintain one woman for each club, are necessarily a public danger as well as a public disgrace and a public nuisance."[40] The Italians, the paper declared, "are the Chinese of our Eastern States."[41]

Basil's appreciation of the picturesque leads him to take an altogether sunnier view of the nation's new arrivals. Basil is sure that one of the chief pleasures of New York life is its quality of foreignness. He sees aspects of immigrant life that Jacob Riis, whose alarmist account of "half" the population was published in the same year as Howells's novel, entirely overlooked. Basil and Isabel are struck by the perfect decorum of Italian restaurants. Basil watches the small Italian children in Washington Square play the newly learned American games of tag and hide-and-whoop while their older brothers practice baseball. Aware of the public fear that some immigrants could never be Americanized, March finds that he likes "the swarthy, strange visages; he found nothing menacing for the future in them" (299).

Basil's outlook allows him to express an optimistic attitude toward aspects of the city— its restlessness, its visual turmoil, its immigration—that others found alarming. But Basil is also uneasily aware that the picturesque is not a universal solvent. His association with the German radical Lindau leads him to question his aesthetic detachment. Basil rides the elevated down the Bowery in Chapter XI of Part Two in order to find Lindau's home. What he sees on the way severely tests the ability of the picturesque outlook to suppress the social disorder it confronts.

In the nineteenth century the Bowery el ran not down the middle of the street but directly over the sidewalks. This arrangement was good for traffic but destructive of architectural effect and appalling for the people who had to walk under the tracks and live or work next to them. Here Basil encounters the full impact of an el that he had managed to find charming.

Appropriately, his first response is to an aesthetic crime. Basil registers alarm at the way in which the el draws "its erasing line across the Corinthian front of an old theatre, almost grazing its fluted pillars, and flouting its dishonored pediment" (183). It is an effect that Howells would have seen every time he visited Harper's offices (Ill. 18).

But this architectural disorder is only the emblem of a moral chaos. Basil senses that the scene before him results from a struggle for survival with the strong persisting over "the

18 ▪ New York Elevated Railroad—View in Franklin Square.
Harper's Weekly, September 7, 1878. Courtesy: The Library Company of Philadelphia.

deformity, the mutilation, the destruction, the decay" of the weak. "The whole at moments seemed to him lawless, godless; the absence of intelligent, comprehensive purpose in the huge disorder, and the violent struggle to subordinate the result to the greater good" (184). This is not a comfortable thought for Basil and he at once retreats into a sentimental appreciation of a Dickensian ballad-seller.

Basil's explorations by elevated bring him just to the edge of New York's area of greatest crowding and poverty. The Manhattan elevated system, laid out on a north-south axis, bypassed the bulge of the Lower East Side. Like the picturesque perspective, the el thus concealed the city at the same time that it revealed it. But Lindau has deliberately chosen to live on the Lower East Side among the city's poorest and he forces Basil to see what might have remained hidden.

Lindau's lifelong moral obduracy will result in his death from a policeman's club in the horsecar strike which provides the novel's conclusion. Just as the trip down the Bowery had led Basil to a vision of a society without any intelligent, comprehensive purpose, so Lindau's death provokes his angry denunciation of "this economic chance-world in which we live," a place where "we go on, pushing and pulling, climbing and crawling, thrusting aside and trampling underfoot; lying, cheating, stealing so that at the end we can come home either to a palace of our own or to the poor-house" (437).

Basil shows far more insight into New York life that his critics have recognized. He sees the relation between the city's physical geography and its state of mind. He learns to face its els and incipient skyscrapers without blinking. He welcomes its immigrants. But the picturesque is a harmonizing vision and Basil is tortured by a conviction that the social arrangements of the city are ultimately anarchic. He never reconciles the two. That is a suspended task at the end of *A Hazard of New Fortunes*—one that Howells himself took up in the Altrurian romances, the works of utopian social criticism that occupied him in the eighteen-nineties.

JOHN SLOAN AND THE TRANSITIONAL CITY

In the art of John Sloan both the el and the streets it dominates begin to appear obsolescent. Sloan came to New York from Philadelphia in 1904, the year the subway opened. The elevateds did not become instant antiques but over the next two decades they increasingly characterized an older New York as against the Wonder City of the subway and skyscraper. Sloan painted the first and largely ignored the second.

Sloan's relation to the transitional city of the el rather than the modern city of the subway may help explain the slightly ambigious place he long held in the canon of American art. Wanda Corn argued in an influential article that the art of the early urban realists was not stylistically equal to the modernity of the city because it did not explore the effects of speed and simultaneity that we find in such modernists as John Marin and Joseph Stella.[42] Interestingly, Mario Maffi makes a somewhat similar objection to *A Hazard of New Fortunes*. Howells's novel has an "unsatisfactory quality," he suggests, because it too much resembles a series of still photographs whereas it is the moving picture, with its movement, time cuts, and time and space telescoping which has the great capacity to portray the modern city.[43]

Corn's objection loses some of its force if we accept that Sloan, like Howells, portrayed New York at a transitional phase in its growth. His rich, complicated city could still be imaginatively grasped by a detached observer moving through it in a leisurely way.

Sloan's New York was geographically distinct from the new city of speed and simultaneity. Because the Manhattan schist on which the skyscrapers are based plunges deep into the ground just north of City Hall, there was a large area of Manhattan between the two skyscraper zones which was not rebuilt in the twentieth century. This was where Sloan lived and worked. The New York he portrayed lay either on the Lower East Side or in the large area bounded by Greenwich Village to the south, Herald Square to the north, and the Second and Ninth Avenue els on the east and west. This was a New York that progress was leaving behind. Sloan painted tenement kitchens, Union Square, the Carmine Theater, a five-cent movie house, the Haymarket dance hall, McSorley's tavern, cheap restaurants, the Jefferson Market Courthouse, and rooftop pigeon coops.

Sloan's choice of urban subjects is also determined by his politics. His only portrayal of the subway before the mid-twenties occurs in a 1911 cartoon for the socialist weekly the *Call*. It shows the skeleton Death drawing workers to the open grave of a subway construction site (Ill. 19). Skyscrapers are lightly sketched in the distance, symbols of the corporate greed

19 ▪ John Sloan. *The Great Subway Contractor—The Promised Loaf.*
1911. Ink and colored crayon on textured, wove paper, 14¹³⁄₁₆ × 22⁷⁄₁₆ in. Georgia Museum of Art, University of Georgia.

20 ▪ Gilbert El Passing in Front of Jefferson Market and Police Court.
Frank Leslie's Illustrated Newspaper, May 25, 1878. Courtesy: Library of Congress.

which mocks workplace safety. By 1911 such artists as the printmakers Joseph Pennell and Anton Schutz were showing the downtown business center on its own self-confident terms. Sloan, by contrast, rejected the New York of capitalist modernity. His art asserts that the city's vitality is to be found in its shabby neighborhoods and crowded streets rather than in the Woolworth Building and the brand-new subway. Real life is lived in the shadow of the el.

The emotional connotations of the el in Sloan's work are as various as the men and women he portrays. An elevated train provides the setting for a sentimental tale of courtship in the illustrations for Harvey J. O'Higgins's story "The Steady" in the 1905 *McClure's*. El tracks block the vista in the restricted urban world of "Innocent Girlish Prattle—Plus Environment" on the cover of the November 1913 issue of *Masses*. They become a hauntingly mysterious shape looming through the mist in *Wet Night on the Bowery* (1911). The elevated structure is cold and menacing in *Sixth Avenue and 30th Street* (1907) but a brightly lit train is a warm and comforting presence in *Six O'Clock, Winter* (1912).

For Sloan, the most evocative characteristic of the el is that it shows signs of age. The comparison of a nineteenth-century view with one of Sloan's is instructive. An engraving in *Frank Leslie's* (Ill. 20) juxtaposes the horizontal el tracks with the picturesque massing of the Jefferson Market Courthouse to show the divided glories of the nineteenth-century city—beauty and structure, architecture and engineering. Sloan treats the same scene in *Jefferson Market, Sixth Avenue* (Ill. 21) but its significance has changed. The courthouse has

21 ▪ John Sloan. *Jefferson Market, Sixth Avenue.*
1917, 1922. Oil on canvas, 32 × 26 in. Pennsylvania Academy of the Fine Arts, Philadelphia, Gilpin Fund Purchase.

become strangely narrow, like a cathedral apse shorn of its transepts and nave, and the el has lost its solidity. Sloan treasures the visual tangle of an aging city.

But aggressive capitalism cannot be kept at bay forever. Sloan's relation to the new metropolis is shown *The City from Greenwich Village* (1922). It is his most elaborate statement on the modern city—one of the few for which he did preparatory studies. Hubert Beck interprets this painting in terms that recall Wanda Corn's comments on the early modern realists as a group. It represents New York, he says, "as an ambivalent juncture of opposites reconciled by the strained formula of older landscape painting rather than by an inherent dialectic of the subject."[44] Opposites are indeed what the painting dramatizes but they are very much part of the inherent dialectic of Sloan's New York.

The City from Greenwich Village explicitly contrasts the Greenwich Village neighborhood with the downtown skyline (Ill. 22). They are arranged on opposite ends of a diagonal that starts with the lights of the driver's cabin of the el train at lower right and leads up through the dark train toward the bright light of the skyscrapers. It does not reach them, however. Sixth Avenue has since been extended southward but in this painting the visual transition from the Village to the downtown skyscrapers is blocked by the band of darkness created by a loft district that was largely deserted at night. The skyscrapers—the shapes of the Singer and Woolworth buildings can be identified—emerge out of the darkness like Oz.

22 ▪ John Sloan. *The City from Greenwich Village.*
1922. Oil on canvas, 26 × 33¾ in. Gift of Helen Farr Sloan, © 1996 Board of Trustees, National Gallery of Art, Washington, D.C.

They could be regarded as an unattainable wonderland but the composition keeps pulling us back to the foreground world of rich shadow and complex lighting effects. Sloan said of the painting that it "makes a record of the beauty of the older city which is giving way to the chopped-out towers of modern New York."[45] It should be regarded as a declaration of love for Sloan's New York and a rejection of the new city that had already arrived.

By the mid-twenties, however, Sloan concluded that that the Skyscraper City had become too insistent to be ignored. It had to be either confronted directly or abandoned altogether. In 1926 he produced the etchings *Subway Stairs* and *Reading in the Subway*. That same year he did an etching entitled *Fashions of the Past* juxtaposing the new flapper dresses with the broad-brimmed hats and full skirts he recalled from his youth. The next year he painted a view into Times Square. Then he turned away from urban subject matter to concentrate on landscape and the female nude.

OBSOLESCENCE AND NOSTALGIA

The contrast between the skyscraper and the el sharpened as the technology of the elevated became more and more archaic and obsolescent. In John Marin's *Downtown, The El* (1921) the tracks could still present an image of speed but to most observers they appeared less as an exemplification of modern dynamism than as a contrast to it. The el appears as a Toonerville Trolley in Howard Norton Cook's woodcut *The Dictator* in contrast to the Equitable Trust Building rising in the background (Ill. 23). It forms a more dynamic double curve in Mark Freeman's lithograph *2nd Ave "El"* (1934), but here too it is contrasted to the towering verticals of the downtown skyscrapers. The movie *King Kong* (1933) offers inadvertent testimony to the differing symbolic roles of el and skyscraper. When the giant ape shakes an el train in the air he is merely brandishing a child's toy; when he climbs to the top of the Empire State Building he is challenging modern civilization.

The elevated tracks over the Bowery defined America's image of urban poverty. The street that had seemed so prosperous in the pages of *Harper's Weekly*, was now, as films like *The Lost Weekend* (1945) told the American public, the place where all alcoholics ended up. When Kirk Douglas staggered and fell in front of the Chatham Square tracks in *Young Man with a Horn* (1950), the skyscrapers in the distance helped us measure the depth of his decline.

Some artists and photographers looked past the poverty and used the els to reveal an unexpected visual order of the city. Stewart Davis, Ralston Crawford, and Francis Criss transformed the pattern of its metal girders into rich abstractions. Berenice Abbott, Todd Webb, and Louis Lozowick portrayed the patterns of light and shadow it threw on the street below. Abbott left a memorable image of an el waiting room with its Victorian woodwork and great pot-bellied stove. In the fifties, when the Third Avenue structure was about to be demolished, Arnold Eagle photographed it as a lovable anachronism in an International Style city, dwelling on its ornament and on the soft light that filtered through the stained glass windows of its waiting rooms.

Not everyone was happy as the els came down. Everett Shinn said that New York streets

23 ▪ Howard Norton Cook.
The Dictator.
N.d. Woodcut on paper, 12 × 18 in.
Culley Collection, Pomona College,
Claremont, California.

had become more monotonous. "I miss the traffic," he told an interviewer. "Now it's all on one level. Automobiles set a specific height, a long monotonous row."[46] John Sloan complained that "automobiles fill the streets."[47] Reginald Marsh lamented: "All the things of the old days were so much better to draw. I hate to go down to Chatham Square where they're tearing down the span; the light and shadow on the characters walking around down there—you can't find anything better to draw."[48] Although the els had become a blight, they remained as picturesque as ever. Symbols of technological modernity when they were first built, they finally became subjects of considerable nostalgia.

CHAPTER THREE

OPENING DAY – AND THE FOLLOWING YEAR

F New York's first subway is regarded as a cultural text, what meanings did contemporaries read in it? It was not, of course, intended to be read at all. It was not like the Statue of Liberty, which had no purpose except communication. It was not even comparable to the Brooklyn Bridge, which served a utilitarian purpose but which was, as Alan Trachtenberg showed in a classic study, embedded from the moment of its conception in a rich network of beliefs about the beneficent power of technology and the westward direction of historical destiny that had been articulated by figures as culturally central as the philosopher Hegel and the poet Walt Whitman.[1] No such visionaries elaborated the significance of the subway, yet few works of engineering have ever revealed so much about the city.

The subway was a statement of resounding optimism. In 1888 Mayor Abram S. Hewitt had called on New Yorkers to construct a transportation system that would allow it to achieve "its imperial destiny as the greatest city of the world."[2] The 1898 consolidation of many scattered communities into the five boroughs of Greater New York demanded an ambitious extension of the transportation system.

On March 24, 1900, Joseph Pulitzer's *New York World* sponsored the official ground-breaking in City Hall Park, with a giant fireworks display and a twenty-one-gun salute. At each volley, the paper reported, "the *World*'s watchword, 'To Harlem in Fifteen Minutes,' ran from lip to lip and swelled into a splendid chorus."[3] The subway was the city's preeminent symbol of unity and hope.

Like any symbol, however, it contained uncertainties and tensions. Urban theorists proclaimed that the subway resolved a contradiction in urban form—it reconciled the economic need for concentration and the human need for dispersal. But while New Yorkers agreed that the subway would make possible the future city, they did not agree on the kind of city they expected to create. While some used the subway to support a dignified vision of the City Beautiful, others employed it to make possible the Skyscraper City of triumphant commerce.

Similar tensions appear in newspaper accounts during construction. To the business-oriented *New York Times* the subway was the creation of far-seeing financier August Belmont and the Rapid Transit Commission's chief engineer William Barclay Parsons. To the popular press, it was built by the honest workman and chief contractor John B. McDonald. This was more than a difference in emphasis. It revealed a bitter class antagonism that was largely submerged in the atmosphere of civic unity but that constantly threatened to break forth.

If the story of the Interborough is told up to its opening on October 27, 1904, it dramatizes accomplishment achieved against heroic odds. If it is extended until the end of the system's first full year of operation, it becomes a tale of unity lost amid competing urban visions, angry class conflict, and mutual recrimination. By the end of 1905 the subway was fast coming to represent not unity and hope but civic discord and social stalemate.

CITY BEAUTIFUL OR SKYSCRAPER CITY?

The 1898 Consolidation focused the public's attention not on what New York was but on what it would become. Imagining the stupendous city of forty, sixty, or a hundred years hence became both an intellectual discipline and a popular delight.

Those who expected the subway to shape and stabilize the spaces of the new city could rely on the most advanced urban theorists. Charles Cooley's classic article "The Theory of Transportation," which occupied an entire issue of the *Publications of the American Economic Association* (1894), and Adna Ferrin Weber's *The Growth of Cities in the Nineteenth Century* (1899) both argued that only low-cost public transportation could resolve the contradictory forces of the modern city.

Cooley saw that industry tended to concentrate itself within limited areas, producing a density that was good for industry but appalling for people who were compelled to live near the factories in which they worked. Inexpensive rapid transit would solve this dilemma by making it possible to have both concentration of industry and dispersal of homes. Adna Weber sums up his own book by quoting Cooley's article: "There is, then, a permanent conflict between the needs of industry and the needs of humanity. Industry says men must aggregate. Humanity says they must not, or if they must, let it be only during working hours and let the necessity not extend to their wives and children. *It is the office of the city railways to reconcile these conflicting requirements.*"[4]

New York seemed to be an extreme example of the city that Cooley and Weber described. Many of its sections were extraordinarily congested while others were ripe for development. In 1905 Manhattan had 122 blocks containing over 750 people per acre and thirty blocks containing over 1,000 per acre.[5] Yet Manhattan north of 134th Street had only 23.4 persons per acre, the central Bronx had only 15.2, and the northern portion of the Bronx had 2.4. Queens had a density of 2.3 per acre.[6] It was easy to conclude that the subway was the solution to the problem of the tenement.

But though all agreed that the subway was the key to the geographical distribution of the city's population, New Yorkers still faced sharply different visions of their future city. The culturally ambitious members of the city's upper and professional classes longed for the City Beautiful. The mass public preferred Skyscraper City.

The City Beautiful movement aimed at the transformation of American cities. Inspired by the Columbian Exposition of 1893, it projected an urban vision derived from ancient Rome and the Italian Renaissance. In contrast to the haphazard streets and mixed architectural styles of the late nineteenth century, the new urban center would be a place of classical order and civic dignity.

The most powerful advocate for the City Beautiful in New York City was the Municipal Art Society. Founded in 1893 as a direct response to the Columbian Exposition, the Society united artists, reformers, civic leaders, and cultivated businessmen in the rebuilding of New York. Its leaders were tortured by the conviction that, as Edwin Blashfield told the group's first public meeting, New York, "more enterprising than any other city," was nevertheless "far behind not only Paris and London, but even tiny provincial towns of France, Italy, Germany, in the possession of an art which should dignify and illustrate the history of her past and present."[7] A contemporary New York magazine went even further when it declared that "we must rival Washington in distances, Paris in beauty, London in all but smoke and fog, and ancient Rome in pre-eminence." Looking at civic improvements elsewhere, it posed the challenge to New Yorkers in the starkest terms: "We cannot afford to be told that the finest street in America is in Cleveland."[8]

The common textbook criticism of the City Beautiful movement is that it dealt only in cosmetic aspects of the urban scene. Peter Hall, for example, in *Cities of Tomorrow*, asserts that it wanted to express pomp, power, and prestige but was innocent of—even hostile to—all wider social purpose.[9] In New York City, at least, this criticism is absurd. Gregory F. Gilmartin shows how the Municipal Art Society rapidly evolved from a charitable group raising private funds for public murals into an advocacy group urging comprehensive city planning. By the late nineties it was clear that any unified approach to the city's problems required detailed attention to its transportation system.

The leadership of the Municipal Art Society included both artists and laymen. The most influential non-artists were upper-middle-class reformers with experience in anti-Tammany politics. The society's president, John DeWitt Warner, was a former Democratic congressman. Its leading spokesmen on transportation were Calvin Tomkins, Milo Maltbie, and John Martin. Tomkins was chairman of the Municipal Art Society's City Plan Committee from 1902 to 1905 and then served as its president. He later became president of the Reform Club and the city's Commissioner of Docks. Maltbie was a strong advocate of public regulation of utilities; as a member of the New York Public Utilities Commission he would be a sharp critic of private transit companies and an advocate of municipal operation. John Martin's practical interests are expressed in the title of his 1909 book on *Rapid Transit: Its Effects on Rents and Living Conditions and How To Get It.*

These three men issued a series of bulletins bringing the principles of the City Beautiful movement to bear on concrete issues of transit planning. They pointed out that a subway would permit the city to remove the ugly elevateds—rather than, as some engineers were now suggesting, equip them with a second layer for additional tracks. They supported a one-fare system that would allow the poor to live far from their congested workplaces. They proposed a crosstown subway near City Hall that would have relieved the Brooklyn Bridge crush by distributing travelers from Brooklyn along the full range of Manhattan's transit lines while permitting the development of a dignified civic center on the ground above. They were sympathetic to municipal ownership and operation of subways. Above all, they urged that the city's new subway be treated as a major work of civic art designed by an outstanding architect and built of the finest materials.

The leaders of the Municipal Art Society expected the subway to provide the underground foundation for the City Beautiful. Although they knew there would be tall buildings in lower Manhattan, they projected New York as a predominantly horizontal city, with all its diverse buildings unified by a neo-classical architectural style and a single cornice line. They were not necessarily hostile to the skyscraper but they did not want to see their city dominated by huge construction projects built on speculation for private profit. They wanted New York, like Washington, D.C., to express its higher purposes through carefully situated, dramatically conspicuous courthouses, libraries, museums, and memorial statues. This vision expressed the aspirations of an upper and upper-middle class eager to display not only its confidence but also, more important, its cultural legitimacy.

If the City Beautiful was a vision of New York's educated elites, expressing their longing for stable traditions and enduring values, the Skyscraper City expressed the man in the street's boomtown optimism. If the City Beautiful was horizontal and dignified, the Skyscraper City was a breathtakingly vertical city-of-the-future.

The city's most ambitious real-estate developers, its less prestigious architects, and its ordinary citizens had been much quicker that its educated elites to realize that the future New York would be dominated by the skyscraper. In 1892 an article in the *Real Estate Record and Builders' Guide*, foreseeing that New York would be symbolized not by its cathedral but by its office towers, proclaimed that "the age has become a commercial one, in which commercial structures [are] designed in a commercial manner for commercial uses."[10] While many observers were timid, accepting sixteen stories but assuring themselves that they would never see thirty, the popular imagination eagerly seized on the possibilities of growth and delighted in a visionary metropolis dominated by towers rising more than a hundred stories into the sky.

Rem Koolhaas observes that the early cartoon skyscrapers that appeared in popular magazines at a time when architectural magazines were still devoted to the Beaux Arts "suggests that early in the century 'the people' intuit the promise of the Skyscraper more profoundly than Manhattan's architects, that there exists a subterranean collective dialogue about the new form from which the official architect is excluded."[11] During the eighteen-nineties such drawings began to appear in the humor and satirical magazines *Puck*, *Judge*, and *Life*. On December 31, 1900, the *World* greeted the new century with two drawings of the Manhattan of 1999 (Ills. 24 & 25). They portray a city of tightly packed skyscrapers, some so

KEY TO TOPOGRAPHICAL
MAP OF NEW YORK IN 1999.

1—Tunnel from Hackensack to Jamaica.
2—Suspension bridges across the Hudson to Peekskill—city limit.
3—Bridge across Long Island Sound.
4—Public parks and recreation piers.
5—Eight new bridges across Newark Bay to Bayonne.
6—Cantilever bridge from New York City to Staten Island.
7—Two suspension bridges across the Narrows.
8—Bridges and tunnels across East River and Blackwell's Island.
9—Canal connecting Newark Bay and New York Bay.
10—Canal connecting Long Island Sound and Jamaica Bay.
11—Bridges across the Kill von Kull. Two tunnels between Staten Island and Brooklyn.
12—Electric railroad across Jamaica Bay.

24 ▪ New York as It Will Be in 1999.

New York World, December 31, 1900. Courtesy: Library of Congress.

25 ▪ The Madison Square of a Century Hence—1999.

New York World, December 31, 1900. Courtesy: Library of Congress.

huge as to cover several city blocks at the base. Moses King's *Handbook* in 1905 published a vision of the future city in which every building in sight had reached the level of the Singer Building.

Clearly the Skyscraper City would demand visionary transportation systems. If, as one expert explained in *The Electrical Review*, "the fundamental cause [of overcrowding] is the combination of the twelve-story city with the one story street," then hundred-story cities would require systems of unheard-of complexity.[12] The *World*'s city-of-the-future is served from without by an elaborate system of docks, railroad tunnels, subways, trolleys, and winged flying machines. Ignatius Donnolly's dystopian novel *Caesar's Columns* (1898) imagined the section of Manhattan now known as SoHo given over to a huge landing field for dirigibles. Moses King's vision featured flying machines, bridges connecting buildings at the fortieth floor, multistory elevateds, and sunken highways.

In spite of all the annoyance caused by its construction, the subway inspired rapturous enthusiasm for the technological wonderland that was being created beneath the city's feet. In 1902 the *World* conceded that parts of Manhattan were "lava-strewn with the eruption of Rapid Transit from its sinuous crater," but insisted that "the dust-brown rubbish that hides the city" was bearable because "already one can see here and there a bit of the glory sticking through."[13]

An article that appeared seven months before the first subway train shows how glorious the transit future appeared in 1904. A future New Yorker, the *World* marveled, would be able to live without ever going outdoors. He would awaken in the recently completed Ansonia Hotel on upper Broadway and ride down in the elevator to the underpass that would connect with the subway that would take him to the elevator that would bring him to his office. During the day he would move about solely by elevator and subway, stopping at an underground newspaper stand, buying flowers from an underground florist, sipping coffee in an underground cafe. He would return to his apartment in the evening without ever having felt the direct rays of the sun.[14]

As opening day approached, few wanted to make trouble for the men who were building the subway. The fact that the subway served two irreconcilable visions of the city was, for a time, overlooked.

THE FINANCIER AS CIVIC SAVIOR

The four men most responsible for New York's first subway were financier August Belmont Jr., builder John B. McDonald, engineer William Barclay Parsons, and architect C. Grant LaFarge. The press was fascinated by the first two. By examining the different ways in which different newspapers treated them, we can trace the class antagonisms which were constantly present in New York life but largely suppressed in the city-wide yearning for a subway. Journalists paid less attention to Parsons and scarcely any to LaFarge. Nevertheless, the engineer and the architect did more than anyone else to shape the actual experience of New York rapid transit.

August Belmont Jr. financed the subway after all other contenders failed—but he almost did something more remarkable. He very nearly raised it above the taint of scandal. That he failed was owing first to his rivalry and, later, to his partnership with a man named Thomas Fortune Ryan.

By the end of the nineteenth century the public had learned to associate transit companies with political corruption, watered stock, and poor management. It was widely believed—and there is evidence to show—that the men who ran New York's horsecars and trolleys gained their 999-year franchises by bribing members of the City Council. They earned huge profits by selling watered stock to investors and by cramming their cars full of suffering fare payers.

Belmont sought to finance the subway without recourse to bribes and without financial shenanigans. He had inherited wealth, social position, and an interest in rapid transit from his father. The first August Belmont had made his fortune as the New York representative of the Rothschild interests. He exchanged his family's inherited Judaism for socially respectable Episcopalianism and sent his boy to Philips Andover and Harvard.

Charming and arrogant, August Belmont Jr. excelled at polo, yachting, and motoring. He served as president of the Jockey Club and helped found both Jerome Park Race Course and Belmont Park. He could have devoted all his energies to racing and high society but a fierce personal pride drove him to excel in finance. He knew that many on Wall Street regarded him as a privileged lightweight and he set out to prove them wrong.

By seeking to finance a subway system, Belmont put himself in competition with the men who controlled the city's elevateds, horsecars, and electric trolleys. Both George Gould of the Manhattan Elevated and Thomas Fortune Ryan and William Whitney of the Metropolitan Street Railway Company tried to keep Belmont from financing the subway. It was Ryan and Whitney who proved most dangerous.

These were men who understood the intricacies of political influence and financial manipulation. William Whitney was a lawyer with good political connections who served in Washington as secretary of the Navy. Thomas Fortune Ryan was a stockbroker from Virginia. The bust that Rodin later did of him, now in the Metropolitan Museum of Art, shows a thin, aristocratic face which gives away nothing of its purposes. Whitney described him as "the most adroit, suave, and noiseless man he had ever known." [15]

Ryan and Whitney established themselves in New York transit in 1884 when they offered thirteen members of the city council a bribe of $750,000 for the street railway franchise in Broadway below 8th Street. When the bribe was rejected, they really showed their mettle. They launched first a whispering campaign, then a press outcry, and finally a legislative anticorruption investigation against their successful rival for the Broadway franchise. When it ended their rival was in disgrace and their cable cars ran on Broadway.

Ryan then began buying up individual transit companies and absorbing them into the Metropolitan Street Railway Company. This is widely regarded by historians as the nation's first holding company. Ryan himself said it was really "a great big tin box." [16] His method of business was to acquire an individual street railway and issue watered stock on it—that is, stock secured by nothing except the promise to pay. No matter how crowded or poorly maintained the cars were, the income from the company was never enough to meet its obligations. The next step was to acquire a new transit company and sell a new round of watered stock which would provide enough money to meet current obligations and provide rich profits from those who controlled the holding company. This worked surprisingly well for some years but it meant that the Metropolitan Street Railway was always in precarious financial condition.

Neither Ryan nor Whitney wanted competition from the new subway. Their maneuvers against Belmont were both powerful and subtle. Reconstructing them has involved historians in a certain amount of speculation but there is agreement on crucial points.

It is certain that the competitive bidding to construct and operate the subway was won by John B. McDonald. It is possible that Belmont was behind McDonald from the beginning. McDonald was a builder. He did not want to operate the new road, as the contract allowed him to do. "Who will it be turned over to?" McDonald said in reply to a reporter from the *Evening Post*. "How do I know? Somebody that knows more about running street-railroads than I do."[17] Belmont probably would have helped with the financing for construction, then stepped forward when it came time to form an operating company.

But the Ryan-Whitney group forced him to declare himself sooner than he had planned. Like any construction contractor, McDonald had to buy surety bonds guaranteeing that the city would be reimbursed if he proved unable to complete his work. Ryan and Whitney used their influence to make this prohibitively expensive.

Belmont moved decisively. Using his family's fortune and his friendships with the city's leading railroad and real estate tycoons, he quickly organized the Rapid Transit Subway Construction Company with a capitalization of $6,000,000 that was intended solely to buy the necessary bond. This removed the obstacle posed by the Ryan-Whitney group and changed McDonald from an independent contractor to a salaried employee. Belmont then organized the Interborough Rapid Transit Company, which quickly bought out all the stock in the construction company.

But this created a legal tangle which enabled Ryan and Whitney to make new trouble for Belmont. He had assumed that his new company could simply take over the operating lease from McDonald. But the Rapid Transit Act provided that the subway contract could only be transferred in its entirety—constructing and operating halves together—and if Belmont's new firm assumed the construction contract, it could no longer act as agent for the surety bonds. It would be in the position of insuring itself. If Belmont could not take over the operating contract he could not run trains over his tracks.

This awkward situation could have been easily resolved by the legislature. A bill was introduced and quickly passed the Assembly. It came to a dead stop in the Senate, almost certainly because of Ryan and Whitney's influence.

Belmont's lawyers discovered that he could operate a subway if he was able to show that his corporation possessed a line already chartered for operation in the city. He quickly bought two defunct street railways in the Bronx—the City Island and Pelham Park lines. He then paid a call on Whitney, told him of his coup, and left with a promise that the legislature would proceed with modifications to the Rapid Transit Act.[18] Belmont now had secure control of a fifty-year lease. The subway was nominally owned by the city but until the fifty years elapsed the operating company was in charge.

This incident had a very happy ending for Belmont. Horace M. Fisher, secretary of the Interborough, later testified before an investigating committee that the company had paid August Belmont $1,500,000 for the Pelham Park and City Island railroad property. $350,000 of this was paid for the railroads themselves. The remaining $1,150,000 was payment to Belmont himself for supplying the "necessary strength" to finance the new subway.[19]

Belmont dealt with other rivals just as decisively. In 1902 he bought out George Gould's 999-year lease for the Manhattan Elevated Railway Company. He must have wanted the company very badly, for he agreed to pay an annual rental of 7 percent on its stock—"more," the *New York Times* observed, "than has ever been paid to stockholders under its present management."[20]

To the business community Belmont's control of the subway was a sign that the bad old days of transit manipulation were over. He was, said the *Commercial Advertiser*, "a very different person, a far more sagacious and public-spirited manager, than either Mr. [Russell]

Sage or Mr. [George] Gould."[21] But Ryan and Whitney had forced Belmont into a position that would ultimately make him a villain to the Pulitzer and Hearst newspapers. The popular press stubbornly insisted that honest John McDonald was the real builder of the subway and that the aristocrat August Belmont was only a financial usurper.

Belmont himself thought otherwise. The subway was one of the proudest achievements of his life. In his attitude toward the Interborough, he combined the decisiveness of an experienced financier with the personal indulgence of a Renaissance prince. He had a special car, the Mineola, fitted out so that he could carry guests from a private track beneath the Hotel Belmont, out onto the subway lines, south to the Long Island Railroad Terminal in Brooklyn, and then to Belmont Park.

Belmont treated the Interborough as an extension of himself. Taking a risk that other financiers had run from, he had shown that subways were profitable. He built a $35,000,000 public work without a hint of scandal. His tombstone at Newport, Rhode Island, proudly identifies him as the man "Under Whose Leadership The Inter-Borough Subway in New York City Was Built."

THE PEOPLE'S BUILDER

If August Belmont was a hero for the business elite, John McDonald was the favorite of the Pulitzer and Hearst newspapers. The son of an Irish laborer who had risen through Tammany ranks to become an alderman, McDonald broke into contracting by building the elevated structure for the New York Central tracks above 96th Street. His greatest achievement had been constructing the Baltimore Belt Railroad which tunneled for 8,350 feet of its seven-mile length under Baltimore's busy Howard Street. Clearly the subway was a challenge that he could meet. "Why," he told the *World*, "there's nothing to this job—but hard work. I tell you it is simply a case of cellar digging on a great scale. Just take all the cellars in this city and string 'em together."[22]

The popular press made McDonald a symbol of city building. His appearance, lovingly detailed in article and interview, took on complex semiotic significance. "To the student of physiognomy," wrote the *Morning Journal* in 1900, "McDonald is [an] interesting study." "Physical strength is shown in every inch of his short, stocky body," the paper reported, "while his face is the picture of resolute strength and splendid energy."[23] "Bright-eyed, rapid in motion as a squirrel, jesting perpetually with stern, business-like lips, betraying force and snap in every move and word, Mr. McDonald once seen is a man to be remembered," agreed the *World*.[24] "There is no sign of the dreamer about him," wrote James Creelman in the *American* (as the *Morning Journal* had been renamed): "His whole personality— the shrewd Celtic face and head, the short stocky muscular figure—all express the man who began life as a rough laborer and rose by intense labor to command thousands of men and millions of dollars, the actual doer of other men's thoughts."[25]

The new visual journalism practiced by the *World* ensured that McDonald's face and body, both expressing his energy and sturdy determination, were instantly recognizable. On January 17, 1900, Pulitzer's editors used a head-and-shoulders sketch under the headline pro-

CONTRACTOR M'DONALD TALKS OF HIS PLANS.

26 ▪ Contractor M'Donald Talks Of His Plans.
New York World, January 18, 1900. Courtesy: Library of Congress.

claiming that he had won the contract. The next day they used a sketch of the contractor in six different but all equally forceful body positions (Ill. 26) as he outlined his plans. Two days after that he appeared as the large, central portrait surrounded by the smaller heads of his presumed backers. When the contract was signed the *World* again used McDonald's head, looking more than ever like a cannonball, as its large central portrait with the minor actors (including August Belmont) arrayed in much smaller portraits around him. The day after construction began on March 24 the *World* used a sketch of McDonald's head again. Flanking him, but only half the size, were August Belmont and William Barclay Parsons.

This glorification of McDonald allowed the popular press to practice a kind of Freudian denial. The editors of the *World* certainly knew that the forces building the subway included high finance. Not far beneath the surface of every portrait of McDonald, however, was an implied opposition between the rough-hewn man of the people and the effete world of financial aristocrats. So long as McDonald was The Man Who Built the Subways, city-building could be presented as a democratic activity.

It was harder to ignore McDonald's connections with Tammany Hall. It was well known that he was a warm friend of Boss Richard Croker. "It is calculated at first thought to give one a shock," said the *Evening Post*, "when he contemplates the idea of a Tammany man getting hold of such an enterprise."[26] The issue was joined at the start of construction when the papers reported a squabble in the Ninth District where the Tammany candidate, challenging a rebel district leader, passed out a circular pointing out that McDonald was a Tammany contractor, that each of the thirty-five district leaders in Manhattan was entitled to three hundred appointments for subway work, and that the Ninth District was unlikely to get its share so long as a rebel held office. Since the loyalist who issued the leaflet was secretary to Boss Croker, he surely knew what he was talking about.

But the *World*, normally a fierce opponent of Tammany, decided to finesse the issue. It headlined McDonald's denial of Tammany control "M'Donald Repulses Croker's Secretary" and gave both a special box and special emphasis on the front page to McDonald's insistence that "I shall run my own business in my own way, and THERE WILL BE NO POLITICS IN THE CONSTRUCTION OF THE RAPID-TRANSIT TUNNEL."[27] Asked directly about subway patronage, the *World* quoted McDonald as replying: "I have no arrangement—positively none—

with Tammany Hall. I hope that I have the friendship of Tammany Hall—it's a good thing to have, hey?"[28] Apparently the twinkle in the eye that accompanied this statement satisfied the reporter.

McDonald emerged in the popular press as a culture hero of the urban miracle, at once powerful and benevolent. Kate Carew, the *World*'s favorite artist/interviewer, pictured "the Titan in tunnels" looking out the twenty-sixth-floor window of a Park Row skyscraper a few days before the subway's official opening, stretching his hand toward "the clustered buildings humming with life and the canyons between in the depths of which trickled streams of curiously foreshortened midgets":

> "These masses"—the Man That Built the Subway is speaking—"not every one realizes the greatness of them, they are so patient. Just consider that the population of this building alone during business hours is 8,000, and that 10,000 pass in and out the doors every day. The bigness of this life of New York is something frightful, appalling—and the hurry of it, and the strain of it.
>
> "The Subway is for these. It will give them more time, more ease. It will carry them to better and cheaper and healthier homes. It will change their very lives."[29]

On October 27, 1904, the day the subway opened, the *World* front page featured a photograph of McDonald flanked by slightly smaller photographs of William Barclay Parsons and manager Frank Hedley. Belmont was routinely slighted in the *World*'s coverage of the subway.

Did this cause jealousies? Reporters were astonished to discover that when the list of speakers for the opening ceremonies was announced, McDonald had been left off. "Belmont ignores M'Donald!" screamed the *American*. "When the dirt is off your shovel," the paper quoted McDonald as saying bitterly, "Wall Street doesn't give a penny for you."

The incident was smoothed over and Belmont made light of it. In his view the importance of McDonald had been much overblown. "The real author of the underground system, the man from whose brain and extensive supervision resulted what is now seen as the finished subway of this city, is forgotten." He insisted that chief engineer William Barclay Parsons was "the real man."[30] To the financier it was brain, not brawn, that ultimately built cities.

LAYING OUT THE STATIONS, DECORATING THE WALLS

However vital financer Belmont and builder McDonald were to the construction of the subway, it was chief engineer Parsons and the architect C. Grant LaFarge who determined what the traveler would actually see and experience. They both understood that for all the optimism that the idea of a completed subway conveyed, the finished project would meet with two difficulties. First, it would be very crowded. Second, the very idea of underground travel would convey at least a suggestion of Subway Hell.

Parsons explained how he would deal with each of these problems in a May 1900 *Scribner's* article on "Rapid Transit in New York." New York, he says, has "a volume of urban travel unparalled as to quantity in any city of the world" and one that is "increasing at an astonishing ratio." [31] At the same time, he conceded, the public will associate underground journeys with veritable approaches to the lower regions. Much of his design addressed one or both of these two problems.

Parsons cited New York's crowds, for example, to justify his decision to keep the tracks close to the surface of the street. He insisted that London's system of deep tubes would be impossible in New York because the necessary system of elevators could never have coped with the congestion of a New York rush hour. He therefore kept his stairways about the same length as those in an ordinary dwelling.

He similarly justified the express-local system by stressing the need to carry large numbers over great distances quickly. "What our musical friends would call the 'motif' of the design," said Parsons, "is the ability to give high speed with the maximum of carrying capacity per track." [32] The unit for measuring distance, he reminded his readers, is the minute and not the yard. Accordingly he laid down a four-track system between Brooklyn Bridge and 96th Street so that he could run both express and local trains in New York's most populated area. Even that proved inadequate. Soon after Parsons's subway opened, New Yorkers realized that it had been a mistake not to build express tracks south of City Hall Park and above 96th Street.

Parsons was equally concerned with the aesthetics of the subway. He was a member of the Municipal Art Society and welcomed its insistence that the subway should be a great work of civic art. During a trip to examine the rapid transit systems of Europe he had paid particular attention to the relative attractiveness of the stations.

The illustrations by Jules Guerin for Parsons's *Scribner's* article were prepared before his architect was hired and therefore show Parsons's intentions for the subway rather than the actual design. They portray spacious platforms where civilized New Yorkers promenade in stiff collars and long skirts. One cross-section (Ill. 27) carefully positions the subway in relation to the city's most obvious monument to culture—the Ruskinian National Academy of Design on 23rd Street.

C. Grant LaFarge, son of the painter John LaFarge, was well equipped to create this kind of environment. Trained in the ideals of the American Renaissance, he never for a moment considered adopting the art nouveau style that Hector Guimard employed for the Paris Métro or Otto Wagner for the Vienna Underground. His design reflects the longing of New York's cultural elite for classical dignity. The *Real Estate Record and Builders' Guide*, predicting that its uplifting effect on popular taste would be enormous, declared that "New York

27 ▪ Jules Guerin. *Station at Twenty-Third Street and Fourth Avenue.*
Scribner's Magazine, 1900. Courtesy: Library of Congress.

SOUVENIR POST CARD CO., NEW YORK.

6078—City Hall Loop, Rapid Transit Tunnel

28 ▪ City Hall Loop—Postcard View.
Author's collection.

can congratulate itself on one specimen of 'Civic Art,' in which a very useful structure has been decorated with the utmost propriety."[33]

Unfortunately, LaFarge's masterpiece, the City Hall station (Ill. 28), is closed—though the New York Transit Museum offers tours and there are plans to reopen it. It was in the city's most prominent location and LaFarge made it the Interborough's jewel with skylights of leaded glass and Romanesque vaults of Guastavino tile—an underground, lower Manhattan echo of the Romanesque cathedral that LaFarge planned for Morningside Heights. Unfortunately when longer cars were introduced, dangerous gaps loomed between their doors and the curving platforms. Though still used as a turnaround for local trains, the City Hall station has been closed to the public since 1945.

The best places to recapture the sensations of 1904 are at the restored Astor Place local stop and at the aboveground control house at 72nd Street and Broadway.

The Astor Place station was located at one of the city's busiest intersections. Cooper Union, in whose auditorium so many meetings demanding rapid transit had been held, is just to the south. Clinton Hall, with its popular lecture auditorium, was to the west and Wanamaker's department store bordered the station. (The closed entrance to the vanished Clinton Hall is visible near the downtown ticket booth; the boarded-up show windows for Wanamaker are along the downtown platform.)

The entrance is proclaimed above ground by a handsome cast-iron and glass kiosk which covers the stairway that leads down to the uptown tracks. These kiosks were Parsons's idea, based on the station entrances to the Budapest subway (which were based, in turn, on the local *kushks* or summer houses) and in part on the iron-and-glass ventilating kiosks he had seen in Paris.

Although the kiosks became a symbol of the subway, they also attracted complaints. They obstructed sidewalks and made it difficult to get a clear view of traffic. The first kiosk was removed a year after the subway opened. Large numbers went in the late thirties and again in the fifties. The last was demolished in 1967. The Astor Place kiosk is actually a re-creation by architect Rolf Ohlhausen, who had been a student at nearby Cooper Union and remembered the original structure with affection.

The restored station below is close to what the New Yorker of 1904 would have seen when he or she walked down the stairs. First there was an underground waiting room containing the ticket booth and the lavatories. Beyond this was the platform proper. In 1904 it was guarded by an agent who manned the "ticket chopper." The original platform can be seen by following the round cast-iron pillars. The columns encased in brick show where the platform was extended at a later date.

LaFarge divided his long expanses of wall both horizontally and vertically by rich ornament. His preferred materials were architectural terra-cotta and faience, a more expensive terra-cotta that has received a special glaze and two firings instead of one.

Horizontally, the wall is divided into three parts. It begins with two and a half feet of Roman brick wainscotting. That is surmounted by the body of the wall, a large area of shiny 3″ by 6″ white tiles. White was chosen to provide maximum illumination underground; the effect was so striking that the city's oculists worried about the effect of glare on travelers' eyes. The wall is topped with a green cornice containing a low-relief design of scrolls and cornucopias.

Vertically the wall is divided into fifteen-foot sections by pilasters of Roman brick. Within each section is a faience tile containing the name of the station. Its blue, green, and ivory colors repeat those of the cornice. At the top of each pilaster is a famous Astor Place beaver. Wherever local associations with a station were strong, LaFarge tried to celebrate the fact with appropriate decoration. The beavers remind us that John Jacob Astor made his first fortune in the fur trade.

LaFarge's Flemish Renaissance control house at 72nd Street was designed to harmonize with the aesthetic taste of turn-of-the-century New York. When the route of the first subway was announced, the price of land below 96th Street rose so dramatically that rows of dignified townhouses quickly gave way to residential hotels and apartment houses, particularly on Broadway itself. The Marie Antoinette (1895) at 66th Street was expanded in 1903. The lavishly ornate Dorilton at 75th Street dates from 1902. The Hotel Belleclaire was completed between 77th and 78th in 1903 and the Ansonia between 73rd and 74th was completed in 1904; it was quickly followed by the Spencer Arms, the Van Dyck, and the Severn, the Astor, and the Apthorp. The *Real Estate Record and Builder's Guide* reported that half the houses on Broadway were replaced by apartment buildings between 1907 and 1912.[34]

LaFarge's ornate structure is so much loved and so often sketched today that it is startling to learn that in 1904 the West Side Association claimed to have a petition of ten thousand signatures demanding that it be rebuilt. Local civic leaders complained that one corner of the building blocked the vista of 72nd Street and, astonishingly, wanted the structure redesigned "with features sufficiently ornamental to harmonize it with the general character of one of the finest residential neighborhoods of New York."[35]

Though engineer Parsons and architect LaFarge were designing for the twentieth century, their work reflects the division between engineering and architecture that characterized so many nineteenth-century public monuments. The split manifests itself in two ways—in attitudes toward materials and in the division of labor between engineer and architect.

In the late Victorian period engineers were innovative about structure but often naive about aesthetics. Architects, by contrast, were devoted to beauty but, because they were trained on historicist principles, often quite conservative about structure. Parsons was extremely proud that he had applied the principles of steel framing to underground construction. LaFarge, by contrast, believed that steel and concrete were dangerous, untried materials. He thought it right to design for new purposes by using terra-cotta and faience according to traditional principles.

Parsons laid out the spaces of his subway stations before he called in an architect to add beauty to them. He did not worry that the low ceilings gave a cramped impression or that the frequent columns between the tracks blocked the view. Both were convenient solutions to engineering problems. As he conceived it, the essential task of the architect was to add beauty to the walls. LaFarge never challenged this division of labor.

Both the faults and virtues of this approach can be seen at the Astor Place station. An observer looking at the walls will be impressed by the craftsmanship and sensitivity that went into their creation. If the same observer turns and looks toward the tracks, he or she will confront an ugly, prison-like grid of steel. Few New Yorkers who have visited the Montreal or Washington, D.C., subways fail to be impressed by the difference between a system where architect and engineer cooperate in shaping space and one where the engineer creates the space and then calls in the architect to decorate the walls. As modern as it clearly was, the first New York subway reflects its nineteenth-century heritage.

A CITY REJOICING

New Yorkers had been eager to see their new toy for weeks. Many had secured "Belmont passes" for a tour of the empty stations.

The opening day ceremonies took place on the steps of City Hall in front of the kiosk leading to the City Hall station. Opening speeches were scheduled to end at precisely 2:00 P.M., at which time each man, woman, and child in town was asked to blow a whistle, fire a salute, ring church bells or in some way make a noise that would usher in the new age of rapid transit. The *World* let the city know precisely when the moment had arrived. It hired tug boats, each flying the *World* flag, to alert incoming ocean liners to the celebration. It stationed a man at City Hall to flash a signal to the roof of the Pulitzer Building where a flag would be lowered as fifteen aerial guns were fired. The enthusiastic speakers talked too long and their words were drowned out when the bands and fireworks started strictly on time. Undaunted, the Mayor and a crowd of dignitaries stepped into the kiosk for the first official ride as Kodaks snapped and vitascope machines whirred.

At seven o'clock the system was thrown open to the public; 150,000 people rode that evening, producing jams worthy of an election night. Enthusiastic journalists recorded the first man to give up his seat to a woman, the first victim of a pickpocket, the first person to recover an object from the lost and found. A ticket agent at Times Square refused an offer of twenty-five dollars for ticket number 1, paying his own nickel instead and keeping the memento for himself.

The subway's hold over the public can by judged by its frequent appearance on neighborhood movie screens. While it was still under construction the American Mutoscope and Biograph Company had produced *Excavation for the Subway* (1903). The camera was placed in a single, elevated position to show cranes, horse-drawn vehicles, and a view of the tunnel at the Union Square construction site.

The next year the Thomas A. Edison Company produced a more sophisticated *City Hall to Harlem in 15 Seconds via the Subway Route*. Filmed by Edwin S. Porter (who directed *The Great Train Robbery* the same year), this utilized four different camera positions—the first showing a man approaching a subway kiosk, the second portraying him descending to the platform, and the third revealing him igniting an explosive which propels him to Harlem in fifteen seconds so that in the final shot he can crash through a roof and land on a woman.

The Edison company made a film dramatizing the October 27th opening ceremonies. Three more films appeared during the Interborough's first months of operation. In February 1905 Biograph cameraman F. S. Armitage made *Across the Subway Viaduct* by mounting his camera on the rear of a subway train and photographing the view as it proceeded over the Harlem Valley. On May 21st cameraman G. W. "Billy" Bitzer (soon to become D. W. Griffith's close collaborator) used a car equipped with special lights to film passengers changing from local to express trains.[36] This was released to theaters in combination with another short film, also photographed by Bitzer, titled *A Rube in the Subway*, which showed a country bumpkin having his pocket picked. Bitzer also filmed *2 A.M. in the Subway* in June 1905, showing a lady and gentlemen behaving scandalously (she raises her voluminous skirt above her knees so that he can tie her shoelace) and being ejected from the train by a guard.

THE BEGINNINGS OF DISILLUSION

On opening day the new subway was a vivid symbol of the city's ability to solve its problems and open up a glorious future of economic power and cultural stability. By the end of its first year it had not yet become what it was to be in the twenties—the city's most vivid symbol of stalemate—but the downward evolution was under way.

Passengers on the second day of operation noticed that holes had been pounded in LaFarge's tile walls so that advertising posters could be put up. Contract One had specified that nothing could interfere with the legibility of the stations' signs, and LaFarge, reasoning that no rider distracted by gaudy advertising would see the plaques bearing station names, had thought that this prohibited advertising. Belmont, reading the law more carefully, took the city by surprise and covered the walls with placards.

Behind the resulting furor over advertising lay a vital cultural principle. It was essential to the City Beautiful that vulgar commercialism be restrained. The Municipal Art Society wanted a pedestrian's eyes to rest on Beaux Arts facades, uplifting decorative schemes, and well-designed street fixtures, not on over-sized tubes of shaving cream. It thought that Contract One forbade such intrusions.

After the fight against Belmont's signs erupted, the society insisted that it was not opposed to advertising in all circumstances. It even devoted a bulletin to showing how advertising might be bearable if restricted to inconspicuous places and placed in properly dignified copper frames. It also led the charge against Belmont's cheap tin frames and gaudy posters. But commercial culture won the day. The advertising agents Ward and Gow claimed that advertising revenue paid nearly one and a half percent of the bonded debt of the subway. Belmont began renting space for gum and candy machines as well.

The next controversy was over "subway air." Within days of the opening reporters found passengers complaining of headaches, attacks of vertigo, dizziness, and occasional fainting spells. The *New York Times* reported on a woman who fainted on a train. "Foul air and nervousness due to the excitement of the trip"[37] was the judgment of a physician who happened to be in the car.

There was a great deal of worry that germs would breed underground and infect the population. An article in the *New York Medical Journal* warned that tuberculosis and pneumonia germs would especially flourish. The Interborough responded by hiring Professor C. F. Chandler of Columbia University to prepare a scientific study. When his report of November 1904 declared the air perfectly safe, the company quickly issued it as a pamphlet. Its cover proudly bore the claim "SUBWAY AIR PURE AS IN YOUR OWN HOME."

But during the first summer the air was not only stuffy but also unbearably hot. Parsons had promised that subway temperatures would be even throughout the year. The *Herald*, however, published figures showing that temperatures on the platforms were from five to twelve degrees warmer than on the street. "This is terrifying if true," said the *New York Times*.[38] The *World* published a story describing "Dante's Visit to New York's Inferno" (Ill. 29). "Do they keep it so hot and stuffy as this all the time?" the poet asks faintly.[39]

George A. Soper, a sanitary engineer, studied both the temperature and bacterial content of the subway air, concluding that the piston action of trains forced stale air out and drew fresh air in through the kiosks as Parsons said it would. He also found that there were only half as many microbes per cubic foot in subway air as on the street. He reported, however, that during July and August of 1905 the subway was on average 5.6 percent hotter than the streets, with the hottest temperatures recorded at Astor Place.

The electrical system generated large amounts of heat and the waterproofing barrier around stations and tunnels kept it from escaping. The company didn't know what to do. It began turning off all but a few incandescent lights in each station. It experimented with ordinary office fans on the Brooklyn Bridge station platforms and then tried large ceiling fans at express stops. It installed small ventilating chambers between stations along upper Broadway so that the air could escape through louvers shaped like Venetian blinds. But each summer New York newspapers still run stories about the unbearably hot subway platforms.

Riders soon discovered that crowding, expected to be bad, was even worse than expected. Within a month of the opening a system designed for 350,000 passengers a day was handling as many as 425,000.[40] It was clear that the situation would only worsen. Skyscrapers, not a major fact of New York life when Parsons first laid out his route in 1896, were concentrating larger and larger workforces around a few subway stops.

At the same time the subway attracted the attention of muckraking journalists. Magazine

DANTE TRIES THE SUBWAY; FINDS THE AIR HOTTER THAN HE FOUND IT IN HADES.

29 ▪ Dante Tries the Subway.

New York World, June 26, 1905. Courtesy: Library of Congress.

exposés of corporate trusts and machine politics became extremely popular while the subway was being built. Lincoln Steffens's famous articles on "The Shame of the Cities," for example, appeared in *McClure's* in 1903. Ida Tarbell's exposés of Standard Oil came out in the same magazine between 1902 and 1904. In spite of this climate of suspicion, it was very hard to find any scandal in Belmont's management of one of the greatest public works of the age.

As the cars grew more crowded during the first hot summer, however, journalists quickly pointed out that a few capitalists were making huge sums of money by packing their fellow citizens into hot metal boxes. Gustavus Myers wrote a long article for the March 13 issue of the *World* on "The Gold Mines of the New York Subway." Ray Stannard Baker wrote an article for the March issue of *McClure's* entitled "The Subway 'Deal'." Baker had not unearthed any great scandal but he used the advertising controversy to symbolize the way in which "the Belmont monopoly" had seized a great public work from its true owners—the citizens of New York.[41]

The nascent hostility toward the capitalist financier Belmont grew when in March 1905 the Knights of Labor called a strike. They nearly shut down the elevateds for a day but the new subway was hardly affected. Nevertheless, the city was polarized. The *New York Times* published sympathetic accounts of Columbia boys singing their school song as they marched into the Interborough offices to volunteer as strikebreakers, but Pulitzer's *World* treated the strikers with dignity. Hearst's *American* and *Evening Journal* went further and passionately embraced their cause.

The passions aroused by the March strike erupted again on September 10th when a southbound Ninth Avenue el car, driven by one of the newly hired strikebreakers, jumped the track at 53rd Street, killing twelve and sending forty-eight injured passengers to the hospital. "MR. AUGUST BELMONT, DON'T YOU THINK 'SCABS' COME A LITTLE HIGH?" asked the headline over the *Evening Journal's* September 13th editorial. The same issue published a full-page drawing of the catastrophe. Held at arm's length, its falling bodies and twisted wreckage suddenly revealed the outlines of a grinning Death's Head.

By the end of 1905, New Yorkers who were growing disillusioned with Belmont and his Interborough agreed that what the city really needed was a vast increase in the number of its subway lines. This is where the city's twentieth-century subway fell victim to the bad transit heritage of the nineteenth century.

Thomas Fortune Ryan once again stepped forward to plague Belmont. He offered to build a far-flung subway system. He hired John McDonald to lend credibility to his proposals. And he offered something that Belmont couldn't possibly match—free transfers from his surface lines to the subway. Historians agree that he was faking.[42] The income of the Metropolitan could not cover the obligations that Ryan had incurred as he and his associates bought, leased, and merged with other street railways, all the while selling the public millions of dollars in watered stock. A merger with the Interborough would be its salvation. Ryan didn't want to build subway lines. He wanted to force Belmont to acquire the nearly bankrupt Metropolitan in order to rid himself of a rival.

Belmont drove the hardest bargain he could but he finally bought a company that he considered almost worthless. His secretary John Hettrick recalled for the Columbia Oral History Project, "All the millionaires who had been trying to cut one another's throats financially for several years met in the spirit of good friendship. They shook hands and told jokes as if it was a reunion of a college fraternity of old graduates."[43]

The Interborough now became the target of all the rhetorical abuse that New Yorkers were accustomed to aim at their transportation companies. The *Evening Post*, a businessman's paper, declared that the plan recalled the stock-watering schemes of Jay Gould and declared that "we are not likely to hear again very soon the assertion which the subway's financial managers have been wont to make with pride, that here at least is a railway enterprise in which capital inflation has played no part."[44]

The *World* used the merger to mount a crusade against the follies of corporate finance. It published a brilliant series of drawings showing the financial costs of the merger (Ill. 30). One showed "What Could Be Done with $108,000,000 'Water' Added to Inter.-Met. [i.e., Interborough-Metropolitan] Stock." Another, "What The Interest On Watered Merger Stock Would Do, Told In Pictures," pointed out the amount of the interest would provide a steak for each New York family every day for three weeks, buy milk for all the babies in New York for one year, and provide enough loaves of bread to circle the globe.

MERGER WITH ITS MILLIONS OF WATERED CAPITAL A BURDEN ON THE WHOLE PEOPLE.

30 ▪ Merger with Its Millions of Watered Capital a Burden on the Whole People.
New York World, January 1906. Courtesy: Library of Congress.

Hearst's papers were even more vitriolic. If the subway had ceased to be a miracle by the end of 1905, it was still a positive symbol of a city where all classes could submerge their antagonisms to solve a common problem. Over the next two decades Hearst would block the kind of civic unity that had made the first subway possible. It was he, more than anyone else, who made the subway a symbol of civic stalemate.

CHAPTER FOUR

WILLIAM RANDOLPH HEARST
AND THE TRACTION TRUST

T H E name of William Randolph Hearst evokes visions of the Neptune Pool in the fairytale castle of San Simeon overlooking the Pacific Ocean, not a subway train roaring under Eighth Avenue. It is possible to tell the story of subway expansion without any reference to Hearst at all. James Blaine Walker, the Public Service Commission official who wrote a history of subways up to the Dual Contracts of 1913, restricted his attention to the engineers, businessmen, and politicians who did the actual work and made only a brief, scornful reference to the "storm of attack" created by "certain newspapers."[1] Clifton Hood's 722 *Miles* gives Hearst more attention, noting his opposition to the Dual Contracts and describing his role as a supporter of Mayor John F. Hylan.

There are good reasons for a longer account. The cheap, mass-circulation newspaper was born with the modern city and was its first great interpreter. While painters and novelists held back, journalists rushed in not only to describe events but also to create the forms—sensational crime reporting, banner headlines, editorial cartoons—which would make an imaginative apprehension of the city possible. At a very early stage in their history New York's newspapers developed a symbiotic relation with its transit system. Naturally they reported on it. It was an easy beat to cover and one sure to interest all their readers. But they went far beyond reporting.

The newspapers intervened very directly in transit development by advocating particular policies and using transit as a means of portraying the larger city. Hearst, for reasons of his own, took these two well-established tendencies to new extremes. He meddled in transit politics more directly than any previous publisher had done. More importantly, he used the subway as a rhetorical frame to dramatize struggles for power in the exploding city—

struggles in which August Belmont and Thomas Fortune Ryan often figured as preposterous villains while Hearst himself invariably emerged as the city's savior.

Though born in San Francisco, Hearst was based in New York from the day he bought the *Morning Journal* in 1894 until he shifted his base back to California in the nineteen-twenties. At a time when all respectable opinion favored private transit companies, Hearst campaigned for municipal operation. When businessmen, transportation experts, and politicians combined behind the Dual Contracts, Hearst's opposition nearly prevented them from being signed. When it became clear that the subways could not generate profit without a fare increase, Hearst fought relentlessly to save the nickel ride. In the process, he doomed private ownership of the transit lines and prepared the way for the publicly owned Independent line.

This sounds like a splendid crusade on behalf of the underprivileged and in some ways it was. But Hearst used the subways to present the city as the site of a never-ending battle between the democratic masses and a secretive elite. He exploited the myth of the Traction Trust demagogically, using it to advance his own political ambitions long after it had lost all correspondence with reality. His long defense of the five-cent fare ensured that the subways would be chronically underfunded. In the end his influence on the subway was largely destructive.

It is difficult to think about Hearst without seeing the sardonic smile of Orson Welles in *Citizen Kane*. The early part of the film tracks Hearst's life very closely, dramatizing his youthful verve supported by his father's almost exhaustless wealth. The film captures his eagerness to use his newspapers as a weapon of the masses against the classes, shows his skillful use of the transit issue (the first headline on a Kane newspaper that we see reads "TRACTION TRUST EXPOSED"), and tracks his growing bitterness and shift to the right.

Even more than his hero and rival Joseph Pulitzer, Hearst was an outsider to New York City's power structures. The son of a genteel schoolmarm mother and a roughneck miner who had struck it fabulously rich in the Comstock lode, young Hearst was sent to Harvard to acquire gentlemanly polish. It didn't suit him. He was more interested in the *Harvard Lampoon* than in his classes and played more college boy pranks than even a tolerant administration could accept. He was finally expelled for sending each of his instructors a large chamber pot with the recipient's name written on the inside bottom.

Instead of wasting his senior year at Harvard, Hearst took a job as a reporter with Pulitzer's *World*. He learned what he needed quickly and soon took over the *San Francisco Examiner*, which his father had accidentally acquired in a business deal. In 1894 he came back to New York and bought a failing sheet called the *New York Journal*. In 1896 he added the *Evening Journal*. In 1901 the *Morning Journal* became the *American*.

The key to Hearst's career is that much as he wanted to be America's most flamboyant publisher, he wanted still more to be its president. In 1902 Hearst was elected to Congress from Manhattan's Eleventh District. In 1904 he received an impressive 263 votes at the Democratic presidential nominating convention. In 1905 he ran for mayor against George McClellan, losing by fewer than 4,000 votes. In 1906 he ran for governor against Charles Evans Hughes, losing by only 58,000 votes out of almost 1,500,000 cast. In 1907 he formed his own political organization, the Independence League, to seek the Democratic nomination for governor. In 1909 he ran for mayor again. Between 1900 and 1925 there was never a time when he was not running for office, angling for a nomination, or maneuvering his supporters into positions of influence.

Hearst's political power was based entirely on his mastery of the new techniques of mass communication. He did everything that Pulitzer did but more of it. He offered the same mix of scandal, crime, and social crusades. He made his news columns a direct conduit to the editorial page. He made each paper a visual feast, with banner headlines (often in red ink), front page sketches and crude photographs, brilliant editorial page cartoons, and some of the best comic strips American journalism has ever seen. A Hearst newspaper didn't even stay on the page. It spilled over into promotional schemes (placard-laden wagons of free coffee), charitable acts (free sweaters for the poor), civic holidays (sponsoring the celebrations for the 1898 Consolidation), and, eventually, election rallies.

Hearst swelled his circulation and advanced his political career by instructing his public in a simple, plausible view of American society. The little people were constantly cheated by the Gas Trust, the Milk Trust, the Oil Trust, the Tobacco Trust, the Light Trust, the Sugar Trust, the Railroad Trust, and, above all, the Traction Trust. Hearst's brilliant artists regularly personified the Trusts as huge, bloated cartoon figures, each one half-thug and half-bon vivant. The remedy was not a return to cutthroat competition. The solution for many industries was government regulation but for the essential few—including mass transit— it was public ownership and municipal operation. This was Progress. This was Patriotic.

New York and its subway provided a particularly vivid instance of this larger view. Hearst's treatment of both may be profitably compared with Pulitzer's. The *World* launched incessant crusades against the city's injustices but in the last analysis it showed New York as a fabulous wonderland. The paper had proudly published O. Henry's stories in the *World Magazine* and for many years afterward it deliberately cultivated O. Henry's sense that New York is the setting for modern Arabian tales, a place where the marvelous is encountered around every corner.

Hearst's vision of New York was both less enchanted and less detailed than Pulitzer's. His Sunday supplements and most of his other features were syndicated to Hearst papers around the country and so they did not make New York their focus. Hearst's vision of New York is expressed primarily in the news columns and on the editorial page. The celebration of New York that we find in Pulitzer's *World Magazine* is entirely absent.

Hearst shows the city as a place where the powerful few are constantly cheating the hardworking many. The subway was one of the perennial scenes of their betrayals. Unlike Pulitzer, Hearst never admits that issues are complicated, that rival points of view might have validity, or that opponents might be motivated by anything except greed and bad faith. And again unlike Pulitzer, Heast never allows rival viewpoints to be expressed in his columns. His pages, with their vivid prose and brilliant cartoons, are like an unending series of advertisements for the same product. His New York is the scene of a vast swindle and his papers express a constant, sullen sense of grievance.

Hearst's creation of the Traction Trust was his most brilliant act of journalistic creativity. In its first years of operation Belmont's subway had proven to be a very profitable operation. As crowding grew worse, New Yorkers became vividly aware that their daily ordeal in hot, noisy trains produced immense dividends for a small group of stockholders. Hearst exploited this resentment and went on doing so long after the profits had begun to fall.

He also pursued a more personal agenda. August Belmont and Thomas Fortune Ryan were leading fundraisers for the eastern, conservative wing of the Democratic party. They were fiercely opposed to Hearst's presidential ambitions and to those of William Jennings Bryan, with whom Hearst was frequently allied. Ryan contributed $450,000 to Hearst's rival for the presidential nomination in 1904. Belmont contributed about $250,000.[2]

Hearst responded with vitriol. Ryan appeared in Hearst cartoons as a cynical puppet master and Belmont was mocked as a servile agent of the international financiers who had invested in his railroad. Noting that Lord Rothschild (who was, improbably, a collector of fleas) had paid $5,000 for two scientifically valuable specimens from the body of an Arctic fox, the *American* (Ill. 31) presented Belmont as simply one more item in the great money man's collection.

No wonder Hearst seized with such avidity on the 1905 merger of Ryan's Metropolitan and Belmont's Interborough. While Pulitzer's *World* tried to explain the economic costs of the arrangement, Hearst assailed personalities. August Belmont and Thomas Fortune Ryan were portrayed as malevolent but high-living grotesques united in their contempt for the

31 ▪ Robert Carter. *For Two Fleas Rothschild Paid $5,000.*
New York American, September 3, 1904. Courtesy: Library of Congress.

FOR TWO FLEAS ROTHSCHILD PAID $5,000.

Too bad he will not allow his agent Belmont to pay decent wages to workmen on the underground railroad. Are fleas so much more precious than engineers?

IN THE MONSTER'S GRASP.

32 ▪ T. S. Sullivan. *In the Monster's Grasp.*
New York American, December 29, 1905. Courtesy: Library of Congress.

common man. "BELMONT, RYAN WELD MERGER WITH A LAUGH," was the *American*'s headline for December 27, 1905. Its cartoon on December 29th showed the Rothschild dragon with Belmont and Ryan as its two heads (Ill. 32). The *Evening Journal* expressed disgust "THAT A LITTLE, SECOND-RATE MAN LIKE AUGUST BELMONT IS ABLE TO RUN ALL THE RAILWAYS OF THE CITY!" [3]

It is hard not to sympathize with Belmont. He thought that he was a civic hero and instead found himself one of the most hated men in New York. He was clearly startled.

THE FIGHT AGAINST THE DUAL CONTRACTS

New York City politics in the first three decades of the twentieth century were dominated by the question of subway expansion. A few days before the first subway opened John B. McDonald sat on one of its new trains with a black cigar in his mouth and told the *American* that New York would be a Subway City within twenty years, with at least three north-south routes, many intersecting subways at the major cross streets, underground arcades where much of the retail business of the city would be transacted and underground connections with most of the large business houses.[4] Five years later William Willcox, Chairman of the Public Service Commission, predicted that by 1930 Manhattan would need subways under every north-south avenue with additional subways or moving platforms under the major cross streets. The lines would penetrate deeply into the other four boroughs with a subway tunnel under the Narrows to Staten Island.[5]

But if New York was to become a Subway City, it would have to find someone other than August Belmont to build it. He had no wish to extend his lines into undeveloped areas that would not contain a significant number of paying customers for many years. After all, studies showed that even the Interborough lost money above 96th Street. On August 14, 1908, Belmont wrote to IRT Chairman T. P. Shonts: "I am confirmed in my opinion that we should not build any more subways. With proper use of the Manhattan Elevated lines as contemplated in the additional tracks New York does not need any more high speed lines for some time to come."[6] His policy was to stand pat. "We're already there," he said. "We've got the lines. If we can't extend them, we'll manage them as best we can."[7]

Meanwhile, transit reformers had offered a proposal of their own—a Triborough subway connecting farflung areas of Brooklyn, Manhattan, and the Bronx. It would compete with the Interborough directly in lower Manhattan while opening up undeveloped areas of Brooklyn and the Bronx for new housing. And while it could have been leased to a private company, it could also be managed by the city.

The 1909 municipal election focused entirely on the fastest way to get to Subway City. The race was three sided. The Fusion ticket consisted of transit reformers. Disgusted at the city administration's failure to build new subways, leading members of a wide range of civic organizations joined to create an independent political force. Their mayoral candidate was a well-connected Republican named Otto T. Bannard. The rest of the ticket included several men who would play important roles in subway development: John Purroy Mitchell for president of the Board of Aldermen, William A. Prendergast for comptroller, and George McAneny for Manhattan Borough president.

The Democratic candidate was Judge William T. Gaynor of Brooklyn. Tammany chief Charles Francis Murphy had turned to him because he need a candidate with a good transit record. Gaynor had earned his public reputation when he intervened as a judge in Brooklyn's 1895 streetcar strike, requiring the companies to maintain service after they had attempted to stop the cars. He had attacked the city's contract with the Interborough for not giving the city treasury a share of the new system's profits.[8] In the summer of 1906, when riots broke out after the Brooklyn Rapid Transit Company tried to charge a double fare for its Coney Island run, Gaynor ruled that only a five-cent fare could be charged. In the spring of 1909 he attacked the Interborough in a *Pearson's Magazine* article on "The Looting of New York." When *Pearson's* tried to advertise the issue in the subway and elevateds, the company refused to post their placards.

Hearst was the third candidate. He had not wanted to run for mayor. Instead, he wanted a friend in City Hall who would support his bid for higher office. But he had broken with the Fusionists when they refused to demand municipal operation of the subway and he was unlikely to get support from a Tammany-allied Gaynor. So he announced an independent candidacy on a hastily invented Civic Alliance ticket. Hearst ran at the head of his ticket but nominated the Fusion candidates Mitchell, Prendergast, and McAneny as his running mates. Though Fusion Candidate Otto T. Bannard came in second on election day, he made little impression in the campaign. So far as public rhetoric went, it was a Gaynor-Hearst race, and an extremely bitter one.

Hearst attacked Gaynor by assailing his Tammany connections. The *American* and *Evening Journal* ran daily assaults on Gaynor's running mates. "TAMMANY'S CITY TICKET GOES TO THE VERY DEPTHS OF DEGRADATION" read an *American* headline on October 7th, and the subhead expanded: "One Protector of Vice, One Leader of Election Crooks, a Third a Parasite, and another a Sullivan dummy."[9]

Since the city's regular Democrats were notorious for their close associations with both August Belmont and Matthew Fortune Ryan, such connections raised questions about Gaynor's ability to carry out a fight for strict municipal control of the subways. "Judge Gaynor says: 'We are now going to fight from the inside,'" Hearst told an interviewer. "That is what the canary said when the cat had swallowed it, but there is no record of the result of that fight, and we independents would like to know just how a fight is to be successfully conducted from the inside of the Tiger."[10]

Gaynor faced the very prickly question of how to respond to a man who was a genius at mass communication. When attacked, Belmont had simply retired into aristocratic isolation. Gaynor had an advantage in that he was a politician and thus by profession accustomed to a discourse which employed outrageous accusations and personal attacks. Where the sober businessman was stiff and dull in public, Gaynor responded with gusto.

His opening campaign speech at the Brooklyn Academy of Music included a detailed assault on Hearst. He accused an unnamed publisher of taking large city contracts for useless advertising. ("What paper was it?" cried a voice from the audience. "Weary Willie's Yellow Journal," another voice promptly answered.) Gaynor then went on to answer Hearst's ad hominem attacks with a more effective personal assault of his own: "The open enemy I honor, but the enemy that sits as an editor, pretending to be for you when he is not in his heart and is only putting a dagger between your ribs, that is an enemy that is despicable."[11]

Out in the open it soon was. Hearst promised new subway lines, insisting that he could pay for them with money that Tammany would no longer be able to steal from the city treasury. Profits from the new city-owned and -operated lines could be used to reduce taxes.

Gaynor was as fierce as Hearst against the transit companies. "By the Eternal!" he exclaimed in a speech that certainly seemed to promise municipal operation; "during the next four years we will build the subways for the city and none of these people will so much as get their little finger into it."[12] He insisted that he had coined the very phrase "municipal ownership and control" before Hearst ever came to New York City.[13]

On election day Gaynor won with 250,387 votes. Hearst came in third with 154,187. All the Fusion candidates were elected. Thus every major city official was suspicious of the Interborough and eager for new subway construction. The stage was set for action.

It might have been expected that the reformers would proceed straight to a vote in favor of the city-constructed Triborough line. Instead, a series of reversals and unexpected events led to the abandonment of the Triborough and the division of the new routes between the Interborough and the Brooklyn Rapid Transit Company—the so-called Dual Contracts. Each of these reversals was reasonable in itself but collectively they allowed Hearst to employ his favority strategy of portraying city affairs as a series of cowardly betrayals.

The first unexpected event was Gaynor's conversion from a critic of the Interborough to its skeptical but nonetheless firm supporter. The company had deliberately set out to win his support. Belmont, suddenly alarmed that his Interborough would be left out of subway expansion altogether, put forward his own plan. He would transform the "S" of the original subway into an "H" by extending the east side line north and the west side line south while keeping the 42nd street tracks as the crossbar.

With a public offer on the table, the Interborough hired Mirabeau Towns, Gaynor's next-door neighbor in Brooklyn, to plead its case in private. He met with the mayor approximately fifty times between October 1909 and April 1910. He arranged to have Interborough President Theodore P. Shonts meet Gaynor at City Hall on January 25, 1910. Afterward the mayor told reporters: "Mr. Shonts seemed to be a man of large and fair views and easy to do business with. No one can get a dividend out of a quarrel and I hope this subway business can be got under way on a reasonable basis pretty soon."[14]

By April 1910 discussions had progressed far enough that Towns arranged to have Shonts visit the mayor at Gaynor's summer home in St. James, Long Island. They found him climbing over a fence toward his cattle and while Towns sat in the automobile, Shonts and Gaynor wore a path in the front yard walking back and forth for three hours. "I told him that I was not as bad as I looked," Shonts said later. "I told him that I didn't wear horns, and that we were on the level, and wanted to convince him."

Shonts explained the virtues of completing a subway system that was already partly there. He argued that the Interborough could built a better subway for $70,000,000 than the city could for $150,000,000. In spite of this, "there seemed to be considerable antagonism on the part of the Mayor, and I told him we were willing to open our books to him and show him we were on the level."[15] Gaynor accepted this, and two of his commissioners spent months poring through the Interborough's records.

Gaynor finally came over to the Interborough's position. Shonts immediately wrote a 3,000-word memorandum on the meeting and sent it to J. P. Morgan Jr. Towns met Gaynor the next morning and accompanied him on his walk across the Brooklyn Bridge to City Hall. The mayor asked Towns how much he had been paid for his services. When Towns figured it at $10,000, Gaynor "stopped and smiled and said it ought to be $750,000 and he had given them a principality." Towns said that he didn't discuss the meaning of the mayor's words, as he considered they might have been "a message or a trap."[16]

Gaynor's position was now that the Interborough was neither the hero nor the villain of New York's subway crisis. "They talk about companies," he said of the Interborough's opponents. "The companies are all the same to me. I never saw one that was any better than any other. They simply work for their stockholders and to make all they can."[17]

Gaynor's change in attitude toward the Interborough had been slow and careful. He had borne in mind that the city had very little money with which to finance a municipal subway. He had ordered his representative to look at the Interborough's books. He had never been so naive as to hope that the company would set aside the quest for profit in order to serve the larger social good but he did become convinced that its plans could be incorporated within the city's.

Hearst presented this slow, complicated process as a sudden act of betrayal. And he simultaneously began assailing Gaynor's character in other areas. In April the *American* and the *Evening Journal* began alleging, inaccurately, that Gaynor had paid off Charles Francis Murphy for his nomination by paying a large legal fee to one of the Tammany boss's friends.

Unlike Belmont, Gaynor was the kind of man who responded to a direct attack with a frontal assault. Speaking before a joint banquet of the American Newspaper Publisher's Association on April 28th, he claimed that these stories were based on both forgery and libel and caused a twenty-minute uproar in the hall by proclaiming: "It is high time that these forgers and libellers were in State's prison, and the time is not far distant when some of them will be there. . . . And just think of a man who is capable of doing things like this being possessed of the notion that he is fit to hold any office from Mayor to President of the United States. Morally speaking, his mind must be a howling wilderness."[18]

The situation was dramatically transformed when, on August 9, 1910, a recently discharged city employee shot Gaynor in the neck. This removed Gaynor from active politics for several months and caused Manhattan Borough President George McAneny to step forward as his replacement on the Transit Committee of the Board of Estimate and Apportionment.

McAneny was well qualified. He had, as president of the City Club between 1906 and 1909, campaigned aggressively for new subway routes. Though he was slow to pick a fight, his relations with Hearst would eventually be as bitter as Gaynor's had been. In his reminiscences for the Columbia Oral History project he recalled Hearst as "a pretty bad man in this town." He remembered bitterly that in 1913, when he was running for Alderman, Hearst reminded his readers that McAneny had been borough president when the Triangle Shirtwaist fire took place and gave an entire front page of the *American* to a picture of frightened girls leaping to their deaths with McAneny's face in the middle and the words "This is the man who is responsible for these yet unexplained fires."[19]

On December 5, 1910, the Interborough judged the time to be right for a new offer. It would complete the "H" as promised and it would give dramatically improved service to the Bronx. Both Ninth Avenue elevated trains and Lexington Avenue subway trains would run up a new elevated structure on Jerome Avenue to Woodlawn Cemetery in the western part of the borough. The existing Interborough line in the central Bronx would be extended to Gun Hill Road. The Third Avenue elevated line would reach to 241st Street. A Pelham Avenue line, similar to that originally proposed for the Triborough, would serve the east Bronx. Most significantly, in terms of future developments, the Interborough announced its willingness to build new lines in Brooklyn.

The Chamber of Commerce, the Merchants' Association, and the Retail Dry Goods Association lined up solidly behind the Interborough plan. Not only would it cost the city less but it would serve the newly opened Pennsylvania Railroad Station, whereas the Triborough route was entirely on the east side of Manhattan.

The showdown between supporters of the rival plans occurred at a January 5, 1911, meeting of the Board of Estimate and Apportionment. John Purroy Mitchell and William Prendergast offered a resolution specifying that the available credit of the city be devoted to the construction of an independent, municipally owned and controlled subway system—that is, the Triborough. No present or future credit could be lent to any other system until the city system had been put in operation. Gaynor opposed it because he thought the Triborough too expensive and preferred the Interborough. McAneny opposed it because he didn't want to preclude further negotiations with the Interborough. The resolution lost by a vote of ten to six.

The Hearst papers reacted with fury. They framed the issue in the simplest terms: a pledge had been violated. The *American* for January 6th spread photos of those who had voted against the resolution across six columns of the first page of the second section under the headline "HOW GAYNOR AND HIS FOLLOWERS HAVE REPUDIATED THEIR PRE-ELECTION PLEDGES FOR A CITY SUBWAY." Immediately below the photos were quotes showing "What They Promised" and below the quotes a description of "What They Did": "Ignoring their personal and party pledges to the people when seeking election, Mayor Gaynor and McAneny, Steers, Miller, Cromwell and Gresser yesterday defeated a resolution calling for the construction of an independent subway system with city money and voted to take the offer of the traction trust in a secret session of the Board of Estimate and Apportionment, from which the public will be barred." [20]

Gaynor received a special battering. The *American* published—and republished almost daily through January, February, and into March—a box headed "The Honor of the Mayor" featuring Gaynor's past statements in favor of municipal subways. A cartoon showed him as Bre'r Rabbit contentedly munching on the lettuce of his earlier campaign promises. Another showed Gaynor and Tammany boss Murphy as puppets sitting on Thomas Fortune Ryan's lap. "GAYNOR URGED PRENDERGAST TO FORGET PLEDGE TO THE PEOPLE" the *American* screamed when it was learned that Gaynor had tried to persuade Triborough backers that they were no longer bound by campaign pledges after a year in office. [21]

Daily stories publicized a mass meeting in support of the Triborough to be held at Cooper Union and subsequent meetings to be held around the city. New Yorkers were described as solidly united behind a city subway. One cartoon presented Gaynor as King Canute trying vainly to hold back the tidal wave of support for municipal operation. A second showed New York as a giant Gulliver tied down by the Lilliputians who defeated the Triborough. A third presented Mrs. Knickerbocker as a dignified matron denied a seat on the subway by the rude politicians who had voted down the Mitchell-Prendergast resolution. Mitchell and Prendergast were "champions" with "the strength of ten thousand men" who led a "fight," a "public uprising," to save the city from a "crisis" brought on by "the lawlessness and rapacity of the Traction Trust." [22]

It was a remarkable performance. Hearst had transformed a complicated issue of transit planning into a simple one of personal integrity. Problems of population dispersal, the difficulty of finding capital, and the varying merits of the different routes were all forgotten. Hearst persuaded his readers that the most independent group of politicians New York had seen in some years had sold out to the shadowy Traction Trust. He simplified the issues, personalized them, and repeated them daily, creating powerful emotions that would spill over into meetings, petitions, and, he hoped, his own election as governor.

During the next few months, however, transit politics took a new direction. The Brooklyn Rapid Transit Company suddenly put forward its own expansion plans. Brooklyn and Manhattan transit companies had traditionally avoided competing with one another but when the Interborough offered to extend its subway under Eastern Parkway and Nostrand Avenue, the BRT felt challenged.

Accordingly, in March 1911, it sent the Public Service Commission a wide-ranging offer. It would build the Fourth Avenue subway in Brooklyn which had been projected for the Triborough. It would convert its steam railroad tracks in Brooklyn—the West End Line, the Culver Line, the Brighton, and the Sea Beach—into rapid transit lines. And most startlingly, it would extend its Fourth Avenue Brooklyn line under the East River at Fulton Street to the Battery, then up Broadway to Times Square. By 1911 it was clear that Manhattan was developing a new business center in midtown. The BRT wanted to be part of it.

In the spring and summer of 1911 the two companies fought a newspaper war for public support. The Interborough insisted that it offered a unified system at a five-cent fare, whereas if the BRT plan was built many riders would have to transfer from one system to another at the cost of an additional nickel. It also pointed out that it was putting up much more of its own money than its rival.

The BRT ads placed a more sophisticated emphasis on city planning. They quoted the editors of *American City* in support of population dispersal and showed little cartoon men with models of homes rushing to south Brooklyn with the caption: "To-morrow—the truck farms are gone. In their place are long lines of streets—gently shaded streets—streets lined with neat residences."[23]

On June 13, 1911, McAneny startled the city by refusing to choose either the Interborough's plan or the BRT's. Instead, he began a complicated series of negotiations that would divide the routes and offer contracts to both companies.

Much of the negotiation soon revolved around what became known as the preferential payments. Since both the companies and the city would be selling bonds for subway expansion, it would have been normal to simply divide the operating revenues between them. Instead, the Brooklyn company insisted that it should receive a payment for its debt servicing and repayment first. Once that was done, the city could then receive the money for its bonds. McAneny thought the arrangement was tolerable because he was sure that ridership would be large enough to produce revenues capable of covering all debt payments and still produce a profit for both company and city. The Interborough, not surprisingly, wanted a similar arrangement.

Hearst was willing to go to extraordinary lengths to keep members of the Board of Estimate from granting the Interborough a preferential payment. Comptroller William Prendergast was a politician who seemed to be wavering. Testimony before the Thompson Committee in 1916 revealed the kind of pressure that was brought to bear.

While dining at home on the evening of July 19, 1911, Prendergast received a call from John H. Weier, a reporter for the *American*, who wanted to set up an immediate meeting on the subway question between Prendergast and *American* editor Bradford Merrill. Prendergast obediently appeared in the *American* offices at about 8:30 P.M. to meet Merrill and Hearst's lawyer Clarence J. Shearn. As they were talking Weier came to the door and handed Prendergast a statement that Mayor Gaynor had just issued. For all his new sympathy for the Interborough, Gaynor objected vehemently to giving it a preferential payment.

Prendergast was now the swing vote. Merrill bluntly asked him whether "he would be a traitor or keep to his word." Prendergast, the editor recalled later, appeared nervous: "He sat down in a chair, fidgeted, jumped up, and sat down several times, and began a long, rambling statement about the advantages of a five-cent fare all over town, as well as the advantages of linking up the new subway with the present one." Finally Prendergast sat down at Mr. Hearst's desk and, picking up a sheet of paper, began to write. "He was so nervous at this point," Merrill recalled later, "that I asked him if his hand shook and he nearly took my head off." Finally, the controller finished his statement opposing the Interborough offer and declared: "Well, there you are. I have written it and you now have it in black and white." Merrill congratulated him for being true to his word and assured him that he was not going down in disgrace.[24] The Interborough offer was rejected.

By the middle of 1911, then, it appeared that the BRT would take charge of subway expansion in New York. On July 31, 1911, construction actually began on the BRT system at the intersection of Lexington Avenue and 67th Street.

But this was an absurd situation. The city would be spending millions of dollars for a Broadway subway that would be only one block from the existing subway in busy areas of Manhattan. Pennsylvania Railroad officials complained vehemently that their new station would be left without direct connection to any rapid transit line. Samuel Rea, vice president of the Pennsylvania Railroad; Seth Low, former president of Columbia University; and representatives of Morgan Bank began a new round of behind-the-scenes negotiations with a meeting at the Century Club. By January 24, 1912, the Interborough had made a new offer and though difficult negotiations still lay ahead, it was clear that the city needed contracts with both the Interborough *and* the BRT.

Hearst fought for more than a year to forestall the Dual Contracts. His most stirring campaigns always depended on a dramatic sense of timing. A story would lie dormant for weeks and months, then suddenly be revived for daily headlines because there was an impending climax in view. Hearst launched several campaigns during 1912 and brought the war to a crisis in January and February 1913. His campaign against the Dual Contracts shows his journalism at its vitriolic best. He transformed the rather technical debate over routes and financing into a struggle between good and evil, dignity and dishonor.

Hearst focused on the persons of Gaynor, McAneny, and Prendergast, presenting their presumed willingness to serve corrupt ends as simply the latest installment in New York's bad tradition of transit misrule. On January 23, 1912, the *American* showed a statue of Boss Tweed, wearing both prison stripes and a huge diamond stickpin, leaping from its pedestal so that Gaynor and Prendergast could take his place. Another *American* cartoon showed large figures of McAneny, Prendergast (who had once again fallen out of Hearst's favor), and Gaynor ridiculing a diminutive Tweed as a mere piker while the former boss exclaims, "And to think they put ME in jail" (Ill. 33).

Hearst laid special stress on the fact that the Dual Contracts had been negotiated in private sessions. An *American* cartoon on February 21, 1912, showed City Hall empty while its officials met with great capitalists in a downtown club. Another of March 25, 1912, showed Gaynor holding a flashlight so that BRT and Interborough lawyers could secretly introduce financial jokers into the contracts. The *Evening Journal* reminded its readers that the negotiations had been "held in the exclusive clubs of the rich, to which no ordinary individual might hope to gain access."[25]

On January 24, 1912, the *American* devoted much of its front page to a huge before-and-after cartoon showing "The Result When Public Officials Go Into Long, Secret, Private Conferences With Powerful Financiers Over Public Contracts." The before version shows huge,

PIKER!

TWEED—"And to think they put ME in jail."

Copyright, 1912, by International News Service

33 ▪ Homer Davenport. *Piker!*

New York American, January 26, 1912. Courtesy: Library of Congress.

powerful city officials glaring down at the Lilliputian representatives of the company. Once the secret sessions have begun the situation is reversed: tiny, bewildered figures of Mc-Aneny and Prendergast are dwarfed by the huge, pot-bellied representatives of capital. Page two showed photographs of "Corporate Bankers Who Have Won and City Officials Who Have Broken Faith." Gaynor, McAneny, and Prendergast were next to the three financiers but only one quarter the size.

Hearst was at pains to show that his three public officials were mere baubles in the hands of the great bankers. A cartoon on January 30th showed J. P. Morgan displaying the latest painting in his art collection. Titled "A Classic of Modern Art," it showed the diminutive McAneny, Prendergast, and Gaynor handing the new subways over to the financier. The *Evening Journal* showed the corpulent Morgan adding a statue of the diminutive Gaynor to his vast collection (Ill. 34). An *American* cartoon caricatured McAneny, Gaynor, and Prendergast as the modern equivalent of the three monkeys who saw, heard, and spoke no evil (Ill. 35).

By January of 1913 it was widely recognized that what was really at stake in Hearst's war against the Dual Contracts was control of the Democratic party. Governor Sulzer, who took office that month, had been elected with both Tammany and Hearst support. Now Hearst wanted him to break with the city's political establishment and line up in the Hearst camp. He could do that by rejecting the Dual Contracts.

The wedge issue was the appointment of a new chairman of the Public Service Commission. William Willcox's term of office would end on January 31st. The new chairman would

34 ▪ Tau, *Most Precious of His Jewels.*
New York Evening Journal, January 30, 1912. Courtesy: Library of Congress.

Most Precious of His Jewels

J. Pierpont Morgan is a great collector. But h e never collected anything as precious or valuable to him as that little, obedient Mayor Gaynor, faithful to the Street Car Trust and obedient.to his master, J. P. M.

DEAF, DUMB AND BLIND TO ALL EVIL

PUBLIC PLEDGES PRIVATELY REPUDIATED

BOROUGH PRES. M'ANENY:

"The city must be kept in the position where it can build its own subways for itself, and where its control of them will be absolutely undisputed. I can conceive of no contingency under which the city would or should be required to do differently."

MAYOR GAYNOR:

"The city will build these subways. * * We do not intend that a single subway or a franchise for it shall be passed over to these men—Mr. Belmont and Mr. Ryan. They have got their clutches into the present subway. * * * They now want to build these subways, and get them and do the same thing over with them. * * * We say Never! Never!!"

COMPTROLLER PRENDERGAST:

"Every benefit offered by the Interboro can be secured to the city by building of AN INDEPENDENT SUBWAY and the GREAT PRINCIPLE FOREVER ESTABLISHED that the citizens of New York SHALL CONTROL THEIR OWN PROPERTY."

35 ▪ Homer Davenport. *Deaf, Dumb and Blind to All Evil.*
New York American, January 27, 1912. Courtesy: Library of Congress.

cast the deciding vote on the Dual Contracts. "CONTROL OF OUR SUBWAYS FOR 53 YEARS WILL BE DECIDED IN A FEW DAYS" proclaimed the *American* on January 29th. Hearst demanded that his attorney, Clarence J. Shearn, be named to the post. He hinted that he was willing to take it himself.

As the decision on Willcox's replacement neared, Hearst headlines grew increasingly frenetic:

—GOV. SULZER OPPOSES PRIVATE MONOPOLY OF SUBWAYS; LIKELY TO ACT DECISIVELY IN CRISIS

—WILLCOX CONFERS SECRETLY WITH MORGAN ALLIES; CRAM DECLARES: "NEW CONTRACTS INFAMOUS IN ROBBERY."

—GOV. SULZER WILL *NOT* LET WILLCOX LINGER; SUBWAY MONOPOLY ALLY TO GO FEB. 1; WALL STREET SYNDICATE WORKING AGAINST TIME

—SUBWAY GRABBERS MAKE IMPORTANT CONCESSIONS TO CITY; MR. HEARST DENOUNCES TREACHERY OF CITY OFFICIALS

—TRACTION TRUST EFFORT TO RUSH GRAB IS FOILED

While these headlines were appearing, Hearst's page one cartoons grew increasingly savage. An *Evening Journal* cartoon of January 26, 1913, showed the Traction Trust as a corpulent lecher pressed against a shrinking New York maiden (Ill. 36).

In the end Sulzer won by throwing off Hearst's timing. When the crucial day arrived he named Chief Justice Edward E. McCall, who promptly announced that, rather than make an immediate decision, he would need several weeks for further study. Hearst could keep his readers in a state of desperate alarm for only so long. A defeat would have commanded gigantic headlines. Rumors of an anticipated defeat several weeks in the future could only lead to an anti-climax. By the time McCall cast the deciding ballot for the Dual Contracts on March 4, 1913, the suspense had gone out of the issue. The *American* bitterly headlined its editorial "SULZER HAS PUT THE JOB THROUGH FOR TAMMANY AND WALL ST." but the drama was flat.

Hearst's battle against the Dual Contracts had no immediate results in terms of its effect on subway expansion. It had very large results, however, in shaping the rhetorical framework within which New Yorkers would think about their city and its complex problems. In Hearst's melodrama, people of divergent views and motives could not come together. There was no room to say, as a reasonable person might well have said, that Belmont was a

36 ▪ H. Hoffman. *The Trust That Treats People Like Swine.* *New York Evening Journal*, January 27, 1913. Courtesy: Library of Congress.

businessman who wanted higher earnings for the Interborough but had no social vision whatever, that McAneny had abundant social vision but wanted route expansion that would not pay dividends for many years, and that the preferential payments were a clumsy but tolerable way of reconciling their quite different goals.

Hearst's outlook allowed no room for the compromises that so complex a mechanism as a city requires on a daily basis. If New York was to solve its problems it needed a rhetoric that would answer that of the *American* and the *Evening Journal*. So far Hearst's opponents had not developed one.

HEARST AND HYLAN

The subway situation changed dramatically in the years following World War I. The Dual Contracts, even though they more than doubled the system's track miles, proved inadequate to the immense throngs that came into the new midtown business and entertainment section. By 1920 there were 2,365,000,000 riders annually on all city transit lines—285,000,000 more than had been packed in the year before and twice as many as all the steam railroads in the country carried. "Every day," exclaimed a startled *New York Times*, "adds 4,100 to the insatiable crowd. On congestion super-congestion accumulates."[26]

The straphanger's suffering became a constant theme not only of news stories and editorials but also of the humor, human interest, and social etiquette features. Bernarr McFadden's tabloid *Evening Graphic*, which campaigned for double-decker subway cars to end the crisis, regularly sent a Miss Courtesy into the subways looking for polite riders. She found two or three each day and gave each one a card explaining how to go to the *Graphic* office to claim a reward. Benjamin De Casseres suggested in the *New York Times* that the subway could be regarded as the National Gym: "The football rush, the strangle hold and the tug-of-war are among the useful sporting exercises for its patrons of the morning and evening rush hours."[27]

Meanwhile, Hearst's political fortunes took an unexpected turn. He had taken a battering during the war because he had opposed entry and was widely suspected of pro-German sympathies. He regained the political initiative when his admirer—almost his hero-worshipper—John Francis Hylan won the mayoral election of 1917. Hearst's presidential ambitions took on new vigor. He still sought local power as a stepping-stone toward the White House and he still found his best weapon in angry crusades against the Traction Trust.

He faced, however, a steady accumulation of enemies. Men who had been targets of his ad hominem attacks nursed bitter grudges. In 1907, while trying to elect one of his political operatives as sheriff, Hearst had vilified the Tammany candidate, "Big Tom" Foley. Now the rising Lower East Side politician Al Smith, who considered Foley his beloved mentor, regarded Hearst with bitter contempt. Famous for his steadfast loyalties, Smith proved no less unswerving in his hatreds.

The 1917 nomination of John Francis Hylan was a direct result of the Hearst–Al Smith feud. Tammany was eager to defeat the reform mayor John Puroy Mitchell. Hearst had initially supported Mitchell, his hero in the fight against the Dual Contracts, but then, for reasons that biographers of the two men have never uncovered, turned violently against him during his first year in office.

The stage was set for a rapprochement between Hearst and Tammany. Boss Charles Frances Murphy was prepared to tell his regulars to nominate Hearst as the party's candidate for mayor. The regulars clearly regarded this as a bitter pill but might have swallowed it. Al Smith, however, exploded. He would withdraw his own candidacy but never in favor of Hearst.

Hylan was a compromise candidate: he had good machine connections in Brooklyn, hated Civil Service reform, and had loudly opposed the Dual Contracts. In 1916 he had become vice president of the Hearst-inspired Society to Recapture the Subway.[28] His opponents dismissed him contemptuously as both a machine puppet and a Hearst stooge. Mitchell fought a hard, dirty campaign, exploiting reports that Hearst had socialized with a German spy and proclaiming that he would save the city from "Hearst, Hylan, and the Hohenzollerns," but on election day Hylan won with a plurality of 170,000 votes.

In Hylan the city had acquired a mayor who used the subway issue as demagogically as Hearst did but with far more personal conviction. To Hearst the transit issue was a useful weapon; to Hylan, by contrast, it was a reminder of a bitter personal humiliation.

A poor boy from a farm in Greene County, Hylan had paid his way through law school by working as an engineer on Brooklyn's Kings County Elevated Railroad. In February 1897, the company fired him for carelessness in rounding a turn too quickly. Hylan's version was that the firing was a cover-up for the negligence of his supervisor. "As I neared the signal tower," he later told the *New York Times*, "Superintendent Barton stepped from behind the tower. Had I been moving fast nothing would have saved him. It was because of the fact that I was not moving rapidly I was able to apply the brakes and thereby save Barton's life." But "someone had to be the goat."[29]

Hylan nursed not only a specific antagonism against the BRT but also a wide-ranging resentment against the opponents who thwarted his ambitions and mocked his intellect. Though his nickname "Red Mike" referred more to his hair than his politics, Hylan eagerly reiterated Hearst's claim that the world was divided between the People and the Trusts. He tied his star to the publisher's, taking his summer vacations in Palm Beach, Florida, to be near his idol. He appointed Marion Davies's father as a city magistrate and named one of the Staten Island ferries *William Randolph Hearst*.

Two dramatic events of 1918 allowed the Hearst papers to position Hylan as defender of the hard-pressed subway rider. The first was a planning and public relations disaster. The second was an accident that cost nearly one hundred lives.

The official opening of the IRT "H" in Manhattan and the first day of the 42nd Street crosstown as a shuttle operation on August 2, 1918, inspired a mood of celebration reminiscent of the opening of the Interborough in 1904. Midtown had arrived as a commercial and entertainment center. Grand Central and Times Square were its twin hubs. The city celebrated its glorious future and then found its transportation system in sudden collapse.

On that first day riders became confused during the walk from the new north-south platforms to the east-west shuttle. Signs were unclear and workmen had left piles of construction debris blocking the passageways. The August weather was hot and humid; the crowd was thick. Riders at Grand Central began milling about, going in the wrong direction, then turning around to find themselves unable to make their way through the opposing stream of traffic.

At Times Square passengers getting off the shuttle failed to realize that they had to go through a tunnel to the new Seventh Avenue–Broadway platform. Instead, they walked up the stairway, then were enraged when denied free reentry into the station. The voices of subway employees, according to the *American*, "were drowned in the wild screams and yells that emanated from the infuriated passengers." Many persons "shouted their bitter denunciations of Interborough and Brooklyn Rapid Transit officials and threats of bodily harm to the transportation heads were numerous." "SUBWAY SYSTEM IN UTTER COLLAPSE," screamed the *American* the next morning.[30]

The Hearst papers seized the opportunity to build up Hylan as the straphangers' champion. As soon as the trouble began he embarked on a tour of the scene with an *American* reporter at his side. The paper presented him as a decisive executive, quick to take action not only against company heads but against unmannerly citizens as well. On the packed shuttle he encountered a young man hogging space by keeping a bundle on the seat beside him while his feet extended a yard into the aisle.

> A modishly dressed girl was crushed in the space in front of the bundle, but the youth ignored her until the Mayor said:
> "Just remove that bundle and let the lady be seated please."
> The young man looked at him and turned away with a half-sneer in silence, and the Mayor, raising his voice slightly, continued:
> "If you haven't the common decency to let a lady sit down, I'll get rid of some of that baggage and put you where you belong."
> The bundle came off the seat abruptly then and the young women sat down, murmuring her thanks.[31]

The authorities solved the problem by placing green and black guidelines on the floor of the station; in 1927 they were replaced by the present strings of colored lights on the ceiling.

Hylan appeared even more heroically aggressive three months later in the aftermath of the Malbone Street disaster. In the morning of November 1, 1918, in the closing days of World War I, the engineers of the BRT went on strike. The company quickly replaced them with inadequately trained employees from other divisions. In the evening rush hour one of the new engineers on the Brighton Line took a curve coming downhill from Crown Heights into a curving tunnel under Malbone Street (now Empire Boulevard). He should have slowed to six miles an hour but he was actually going over forty. The first car left the rails, rammed into a concrete partition, and was thrown across the roadbed in front of the entrance to the tunnel. The other four cars of the train smashed right through it and came to a stop two hundred feet down the tracks inside the tunnel. The third rail was at once switched off but, because of a faulty communications system, was switched back on as passengers were groping through dark tunnel. Ninety-three people died that night and many more were taken to hospitals.

The *American* and *Evening Journal* showed Hylan arriving quickly at the accident scene, talking to survivors, intervening to get additional nurses, demanding the prosecution not just of the motorman but of the higher-ups, and seizing on the little-known power of the mayor to intervene as chief magistrate and hold hearings to fix responsibility. Just as the Hearst press had relentlessly presented Gaynor as a Judas, a sneering betrayer of the common man, so it now built up Hylan as the champion of the little guy ready to fight the big fight against the transit dragons who ruled the city.

YELLOW JOURNALISM VERSUS PUBLIC RELATIONS

Meanwhile the IRT and the BRT, as the Interborough and Brooklyn Rapid Transit companies now began to be called, were in crisis. The Dual Contracts locked them into a five-cent fare but postwar inflation had both reduced the value of the nickel and increased the cost of labor and materials. Companies that had been highly profitable went into receivership. (When the BRT emerged it was reorganized as the Brooklyn Manhattan Transit Company or BMT.)

Hearst and Hylan regarded the transit companies' pleas for a higher fare with contempt. Their attitude was concisely expressed in the headline over a September 12, 1918, *American* editorial: "TRACTION TRUSTS HAVE DANCED, NOW LET THEM PAY THE FIDDLER." In these circumstances, the companies began looking for new ways to communicate with a skeptical public.

The problem that the so-called Traction Trust faced was not greatly different from that of American business as a whole. The first response of businessmen to the assaults of progressives and muckrackers had been to cultivate secrecy. By the postwar period, however, American capitalism was fast acquiring a new sophistication and many companies turned to the first man ever to offer regular public relations counseling on a fee basis—Ivy Ledbetter Lee.

Born in Cedartown, Georgia, in 1877, educated at Emory College and Princeton, Lee had started in New York City as a journalist. Ironically, he worked briefly for Hearst as well as for the *Sun*, the *New York Times*, and the *World*. He began his career as a publicist in anti-Tammany politics but soon turned to business clients. He represented the Rockefeller family exclusively until 1917, when he expanded his client list to include the Pennsylvania Railroad, Bethlehem Steel, the International Sugar Council, and the Guggenheim and Chrysler interests.

Lee worked for individual companies but he conceived himself to be serving American capitalism as a whole. His lifelong purpose was to give the modern corporation a human face. As a result of Lee's pioneering efforts, many Americans who had worried about the rapacity of the giant Trusts now found themselves impressed by the sincerity of public service corporations.

In 1916, as Lee was about to leave his exclusive service to the Rockefellers, the directors of the IRT asked him to reshape their public image as well. He was hired at an annual retainer. Ten years later he testified before the Transit Commission that he had been paid a total of $212,954 and Samuel Untermeyer, the Commission's special counsel, estimated that when printing and other expenses were added in the total came to over $300,000.[32]

He set about winning over the newspapers. Oswald Garrison Villard, publisher of the

Evening Post, said of him: "He knew the ways of newspaper men, what they could do and could not do, and how to present the facts of a matter which he wished taken up. The result was that he was a welcome visitor who often aided editorial writers by calling their attention to matters of public moment and giving them material on which to base their comments."[33] Lee began issuing a stream of press releases designed to prompt admiration for the subway with odd, attention-catching facts. One for July 2, 1916, relates that five tons of newspapers and seven and a half tons of dirt are cleaned off the steps and platforms of the subway stations each day. Others point to such technological improvements as the moving platforms being installed to eliminate dangerous gaps between platform and car at the curved Union Square station.

These press releases presented the IRT as a big company with a small-town personality, one that struggled valiantly under difficult conditions to carry more people quickly and safely than all the other railroads in America put together. These releases are preserved in the Ivy Lee papers at Princeton University as are clippings of the newspapers stories they inspired. To an amazing degree the newspapers simply picked up Lee's viewpoint and often his precise words.

But though he used the newspapers brilliantly, Lee sought more direct means of communicating with the public. In 1917 he launched his famous "We Ask Your Help" campaign in which IRT president Theodore P. Shonts appealed directly for suggestions from ordinary straphangers as to how service could be improved. The purpose was not to get advice but to establish a human relation between corporation and public.

As the *Electric Railway Journal* commented approvingly, "Antagonism melts the moment a man says, 'I'm doing all I can, but I know I'm not perfect; tell me of your criticism, and I'll do my best to profit by it.'"[34] An astonishing seven thousand letters were received in February and March alone. Lee made sure that each correspondent was answered individually—no form letters were used. In 1917 and 1918 he distributed a newsletter titled *Rapid Transit* which summarized the public's suggestions and quoted Shonts's replies.

Lee's most visible contribution to the daily life of New Yorkers was a series of posters with a newspaper format called the *Subway Sun* which were displayed in each car. These too presented the IRT's new, friendly face. The purpose, which Lee thought more effective than mere propaganda, was to touch on little things—to give notes on the city's recreational facilities, to offer illustrated glimpses of old New York, and to make suggestions toward more comfortable riding. "Such bulletins cannot help being interesting," Lee said, "and their interest is bound to be reflected in goodwill for the company."[35]

Typical *Subway Suns* praised the company's safety record or described its technological improvements.[36] The *Subway Sun* and its twin *The Elevated Express* helped persuade the public that the switch from "old-fashioned" ticket choppers to the new "Feather Weight Pressure" turnstiles. A series entitled "Why I Use the Interborough" featured a variety of New Yorkers, including Negro writer James Weldon Johnson, explaining how the subway made their lives easier (Ill. 37).

But the *Subway Sun*'s most important goal was to convince the riding public to accept a fare increase. Lee tried to shift attention from the cost of a ride to those two other bugaboos of an average New Yorker—rents and taxes. A 1919 poster argued that the inadequate fare

Our Men Know Their Jobs

The Subway Sun

PUBLISHED NOW AND THEN BY THE INTERBOROUGH RAPID TRANSIT COMPANY

Safest Railroad In the World

No. 34

Why I Use the Interborough

—*From the Secretary, the National Association for the Advancement of Colored People*

I USE the Interborough because it enables me to spend fifteen minutes longer over my breakfast table uptown and fifteen minutes longer at my desk downtown, without being late going or coming.

JAMES WELDON JOHNSON

37 ▪ "Why I Use the Interborough."

The Subway Sun. Ivy Lee Papers, Manuscripts Division, Department of Rare Books and Special Collections, Princeton University Libraries.

The Subway Sun

PUBLISHED NOW AND THEN BY THE INTERBOROUGH RAPID TRANSIT COMPANY

World's Safest Railroad

VOLUME II   MARCH 29, 1919   NUMBER 4

Crowds, Taxes and Rents

New York was never so congested as now. No wonder rents are going up!

Two million strangers, the papers say, were in town to see the Twenty-Seventh parade. Half a million commuters and other outsiders are here every day.

Every one of them riding on the Subways and Elevated is carried at a loss, and New York City must help pay the bill.

The City has $250,000,000 invested in Subways and the 5-cent fare does not pay the cost of the service these strangers receive.

Unless the fare is increased to give the City—out of Subway earnings—interest, etc. on its investment (about $13,000,000 a year,) it must be raised by taxation.

INTERBOROUGH RAPID TRANSIT COMPANY

Theodore P. Shonts
President

38 ▪ "Crowds, Taxes, and Rents."

The Subway Sun. Ivy Lee Papers, Manuscripts Division, Department of Rare Books and Special Collections, Princeton University Libraries.

prevented payments to the city treasury and so resulted in a higher tax bill (Ill. 38). A 1921 issue of the *Elevated Express* quoted a Chamber of Commerce report which argued that a higher fare would result in new subway lines, new apartment building, less congestion, and, ultimately, lower rents for each apartment.

Hearst could not permit Lee's campaign to pass unopposed. During the great war over the five-cent fare Hearst's editors, writers, and cartoonists made the *Subway Sun* a continual butt of their mockery.

Tom Powers and Winsor McKaye made Lee a special target. Powers had been with Hearst since the days of the Spanish-American War and his political cartoons belonged to the same funny-paper world as the Yellow Kid and Foxy Grandpa. He was fascinated by the sudden appearance of the anonymous posters and soon his drawings were enlivened by parodies

Great Subway Mystery

Who Is the Editor of the Subway Sun? By T. E. Powers

39 ▪ Tom Powers.
Great Subway Mystery.
New York Evening Journal,
December 28, 1920.
Courtesy: Library of
Congress.

bearing such earnest messages from the IRT directors as "Don't Get Off the Express Between Stations" and "You Would Be Surprised To Know How Many Flat Wheels We Are Using." He was also intrigued by the fact that the posters were unsigned. "Who is the Editor of the Subway Sun?" Powers asked in a series of cartoons portraying a mysterious bearded figure stalking through the world of subterranean journalism (Ill. 39).

Powers made savage fun of Lee's almost totally ineffective pleas for public acceptance of a fare increase. One of his best cartoons features a bug-eyed straphanger staring astonished at the IRT's specious reasoning (Ill. 40). For the most part Lee absorbed this attack without complaint but in April 1920 he couldn't resist issuing three *Subway Suns* pointing out that Hearst's justifications for an increased newspaper price applied with equal force to the subway fare (Ill. 41).

Hearst's other major cartoonist of the postwar period, Winsor McCay, responded to Lee's public relations campaigns in a quite different style. McCay was a vaudevillian as well as a cartoonist. He began drawing *Little Nemo in Slumberland* in 1905 but his major contribution to the mass media came in 1909 when he produced more than ten thousand pencil sketches to animate five minutes of film in *Gertie the Trained Dinosaur*—the first animated cartoon to feature an animal.

Although McCay introduced Little Nemo for the *Herald*, he moved to the better-paying

If So, Why Not?   ∴   ∴   ∴   **By T. E. Powers**

40 ▪ Tom Powers.
If So, Why Not?
New York Evening Journal,
December 3, 1920.
Courtesy: Library of
Congress.

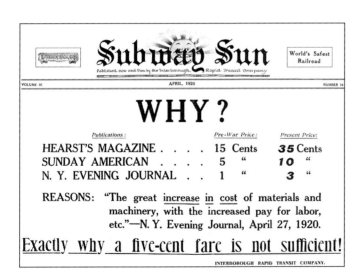

41 ▪ "Why?"
The Subway Sun. Ivy Lee
Papers, Manuscripts
Division, Department of
Rare Books and Special
Collections, Princeton
University Libraries.

BAD DREAMS

42 ▪ Winsor McCay.
Bad Dreams.
New York American, October 26,
1921. Courtesy: Library of
Congress.

Hearst papers and began producing first humorous drawings and then, as World War I came to an end, a brilliant series of political cartoons. In contrast to Powers, who felt most comfortable with a sketchy style that filled every bit of a strip of drawings with some satirical jab, McCay favored single images with bold areas of black and white. It was a manner brilliantly calculated to capture the physical menace of the bloated Traction Trust (Ill. 42).

By 1922 Lee had admitted that the public relations campaign for a fare increase had been a total failure. If the fare were to rise, it would never be with the acquiescence of the riders.

THE FIVE-CENT FARE AND THE IND

The subway crisis continued to dominate city politics. Hearst and Hylan had staked their political futures on preserving the five-cent fare while somehow still finding means to expand the system. They quickly found themselves battling both the city's business leaders and its most popular Democratic politician—Governor Al Smith.

Hearst and Al Smith had competed for the gubernatorial nomination in 1918. Smith had won at the Democratic convention and had gone on to win a two-year term as governor. Hearst's newspapers had supported him after he made a brief statement supporting municipal ownership and operation of utilities—including the subway. But the two men remained bitter rivals behind the scenes.

Hearst had to strike at Governor Smith in order to preserve his own prospects within the Democratic party. He found his opportunity in 1919 when New York's milk producers went on strike. The price of milk rose to eighteen cents a quart and stayed there after the strike ended—a perfect issue for Hearst, combining as it did bitter social resentment against price-fixing with sentimental tears for starving babies. Throughout August and September of 1919 Hearst's headlines, editorials, and cartoons featured daily diatribes against the Milk Trust and its lackey Smith.

The governor followed Mayor Gaynor's example by replying to the master of personal attacks with a bitterly personal assault of his own. Hearst was "a mean man," a "particularly low type of man" and, worst of all according to the Tammany code, "a man who has been loyal to nobody." "Of course that foolish attack in *The New York Evening Journal*," Smith told a meeting of the Woman's Democratic League, "would never have been made on me if I had shown the proper degree of subservience to the owner of the paper."[37] On the evening of October 29, 1919, Smith hired Carnegie Hall to defend his record and assail Hearst as "the pestilence that walks in the dark" before four thousand flag-waving Democrats.[38]

In November 1920 Smith lost his bid for reelection in the Harding-Coolidge landslide. It was a narrow defeat and Smith remained widely popular. It was assumed that he would be back in Albany as soon as Governor Nathan L. Miller's two-year term in office was completed. This proved to be the case. In the meantime, however, the Republican Miller had a chance to solve the subway mess.

In January 1921 Miller appointed his Transit Commission. The three commissioners were George McAneny, who had represented the city in the Dual Contract negotiations; Leroy Harkness, who had been assistant counsel for the Public Service Commission when the Dual Contracts were drawn up; and General John F. O'Ryan, who had already directed an internal reorganization of the Interborough. They set out to both restructure the subway companies and plan ambitious new routes.

A serious attempt to restructure transit finances and bureaucracy, the Transit Commission's plan was also a thoroughgoing effort to transform the semiotics of the subway. Everything that had become a sign of corruption was to be eliminated. There would be no more watered stock. There would be no more preferential payments. The barest mention of New York transit would no longer raise mental images of Boss Tweed and bloated Wall Street speculators. "In so far as the crimes and blunders of the past can be wiped out," said the *World*, "the commission purposes to do so and start with a clean slate."[39]

The commissioners also tried to remove fare increases from public debate by making them entirely a matter of technical calculation. Once operating expenses and interest on bonds had been paid, transit revenues would be placed in a so-called Barometer Fund. If the fund went above a specified level, the fare could be lowered. If it fell below that level the fare would be raised. The whole thing could be done with a slide rule.

The Transit Commission plan dominated the 1921 mayoralty race. Manhattan borough president Henry Curran faced an impossible task in opposing Hylan. As a Republican, he could not repudiate the governor's efforts at transit reform. He equivocated, accepted the Transit Commission plan as a first step, but insisted that he had important ideas of his own.

Meanwhile Hearst and Hylan focused relentlessly on the five-cent fare. Their strategy was

TAG, HENRY, YOU'RE IT!

Copyright. 1921. by Star Company.

The Subway Son

CURRAN

HE fell heir to this label when he consented to lead the Traction Trust-Miller-Upstate drive against Home Rule in New York.
He is not only the Subway Son but the favorite son.
See editorial.

43 ▪ Winsor McCay.
Tag, Henry, You're It.
New York Evening Journal,
October 27, 1921. Courtesy:
Library of Congress.

to portray Curran as yet another tool of the Traction Trust. Winsor McCay hung the label The Subway Son around Curran's neck (Ill. 43) and Hearst's editorial writers explained what it implied:

> Papa and Mamma Traction Trust have another child.
> "THE SUBWAY SON."
> Godfather, Ivy Lee. No, Ivy is not a lady. Ivy is a male person. Press agent for the Traction Trust or any other old trust that pays him. Ivy says the latest addition to the Trust family is just real sweet and always does everything that Papa and Mamma Traction Trust want him to do.
> "THE SUBWAY SON."
> Child of Mr. B.R.T. and Mrs. I.R.T. Traction Trust. Mamma doing nicely and Papa tickled pink. Says they never had a son who gave them so little Trouble.[40]

This convicted Curran of the major charges in the Hearst arsenal of vices: servility, unmanliness, and sympathy for the traction companies.

In the final days of the campaign Curran campaigned more against Hearst than against Hylan. He attacked him as "the meanest man in public life."[41] "Will you Democrats forget how he attacked Al Smith," he demanded.[42] In his final speech of the campaign, delivered over the new "wireless telephone" from the De Forest Radio Telephone and Telegraph Company at 181st Street and Sedgwick Avenue in the Bronx, Curran declared that the sole issue was "whether we are to have four years more of Hearst, by Hearst, and for Hearst, through the agency of Hylan, his overseer."[43]

It was a good rhetorical point, but Curran didn't have a chance. Hearst and Hylan mounted a brilliantly effective campaign against Wall Street, Standard Oil, the BRT, the IRT, and the twice-daily misery of the rush hour. Hylan, "the 5 cent mayor," won reelection with a huge plurality.

If the 1921 mayoral race was dominated by the Transit Commission reorganization plan, the next year's battle for the gubernatorial nomination between Hearst and Smith provided the setting for dramatic promises of new subway routes.

In May of 1922 the Transit Commission offered an ambitious expansion plan, including extension of the Seventh Avenue line up Central Park West, a new line on Eighth and Amsterdam Avenues, a crosstown line from Long Island City through Brooklyn, an extension of the Corona-Flushing subway, and a subway line under the Narrows from Bay Ridge to Staten Island. It publicized its plans with a short film shown in 150 theaters, *Standing Room Only*, in which Father Knickerbocker used pictures and animated drawings to argue for new routes.

Hylan countered the Transit Commission's proposals with his own just in time to give Hearst an issue. At its center was the call which Hearst had been repeating since the 1890s for municipal ownership, municipal construction, and, above all, municipal operation. The city would plan, build, and run new lines. It would "recapture" the old lines and merge them with a new city system.

Hylan's plan also contained a grandiose scheme of route expansion. If the Transit Commission proposed to spend a mere $218,000,000 on new subways, Hylan offered to invest an astounding $600,000,000 in 126 miles of city-owned subways. They would be financed partly by municipal bonds, partly by what Hylan loudly insisted were the hidden profits of the existing lines. The profits from the new lines would permit still further subway construction and New York would at last become a true Subway City without a fare increase, without higher taxes, without pain. Hylan's plan was announced on August 27th, just as the gubernatorial nominating convention approached.

Smith wanted the nomination. So did Hearst. He told reporters that Smith was qualified "to lead the Democratic Party, if it is to be a conservative party" and hinted broadly that he was ready to run on a third-party ticket.[44] Party bosses desperately feared a split. Then, unexpectedly, Hearst offered them an ideal solution: he would endorse Smith for governor if he himself were nominated for senator.

Smith rejected this deal with savage contempt. He threatened to repeat all his previous attacks on Hearst on the convention floor and announced he would walk out of the hall rather than run on the same ticket with Hearst. In the end he prevailed. The day after the November election the *World* congratulated Smith for overwhelming "the Hearst money-bags"[45] and the *Tribune* declared enthusiastically that Smith had "rid his party forever of the menacing candidacy of William R. Hearst."[46]

With Hearst losing interest in New York politics, Hylan's position was weak. The knives were being sharpened. What was needed was a dramatic appeal to public opinion and the city's mercantile establishment made one.

The Merchants Association could not help despising Hylan. Its members, executives in banking, real estate, insurance, utilities, and manufacturing, were deeply concerned with municipal frugality, low tax rates, and private enterprise. They wanted healthy transit companies, privately owned, and new subway construction.

In 1923 the Association launched a full-scale public relations offensive by organizing a Committee of One Thousand to circulate a petition throughout the city demanding immediate subway relief. Its organizers picked on two routes common to both the Transit Commission proposals and the Hylan plan and demanded that construction begin without further delay. On the surface "Say It With Shovels" looked like a neutral slogan but the entire city understood that Hylan alone was being blamed for blocking rapid transit progress.

The campaign's official leader was the fountain pen manufacturer Frank B. Waterman, though Lewis E. Pierson, president of the Merchants Association, did most of the practical work. Waterman and Pierson wisely launched their drive in July, since a hot, uncomfortable summer was sure to make New Yorkers discontented. A placard appeared in the subway cars declaring:

* *
FELLOW STRAP * HANGERS: We are crowded worse each day. While officials delay, WE
suffer. Ask the Board of Estimate to Act. SIGN THE SUBWAY PETITION.
* *

The *World*, the *Times*, and other newspapers enthusiastically joined in the campaign and published daily stories on eager volunteers who were accumulating vast quantities of signatures.

The organizers presented themselves as practical men who had no time for the Hearst-Hylan bogey of the Transit Trust. Pierson told the *World* that though some might call his petitioners "the interests," they were really "plain business men of the sort one meets in the subways."[47] Waterman told his volunteers that they were representative of all those employers who were "tired of having their stenographers arrive late and with their clothes torn." He also told them that "The Mayor is so jumpy about the 'interests' that he sees a traction-goblin behind every lamppost."[48]

Hylan and the Hearst papers fought back by pointing out that several years before Waterman had maintained a Protestants-only hiring policy at his Fountain Pen factory. Hylan declared that what he scornfully called "the fountain pen petition" was "conceived in iniquity and born in sin."[49]

In 1924 the struggle between Hylan and the Transit establishment moved into a popular new medium of communication. Radio had become a national craze after World War I with thousands of amateurs broadcasting and receiving on homemade crystal sets. By 1920, the year of the first regularly scheduled broadcast, there were four thousand stations in America. Most of these were small affairs, set up by individual enthusiasts. New York City established a municipally owned station, WNYC, to broadcast fire reports and police bulletins.

Hylan and his advisors were quick to see that radio offered a new means to circumvent newspapers that they loudly insisted were controlled by the Traction Trust. On September 30th, Hylan spent an hour on the city station denouncing his opponents as "organ grinders and tomtom beaters of the transit corporations."[50]

Major General John F. O'Ryan was offered time to reply but only if he submitted his text in advance to an editing board. O'Ryan called this censorship and attacked Hylan for perverting WNYC to political ends. "The city radio station is not being used for political purposes, as the Major General says," Hylan indignantly replied. "It is being used to tell the truth about politicians who are working against the interests of people in both parties."[51]

O'Ryan did speak on October 20, but only after his manuscript had passed inspection by Commissioner Mills of the Department of Plant and Structures which controlled the radio station. Not surprisingly, O'Ryan gave a moderately phrased defense of the commission.

On October 26 Hylan was back on the radio assailing George McAneny, "Jerry" Dahl of the B.M.T., and "the transit profiteers" who were making what Hylan continued to insist were great profits out of the nickel fare.

O'Ryan's reply to this new provocation came not on WNYC but on the *Brooklyn Eagle*'s radio station, WARG. O'Ryan tried to raise the discussion from attacks on Hylan himself to a broader consideration of Hylanism and the failure of democracy it represented.

The current mayor of New York, he told his listeners, was merely the latest representative of that tendency toward demagoguery which had plagued democracy since the Greeks. The ancient crowd had now become mass man, susceptible to appeals not only from individual demagogues but also from sensational newspapers and radio:

> It is this mass of us, concerned with our own affairs, that are peculiarly susceptible to infection by the bacillus of Hylanism. In reading the morning papers we turn aside from a detailed and authoritative explanation of some public matter of importance, given by some experienced man of character, in order to read the more exciting headlines and matter that make appeal to our emotions. We don't stop to analyze the emptiness of an appeal of that character.

O'Ryan cited Hylan's statements about the exorbitant profits earned by the companies as demagogic appeals to resentment and passion. "Do you not resent the misstatements of the Mayor?" O'Ryan demanded. "Hylanism evidently acts upon the theory that its muddled and deceiving statements about the 'swollen profits,' 'pockets of the people,' and that sort of thing, if repeated often enough, will so muddle your understanding of the whole matter that, at least, you will conclude to let bad enough alone, which means him."[52]

Hylan at once took to the city radio waves, assuring citizens that he was not in the least affected by "the poison of abuse poured out by squirming traction toadies."[53] He seemed to be winning his transit fight. The legislature, under Governor Smith's prodding, had granted the city the powers to plan and construct its own subways and, though the state Transit Commission had not been abolished, the city's Board of Transportation had began work on the Sixth and Eighth Avenue lines. Hylan was considered a shoo-in for a third term.

He made his crucial misstep on October 17, 1924. Two BMT trains had crashed near the Ocean Parkway station of the Brighton Beach line, causing one death and thirty injuries. Hylan thought he saw an opening. He persuaded the Board of Estimate to demand that Governor Smith remove Transit Commissioners McAneny, Harkness, and O'Ryan on grounds of malfeasance in office. But Hylan wanted more than the removal of the commissioners. He wanted a hearing which would be, in effect, a public trial.

That is what he got, only he was the defendant. Hylan was now the central figure not only in the city's subway crisis but also in a power struggle within the Democratic party. Longtime Tammany boss John Francis Murphy had died. Who would seize his power? Governor Al Smith later commented mildly in his autobiography that "the rank and file of the party had become definitely convinced that Hylan was under the domination of Hearst and that Hearst was in reality the leader after the death of Murphy."[54] This Smith would never tolerate. Hylan's charges against the Transit Commissioners gave him an opportunity to get rid of Hearst and Hylan forever and to assert his own dominance over the New York Democratic party.

Smith initiated a general transit investigation to be conducted by Associate Justice John V. McAvoy of the Appellate Division of the Supreme Court. A long parade of experts came to testify that Hylan was the major source of transit ills. He had obstructed efforts to complete work under the Dual Contracts. He had blocked efforts to improve shops and yards for repair work. He had made it impossible to acquire new cars. He was chiefly responsible for the delay in building subways and for the resulting congestion.

The Hearst papers replied with headlines showing Hylan as the subway activist:

—HYLAN ASSAILS SMITH TRANSIT INQUIRY

—HYLAN WINS STEP FOR 4-BORO SUBWAY

—HYLAN TRANSIT STAND PRAISED

—MAYOR DIRECTS ACTION TO END B.M.T. JAM

—HYLAN WINS SUBWAY FIGHT FOR PEOPLE

—HYLAN CHARGES TRANSIT BOARD DELAY

But for once the Hearst papers were drowned out in the public clamor. When McAvoy issued his report condemning Hylan on all counts, the *World* concluded that the Democratic party "must either dissociate itself entirely from the Hylan record or surrender body and soul to Hylan and Hearst and go down with them."[55] It chose the first course. Smith picked Jimmy Walker to oppose Frank Waterman in the next mayoral election and although the city pressed ahead with the municipal or "Independent" subway system, Hylan's political career was finished.

William Randolph Hearst's impact on the New York City subway system came to an end when Hylan left City Hall. Transit stories had dominated Hearst's front pages since he acquired the *Morning Journal* in 1894. They had built his circulation and given him his most powerful political weapon for thirty years. Now he had failed to become president, governor, or senator. He had not even reached Gracie Mansion.

What had the city gained from Hearst's long battle? It had certainly acquired a municipally owned and operated subway system. And, until 1947, it enjoyed a five-cent fare.

These accomplishments, however, came at great cost. Hearst had a disastrous impact on the politics and economics of the subway. By insisting that the private companies weren't losing money at all but were merely hiding immense profits by clever bookkeeping tricks, Hearst maintained that it was possible to operate and expand the subway within the limits of the five-cent fare. Yet when the IND opened for service it was discovered that it could be self-sustaining only if it charged eight cents a ride. New York transit politics entered a make-believe phase as city leaders pretended that a five-cent fare was still reasonable for the private lines and that the IND would balance its books after a brief (though constantly extended) period of subsidy. Hearst had enabled the public to do something that it is all too willing to do: demand a rising level of government service while ignoring the fact that someone's taxes are going to have to go up.

But Hearst did something worse than embitter the subway's politics and confuse its finances. He reinforced the growing suspicion that New York was a giant, intricate mechanism that could never work to the benefit of its ordinary citizens. If New Yorkers of 1904 had felt such a fear they easily put it aside and pointed to the success of the subway in doing so. Twenty years later acrimony in city politics and crowding in the trains suggested that there was something inherently wrong with the very idea of a Subway City. In Chapter Five we will watch this suspicion dawning among politicians, architects, and city planners. In Chapter Six it will spread to an artist, a playwright, a novelist, and a poet.

CHAPTER FIVE

SKYSCRAPER AND SUBWAY

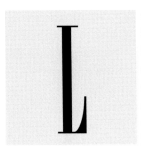 O O K I N G at the growth of New York City in 1929, twenty-five years after the opening of the Interborough, William Barclay Parsons declared that the most "spectacular consequence of the subway has been the skyscraper."[1] What is surprising in retrospect is that Parsons should have been so surprised. From the mid-nineteenth century New Yorkers had witnessed the outlines of a new kind of city emerging all about them—a city of unbelievably immense crowds and astonishingly tall buildings. The same years that saw the construction of the subway saw the erection of the Flatiron Building (1902) and the Times Tower (1904), but few anticipated the size or the numbers of the skyscrapers to come. For Parsons and millions of his fellow New Yorkers enthusiasm mingled with stunned disbelief. Surely the congestion could be dispersed; surely the skyscrapers would stop their upward thrust. But as New York spread outward at its base, its drive for height did not abate in the least.

The skyscraper was profoundly destabilizing to the nineteenth-century ideal of the city promoted by the City Beautiful movement. The Municipal Art Society envisioned a largely horizontal city of orderly streets punctuated by sculpture, courthouses, and other expressions of civic order. The skyscraper, however, implied a vertical city, with dark, congested canyons below and the material expression of the profit motive soaring overhead.

New Yorkers required a new vision of the city to direct its growth. Did their dramatic skyline represent the triumph of enlightened business leadership or was it the chaotic result of private greed? Was New York the Wonder City or a new form of urban hell?

A vision that could embrace the diversity of the new city would have to be founded on a dialectical opposition. The most obvious was that between skyscraper and subway. Civic boosters proclaimed that the symbiotic relation between them had given the city not only its soaring skyline but also its constantly rising real estate values.

But subway crowding was the blot on this glorious vision. If the skyline symbolized the glorious aspirations of the Wonder City, the subway increasingly came to represent its oppressive day-to-day reality. Henry Curran, Harvey Wiley Corbett, Hugh Ferriss, Lewis Mumford, and the men who produced the Regional Plan of 1929 all attempted to deal with the contradiction between the rich promise of the Wonder City and its appalling congestion.

As they did, an odd and fateful shift occurred in thinking about the city. While some still insisted that the answer to subway congestion was more and better subways, others replied that more subways would only produce more skyscrapers, more apartment blocks, and more congestion. Instead of better urban infrastructure, they urged the decentralization of cities. The skyscraper-and-subway city suddenly looked like a huge mistake.

THE WONDER CITY

In 1913 Edward E. McCall, chairman of the Public Service Commission, extolled the Wonder City in an interview with the *New York Times* and praised the subway's role in creating it.[2] McCall's New York is a place of accelerating and bewildering but still glorious change. Only old New Yorkers who could remember the city of horsecars and five-story buildings could grasp the magnitude of the city's transformations. McCall cites "a group of downtown buildings which, within the memory of a child born fifteen years ago, were subjects for the stranger's drop-jawed stare and for the native's boasting." Now the same buildings look "like a little company of dwarfs set down amid a giant's concourse."

Changes in the city were so rapid and so vast that they produce a kind of vertigo for the imagination. "We make new records every year," McCall said. "New Yorkers," he added proudly "cannot keep up with New York."

McCall's confidence rested on two widely shared principles: first, that progress can be measured in terms of rising land values and, second, that the subway increases the value of land. R. L. Duffus expressed the conventional wisdom in 1929 when he wrote that "an elevated will approximately double neighboring land prices while a subway will multiply them four to twelve times."[3] Edwin H. Spengler's *Land Values in New York in Relation to Transit Facilities* (1930) suggested that rising values were neither so certain nor so uniform as had been believed but also showed that the subway was very definitely a major contributor to the city's massive real estate boom.

Only one area seemed to decline as a result of underground rapid transit. That was the drygoods section that ran from just north of City Hall to Houston Street. The subway encouraged a movement northward to sprinkler-equipped loft buildings north of Union Square, a movement which accelerated when fire insurance rates rose dramatically after the 1906 San Francisco earthquake and fire. In 1913 the dark blocks between Chambers and Houston provided the one spot of gloom in Edward McCall's view of his booming city.

The area remained depressed for decades before reviving in the sixties. In 1913 the loss of real estate value there following subway construction was, according to McCall, "a towering tragedy."

The rest of New York, on the other hand, showed "subway magic." The midtown area between 42nd Street and 57th saw New York's most explosive growth. Spengler noted that when a well-known real estate developer listed the ten most valuable sites in the city, eight were between 41st Street and 59th.[4]

The legitimate theaters that had followed the Interborough to Times Square were joined by motion picture palaces along 42nd Street and along Broadway. Adolf Zukor proclaimed in 1926 that the motion picture theaters, "with the moderate prices, prices within the reach of all, brought to Broadway hundreds of thousands of people who before that time had found their amusement elsewhere."[5]

The rest of midtown saw real estate promoters and architects join in a frantic race to build the world's tallest skyscraper. Deems Taylor wrote in a 1929 issue of *Vanity Fair* that in the limited area around the Grand Central Station tower the fifty-two-story Chanin Building, the thirty-story Pershing Square Building, the sixty-two-story Reynolds Buildings, and a fifty-three-story building rising next to the Hotel Belmont were either recently completed or under construction. "About you, in other words, in a district less than 200 yards square, stands—or will stand, shortly—a group of skyscrapers whose floor space totals nearly 100 acres and whose tenants outnumber the combined population of Cheyenne, Wyoming; Brownsville, Texas; Reno, Nevada; Emporia, Kansas; and Albuquerque, New Mexico."[6]

The real estate boom in the outlying sections of the city matched that in the central core. Three quarters of the land in Manhattan north of 134th Street had been vacant before the first subway was built. In the early years of the century young men rode to Dyckman Street to play softball in the undeveloped fields around the station. Now all of Manhattan north of Harlem was rapidly subdivided and developed with five-story walk-ups and taller elevator apartment buildings. Edward McCall cited the area along Tenth Avenue near Trinity Cemetery at 153rd Street to show the impact of rapid transit: "Not many years ago it was a desert waste. Then came the subway. Now look at it! It is solid city, raised layer upon layer, housing in magnificent buildings mighty multitudes."[7]

The same story was repeated in large sections of the Bronx. James R. Murphy, a Bronx real estate dealer, credited the express service along Jerome Avenue with converting that part of the west Bronx "from a sparsely settled one-family dwelling neighborhood to a fully built apartment house district."[8] Real estate auctioneer Joseph P. Day listed twenty large estates that his firm had auctioned off during the nineteen-twenties and declared that new subway facilities were not merely a good thing—"They are an absolute necessity."[9]

This building boom inevitably caused subway crowding. "New York transforms herself more swiftly than the imagination can follow," an enthusiast declared in 1927 and then added with slightly more irony: "It has crowded more people into a given area and also into a given subway car than any other city since the dawn of time."[10]

The Transit Commission, comparing travel patterns in 1913 and 1923, found a 40 percent passenger increase for the downtown district but a 154 percent increase for midtown.[11] In 1922 the busiest stop in the system was still the Brooklyn Bridge station where thousands of commuters who came across the bridge in trolleys transferred to the subway. By

1923, however, the Times Square station had moved decisively into first place, collecting a million more fares than Brooklyn Bridge.[12] "At any hour of the day," the *New York Times* reported, "it is something in the nature of a riotous adventure to get through it; but in the morning and in the evening, when from every point of the compass endless legions of passengers in mass formations make one vast football game of the place, with both sides in possession of a hypothetical ball and one down to go, and all rules abolished, the place becomes a maelstrom."[13]

Moreover, while all agreed that the subway had reduced congestion on the Lower East Side by enabling vast numbers of families to escape northward, it had led to new, admittedly less severe, congestion in the Bronx. In 1928 the Regional Plan Association's survey of *Transit and Transportation* (1928) discovered that most of the residents in areas served by rapid transit clustered within a quarter mile of the tracks. Thus the subway helped create the neighborhood that Kate Simon describes in *Bronx Primitive* where immigrant mothers kept spotless apartments while their husbands traveled to the garment center and returned home exhausted from both the long workday and the wearying ride in packed trains.

The subway-supported real estate boom of the twenties was so prolonged that many real estate men became convinced that it would never end. Developer Louis Tishman maintained in 1928 that the concept of boom-and-bust was irrelevant to New York. The city was simply unique. "What is sensational news in the real estate world somewhere else," he said, "becomes a conservative statement of action here. What would be a 'wild' speculation elsewhere is simply a sane, sound investment in New York."[14]

THE VICIOUS CIRCLE

If real estate men saw any threat at all to the endless boom, it was not from the stock market but from the subway system's inability to cope with the constantly growing demands that the skyscraper put on it. Robert Brown, president of Empire State, Inc., pointed out that it had been necessary to close the Grand Central platforms eleven times during the first three months of 1930, leaving the crowds milling about outside, because the danger to human life had become too great within. Yet buildings currently under construction in the area were expected to bring in another 180,000 people. If only half of these used the Lexington Avenue subway, they would absorb all the added capacity that the Transit Commission hoped to supply with an ambitious program of station improvements.[15]

Even the most ardent civic boosters recognized that New York was in serious danger of choking on its own growth. This produced a situation where experts first sought palliatives and then, slowly, began to fear that the crisis was insoluble.

One possible solution to subway crowding was to stagger work hours. In 1926 Health Commissioner Louis I. Harris began gathering information on riding patterns according to geographical locations and type of economic activity. More than a million and a half questionnaires were distributed throughout the city. After the returns had been analyzed Harris began visiting businessmen's groups, trying to persuade the leaders of twenty-two key industries to arrange their hours so that riders would be spread more evenly during the morning and evening rush hours.

The businessmen proved recalcitrant. Theater managers were willing to end their matinees by 4:45 but resisted shifting their evening curtains. The Metropolitan Life Insurance Company agreed to staggered hours for the army of clerical workers in its Madison Square skyscraper, but by 1930 only about 21,272 of the approximately 500,000 persons working in the Grand Central zone were participating in the plan.[16]

Daniel L. Turner led the search for more radical solutions. One of the talented young men hired for the first subway by William Barclay Parsons, he had begun his career serving as liaison between Parsons and architect Grant LaFarge. By 1927 he had worked with every agency that had supervised New York subways. He had helped lay out the Dual Contract lines. He was advising on the new Independent system. He was the man journalists turned to for an expert view of New York's transit problems.

In 1924 Turner had proposed building new superstreets through the middle of blocks, one on the East Side between Second and Third Avenues and one on the West Side between Ninth and Tenth. These would have been triple decked, with a four-track subway below and two levels of roadway for local and long distance automobile traffic (Ill. 44).

He also wanted to rebuild the midtown subway stations. Both Grand Central and Times Square would be reconstructed to have two express platforms in each direction as well as a local platform. This would dramatically increase the number of express trains that could be run.

But by 1927 Turner became convinced that not even the most ambitious construction

44 ▪ Superstreets.

Thomas Adams, *The Building of the City.* New York: Regional Plan of New York and its Environs, 1931. Courtesy: Library of Congress.

projects could end New York's transit woes. Not by temperament a prophet of doom, he described his doubts in a characteristically brief, logical, and dispassionate address to the Snag Club—an informal group that met "now and then to talk over various methods of getting rid of snags." [17] His title was "Is There a Vicious Circle of Transit Development and City Congestion?"

His answer was yes and his argument was simple. The fault of New York's transit lines was that they were designed to run through areas that were already congested. Their designers expected that they would relieve the congestion and so they did—briefly. But they made possible the construction of new skyscrapers in the central business zone and long rows of elevator apartment buildings outside it. They also encouraged the public to expand its riding habit. Within a very brief time the new lines were as congested as the old had been.

This had happened three times in the brief history of New York's subway system. In 1905 an average New Yorker took 98 rides per year. By 1913 he or she took 161 rides per year. "The new subway, instead of relieving the congestion, accelerated the traffic increase and in a short time created worse congestion than before." [18]

The same thing happened when the Dual Contract subways were built. Congestion was relieved for a time as each new line opened but then worsened as each New Yorker used the subway more and more often. The 161 rides of 1913 rose to 276 in 1925.

As Turner spoke, the city was embarking on the third major phase of its transit development—the Independent line. At some points in Manhattan the Independent tracks were only two hundred feet away from one of the existing lines. The Independent line on the Grand Concourse was only three blocks away from the IRT's Jerome Avenue line. The result, Turner insisted, was that history could only repeat itself. Congestion would be relieved for a short time, but new construction and new riders would soon swamp the new lines as they already had the old.

There was something fundamentally wrong with the Wonder City.

SKYSCRAPER VERSUS SUBWAY

Turner's pessimistic account of the relation between subway and skyscraper provided the basis for a series of exchanges between the civic leader Henry Curran and the architect Harvey Wiley Corbett. Curran's proposal that skyscrapers be banned in Manhattan is often portrayed as a cranky rearguard movement against one of the great architectural forms of this century. But Curran was not primarily concerned with skyscrapers at all. He was trying to end subway crowding.

Curran's campaign against Hylan in the 1921 mayoralty election had shown him the awesome complexities of the transit question. In 1926 he agreed to serve as legal counsel to the City Club of New York. The club had always been a powerful advocate of transit development and city planning. It expected its new counsel to lead a major assault on the congestion that threatened to choke the city's growth.

Curran's proposal was bold enough to command headlines and provoke debate: restrict building heights to six stories on side streets and ten stories on the avenues. If New York

City's congestion was caused by "the vicious interbreeding of subways and skyscrapers," abolish the skyscraper.[19]

This is less unrealistic than it may seem in retrospect. If business activities were spread out evenly, they could indeed have been housed within Curran's limits. He ignored deep social tendencies toward concentration in certain preferred locations, but his arithmetic was sound.

It was the congestion in the downtown and midtown commercial zones that Curran wanted to end. He readily conceded that individual skyscrapers were indeed beautiful. It was the massing of them, he insisted, that gave New York "structural indigestion." Midtown had taken on "the appearance of a baggage room after a holiday, with all the trunks and cracker boxes up-ended on a giant scale." The crowding on 42nd Street was already unbearable and the prospective opening of the Eighth Avenue subway three or four years in the future had already brought a chain of skyscrapers to the avenue so that the trains were sure to be packed as soon as they started running. In rush hours "every subway platform within reach, every elevated station and corner stopping place becomes a football field."

The result was a wretched kind of life for millions: "We burrow under the ground horizontally like moles for miles, and then we turn a sharp right angle and go up vertically through the dark interior of a vertical skyscraper. . . . We have reached the limit of this form of municipal stupidity. The skyscraper must go."[20]

Curran's assault provoked a passionate defense by the two most powerful spokesmen for the setback skyscraper—Harvey Wiley Corbett and Hugh Ferriss. Corbett was the designer of the Bush Tower (1918) and an entertaining polemicist. Ferriss was the architectural profession's best-known delineator of perspective drawings. Neither had any patience with those who denounced tall buildings and called for the decentralization of cities. "Concentration has become a commercial necessity," Corbett told readers of the *Saturday Evening Post*, "and the skyscraper is the acme of concentration."[21]

Although Corbett and Ferriss clothed their ideas in sleek modernism, they expressed the New Yorker's traditional delight in the culture of crowds. "Cities are built because people like to be together," Corbett insisted. "They are a manifestation of the group instinct." As proof, he offered the example of two teenage girls from San Francisco who, asked what interested them most about the city, chimed in unison "The Subway!"[22] People liked busy streets, crowded theaters, and great apartment buildings. Curran and Ferriss looked forward to vast superblocks which would contain not only offices but also promenades, theaters, apartments, gymnasiums, and swimming pools. "We are not contemplating the new architecture of a city," said Ferriss. "We are contemplating the new architecture of a civilization."[23]

Inevitably, Corbett became the city's most eloquent opponent of Curran's call for height limitations. He and Curran debated on several occasions—at a 1926 meeting of the New York Building Congress, in the pages of the December 5, 1926, issue of the *New York Times Magazine*, at a 1927 meeting of the Architectural and Allied Arts Exposition, and at a 1927 meeting of the Civic Development Department of the U.S. Chamber of Commerce. When Corbett wrote an article titled "Up With the Skyscraper" for the February 1927 issue of the *National Municipal Review*, Curran replied in the April issue with one insisting that "The Skyscraper Does Cause Congestion."

Corbett was unmoved. He not only didn't think that skyscrapers caused traffic congestion, he was sure that they actually reduced it. If a huge corporation spread its personnel in several small structures—even ten-story ones—they would be constantly traveling from one to the other in order to transact their affairs. If they were housed in a single huge building, by contrast, employees would enter it at nine in the morning and be off the streets till five. It was a mistake to become fixated on the number of people on each square acre of land.

The real problem was to imagine a city so organized that it could accommodate crowds without the miseries of overcrowding. Hugh Ferriss tried to do this in his remarkable 1929 book, *The Metropolis of Tomorrow*. The date is of course unfortunate—this vision of reconstructed cities was published just when money for new construction was about to disappear. But Ferriss's vision remains deeply compelling.

His goal is to redeem the modern city by reasserting human power over it. He wants to plan concentration on rational principles. Accordingly, he explores the potential of multi-level streets, glass-walled buildings, and the use of rooftops for penthouse apartments, gardens, and even open-air theaters.

The book ends with a utopian vision showing a city in which the vast majority of buildings would have pleased Henry Curran—they are only six stories high, no taller than the width of the streets they face. But if most of the city is low, a few huge office blocks concentrate the activities of art, science, and commerce. They are much larger than any building in the New York of the twenties, several blocks wide at the base and rising one thousand feet or more into the air. Ferriss hopes to get all the virtues and none of the faults of huge buildings by locating them according to a definite plan. Each is placed half a mile from the others and located at the intersection of major transit arteries. Thus each has adequate light and air. Movement between them proceeds smoothly along transit ways which are divided into separate levels for pedestrians, automobiles, and subways.

It often appears that Corbett and Ferriss are giving the best possible defense of the skyscraper and subway city, but a careful student of their work will notice that while the skyscraper engages their imaginations, the subway does not. They are much more fascinated by the automobile. To be sure, Corbett noted the miseries of subway crowding and Ferriss carefully located his skyscrapers blocks a full express stop apart from one another. But while Curran talked subways, subways, subways, Corbett replied with proposals to speed circulation by making the city more accommodating to automobiles.

Curran noted this and tried to draw Corbett back to the main topic:

I never bought an automobile [he said in reply to one of Corbett's arguments]. I never owned one, or borrowed one or stole one. I never had one, in any way, shape or manner. My only automobile is the subway, where I find a surplus of company and a deficit of comfort. While Mr. Corbett rides above ground in his expensive limousine, and, as he looks up in the air, counts his profits from building skyscrapers, I am being hauled to and fro below the ground through a dark tube like a mole.[24]

Corbett discussed congestion as if it were entirely a matter of automobile traffic and while he and Ferriss enthusiastically proposed many plans for multilevel highways, they were silent on improved subway facilities. A fateful juncture had been reached. The subway was losing its hold on the imaginations of urban planners. It was being replaced by the automobile.

THE ASSAULT ON THE WONDER CITY

Corbett and Ferriss's vision of New York as the world's shining megalopolis was countered by Lewis Mumford and the small group of planners, architects, and social critics who organized the Regional Planning Association of America. Mumford was later to emerge as a savage critic of America's highway systems, but during the twenties he argued that the automobile would be a decentralizing force that would lead to the necessary breakup of the skyscraper and subway city.

If Daniel Turner's outlook was that of the engineer, Henry Curran's that of the civic leader, and Harvey Wiley Corbett's that of the booster-visionary, Mumford represented the intellectuals who emerged during the nineteen-twenties as sharp critics of American civilization. His first book, *The Story of Utopias* (1922), was a survey of social thought, his second, *Sticks and Stones* (1924), a pioneering study of American architecture, and his third, *The Golden Day* (1926), a survey of what was best in the American past. Author of such major studies as *The Culture of Cities* and *The City in History*, Mumford has had a powerful, enduring impact on the ways in which Americans look at their cities.

Mumford loved New York and hated the Wonder City. Both feelings are rooted in his early experiences. Born in Flushing and raised on the west side of Manhattan, Mumford encountered a city of vaudeville theaters and museums, lively neighborhoods and green parks first as a child on long walks with his grandfather, then as a young man in explorations by foot, trolley, and double-decker bus. But while he loved the New York of his youth, Mumford was appalled by the newer city he encountered as a young man.

In the summer of 1916 Mumford found a job as an investigator for the dress and waist industry's Joint Arbitration Board. He spent six weeks darting between racks of clothing in the city's congested garment district and climbing stairs in loft buildings that reminded most observers of rows of packing boxes. He watched the transformation of midtown Manhattan into a skyscraper zone; writing later in "A New York Adolescence," he recalled the "openness of the midtown district . . . , its low buildings and the vast unbuilt spaces on Park Avenue," with its gracious pedestrian promenade down the large, grassy space in the middle.[25] New York, he felt, had become "the center of a furious decay, which [is] called growth, enterprise, and greatness."[26]

By the end of 1916, influenced by his own experiences as well as by such classics of the English Garden City movement as Ebenezer Howard's *Garden Cities of Tomorrow* and Patrick Geddes's *City Development*, he was laying out plans to decentralize New York.

Mumford's hostility toward the Corbett-Ferriss vision of New York is expressed in a cartoon he did for the December 1925 issue of the progressive magazine *Survey*. It is clearly a response to Hugh Ferriss's "An Imposing Glimpse of New York as It Will be Fifty Years Hence" which appeared in the February 1924 issue of *Vanity Fair* (Ill. 45). Ferriss's drawing shows his visionary gazing up at a future city of densely clustered towers. Mumford's parody

45 ■ Hugh Ferriss. *An Imposing Glimpse of New York as It Will Be Fifty Years Hence.*
Vanity Fair, February 1924. Courtesy: Library of Congress.

shows two Lilliputian figures at the top of a huge building looking up at the still huger buildings that dwarf them (Ill. 46). "Yes, sir," says one, "that's the city of the future! Two hundred-story skyscrapers! Air pumped in from the country. Every cubic foot of space used day and night. Mechanically perfect!" "Magnificent!" the other responds and then asks, "Will any one *live* there?" When Ferriss's *The Metropolis of Tomorrow* was published, Mumford said that its seductive drawings expressed the "painfully childish romanticism of our modern financial leaders."[27]

Mumford wanted to replace megalopolis by a series of regional cities, none larger than 300,000 people, which would contain all that was necessary for healthy work and a satisfying life. He hoped that the technological basis for regional development would be provided by the electrical power line and by the automobile. "The tendency of the automobile is within limits to disperse population rather than concentrate it," he wrote. "Any projects which may be put forward for concentrating people in greater city areas blindly run against the opportunities the automobile holds out."[28]

Many years later Mumford would argue bitterly that much of the promise of automobile had been lost. In his 1961 book *The City in History* he lamented that "we have sold our urban birthright for a sorry mess of motor cars"[29] and heaped scorn on the engineers and planners who had allowed mass transportation to deteriorate. Nevertheless, it can be argued that his early writings did something to bring that result about.

Mumford and the regional planners transformed the way people thought about cities. Since before the Civil War, New York's growth had been fueled by the real estate man's pursuit of rising land values and by the average citizen's hope for a home removed from the central core yet tied to it by transit lines. Now Mumford, like Daniel Turner, argued

By Lewis Mumford

Yes, sir, that's the city of the future! Two-
hundred-story skyscrapers! Air pumped in from
the country. Every cubic foot of space used day
and night. Mechanically perfect!

Magnificent! Will any one *live* there?

46 ■ Lewis Mumford. *Yes, Sir,
That's the City of The Future!*
Survey, December 15, 1925.
Courtesy: Library of Congress.

that the skyscraper and the subway were parts of a vicious circle. The subways increased land values. Real estate promotors, to make their more expensive land pay, built taller buildings. The new towers required more subways to bring office workers which further increased land values. Now that the land was even more fabulously expensive, skyscrapers had to be even taller in order to be profitable and this led to even more congested subways.

For Mumford the mere existence of a subway becomes a sure sign of urban failure. In an article on "The Intolerable City" he cites "the Swedish massage" of the subway guard[30] and "the pulping mill of the subway"[31] in order to mock those who issue weekly bulletins "of plans for doing away with traffic congestion by sinking endless millions into ingenious feats of engineering."[32] In a remarkably gloomy article for the *Journal of the American Institute of Architects*, he declares that cities like New York represent the final, megalopolitan stage in Oswald Spengler's vision of the rise and decline of civilizations. "The megalopolitans are those who regard double-entry bookkeeping, subways, root-canal dentistry, clinical medicine, metropolitan operas and motion pictures, and mechanized recreation as the essence of a life-abundant."[33] With Mumford the subway that was hailed in 1904 as the sure foundation for New York's glorious future has become its preeminent symbol of economic and spiritual malaise.

THE REGIONAL PLAN

By the mid-1920s students of the city faced two different models of the urban future. One was the centralized city with a downtown business and shopping core tied by rapid transit lines to outlying residential districts. The other was a regional network of small, uncongested cities, each surrounded by a greenbelt, each containing home and work in comfortable proximity to one another. The Regional Plan of New York was an uneasy compromise between these opposed visions.

Its first volume, *The Graphic Regional Plan* (1929) explained how the skyscraper-and-subway city could be reshaped. It consisted of more than four hundred recommended projects, including bridges, parkways, and forty-two airports. The second volume, Thomas Adams's *The Building of the City* (1931), set forth the philosophy of growth that would guide the New York region for years to come.

Where Mumford and the team of Corbett and Ferriss were radicals, the men of the regional plan were compromisers. They specialized in the shining vision and the vague statement. Faced with an irreconcilable conflict between praise of the centralized city and calls for regional dispersal, they carefully consulted both sides and sought a compromise. "It is probable," said Thomas Adams blandly in *The Building of the City*, "that the Utopia of the perfect 'garden city' will influence future urban growth in the New York region at least as much as the Utopia of the perfect 'skyscraper city' and that the expansion of the city-region will evolve along lines that will show an attempt, at least, to embrace the best features of both."[34]

The regional planners understood that transportation was the key to shaping cities. The trouble with New York, they concluded, was that it was too much like a funnel—all traffic converged on the central point of Manhattan below 59th Street. In order to travel from Newark, New Jersey, to Flushing, Queens, or from Coney Island in Brooklyn to Gun Hill Road in the Bronx you had to pass through New York's area of greatest congestion. Their solution was to recommend great belt lines for both automobiles and railroads. This would both relieve congestion at the core and permit the development of regional centers for both housing, offices, and industry.

The Regional Plan left specific projects for the New York subways to the state's Transit Commission and the city's Board of Transportation but it set forth guiding policies for underground development. It endorsed efforts already underway to unify the three systems, backed special assessments to pay for new construction, supported public ownership, and declared that, in view of the benefits that flowed to the owners of property surrounding rapid transit lines, it was unjust to require riders to bear the full expense of the system. The 1928 Regional Survey volume on *Transit and Transportation* endorsed an impressive series of plans to extend the existing lines, some of them already adopted by the Board of Estimate and Apportionment.

Above all, the Regional Plan urged that the city system be integrated with Corbett's multi-level highways and with the regional commuter rail system. Its sketch of a Second Avenue speedway shows these principles in action. The Second Avenue el would be replaced by a new, four-level speedway (Ill. 47). At the bottom level were four tracks—the inner two for long-distance suburban trains and the outer two for city express trains. Above that was a cross-over permitting riders to switch from local to express and pedestrians to cross from one side of the avenue to the other. At the center of the next level was a highway for long-distance automobile and truck traffic. To the right and left of this road were galleries for sub-surface utilities. On either side of the utility galleries were tracks and platforms for local trains. Above that would be a broad avenue for local automobile traffic. Its middle would be pierced with openings so that light could penetrate the street below. There would be two-level sidewalks incorporated into arcades beneath the buildings.

The most eye-popping feature of this new speedway was to come at its southern end (Ill. 48). The city had acquired a strip of land just south of Second Avenue between Christie and Forsyth Streets for slum clearance. It was too narrow for housing but just the right size

47 ▪ Proposed Development of 2nd Avenue.
Thomas Adams, *The Building of the City*. New York: Regional Plan of New York and its Environs, 1931. Courtesy: Library of Congress.

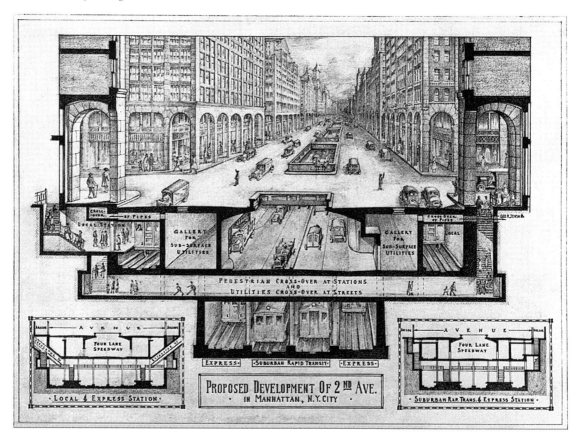

48 ■ Christie Street
Expressway.

Thomas Adams, *The Building of the City*. New York: Regional Plan of New York and its Environs, 1931. Courtesy: Library of Congress.

for a grand parkway lined with Corbett's beloved apartment house skyscrapers. The result is a splendid science fiction vision of the city that might have been.

Clearly the Second Avenue Speedway and the Christie-Forsyth Parkway represented Corbett's dream and Mumford's nightmare. Not surprisingly, Mumford assailed the Regional Plan in two long articles in the June 15 and June 22, 1932, issues of *The New Republic*.

The planner's basic sin, he charged, was economic: they had treated New York as a giant real estate speculation. The ultimate purpose of all their projects was to inflate land values so that property owners might profit from pyramiding ground rents. Soaring land values increased pressure for huge skyscrapers and zones of elevator apartment buildings that could be reached only by packed subway trains. Denouncing "the colossal highway and rapid-transit schemes outlined by the Regional Plan," he assailed "the weird mathematics and logic by which Messrs. [Raymond] Hood and Corbett have undertaken to defend skyscrapers as an aid in relieving congestion."[35] The skyscraper and subway city was not, in Mumford's view, a machine that would run better with a few improvements. Its miseries were built in.

There is a widespread belief among Americans that the turn away from mass transit resulted from a plot by automobile manufacturers. This is even enshrined in a popular film, *Who Framed Roger Rabbit?*, where the evil Judge Doom, sole stockholder in Cloverleaf Industries, sets out to destroy Los Angeles's trolley cars so that he can replace them by freeways lined by gas stations, motels, automobile dealerships, and billboards. This paranoid vision of Los Angeles transit history has been refuted by careful historical analysis.[36] It is equally inapplicable to New York.

Yet it is clear that between the wars political leaders and urban planners gradually averted their eyes from subways and began to fasten them with great longing on freeways and expressways. This was a national trend, not a local one, and there is no simple explanation for it. In the particular case of New York City, however, it is possible to isolate two causes—one political, the other conceptual.

The political cause is that Hearst and Hylan had left subway financing in a shambles. They had argued that the IRT and BMT were earning and concealing large profits. If this was true, then it was possible to run the system and build new lines without a subsidy from the taxpayers. But it was not true. It was necessary either to raise the fare or provide a permanent, adequate subsidy. Either alternative would lose votes. Until William Gaynor mayors had made the subway the centerpiece of their programs. After Hylan they distanced themselves from it. Fiorello La Guardia encouraged the arduous process of transit unification but his only other major contribution to transit reform was an angry crusade against trolleys on the grounds that they impeded automobile traffic.

The conceptual cause for the subway's difficulties is that city planners became increasingly convinced that subways were a feature of the wrong kind of city. John Ihlder, manager of the Civic Development Department of the U.S. Chamber of Commerce, expressed this view in 1927. Admitting that advocates of decentralization could as yet point to no stunning success, he nevertheless praised their negative arguments against the centralized city. Their "most telling illustrations are of things that should *not* be done *again*—the subways, for example on which New York spends so much of its resources to no perceptible end." The subway was, like the outside iron fire escape, "a confession of failure to build properly."[37] John Nolan, one of America's most active city planners, made the same point when he said in 1931: "Subways are evidence of an unsuccessfully planned city. They may be a necessary evil, but they represent the failure of planning."[38]

The new thinking was dramatized at the World's Fair in 1939. Hundreds of thousands of New Yorkers came to the fair by a specially built subway line but what they found there was a vision of the future based on the automobile. This was especially clear in two exhibits that dealt explicitly with city planning.

One, organized by the American City Planning Institute, presented Pare Lorentz's film *The City*, with a script by Lewis Mumford, direction and camera work by Ralph Steiner and Willard Van Dyke, and a score by Aaron Copland. It presented the future according to the regionalists, contrasting the bad old city of smoke, skyscrapers, and crowds with the good new world of lawns, bicycle rides, and softball games. A sophisticated fairgoer who knew Mumford's work would have recognized the plea for regional cities, limited in size and containing both workplaces and homes. A more hurried and less sophisticated fairgoer could have quite forgivably misinterpreted it as a hymn to the suburb. In either case, the film showed an America that had no need for subways.

The other exhibit was the incredibly popular General Motors Futurama designed by Norman Bel Geddes, a brilliant stage designer who had already redesigned America's corporate products and was now ready to reshape America itself.[39]

As many as 28,000 people a day waited patiently on the pavilion's streamlined ramps for admission to Futurama. Once inside, they were transported into the world of the 1960s. Seated in his or her own chair, equipped with an individual loudspeaker and attached to a conveyor, the fairgoer floated for fifteen minutes over the city of the future. The outer fringes of it, which contained both factories and housing, may have reminded some of Mumford's world but the core consisted of widely separated towers, each covering a full block and rising as much as 150 stories into the air. The large stretches between the towers were devoted to low buildings, generous parks, and, above all, automobile expressways. These were incredibly wide, with separate lanes for cars traveling at fifty, seventy, and one hundred miles an hour.

The rise of the automobile was confirmed in an unexpected way in the career of Robert Moses. He had begun his career in the twenties at the feet of Al Smith. One of his first published articles was a contemptuous account of the Hearst-Hylan strategy against Henry Curran in the 1921 mayoral race—an article which showed a clear-eyed understanding of how politically destructive the transit issue could be.[40] He determined to avoid it.

This might have made sense if Moses had been a regional planner who wanted to destroy what planner Clarence Stein called Dinosaur Cities with their "slow-moving crowds of people clambering into street-cars, elevateds, subways, their arms pinioned to their sides, pushed and packed like cattle in ill-smelling cars."[41] In fact Moses was an enthusiastic defender of the city as New Yorkers had conceived it since the middle of the nineteenth century. He assailed Lewis Mumford, Frank Lloyd Wright, Rexford Guy Tugwell, and other advocates of greenbelt communities. He pointed out that for all the propaganda in favor of decentralization, the average American continued to believe that his ambitions were most likely to be realized in a city and that "with this spur he is apparently willing to put up with incredible discomforts in order to live and work in crowds."[42]

Moses epitomizes the inconsistencies of the postwar faith in the automobile. Even though much of his career would be devoted to New York's traffic problems, he absolutely refused to integrate mass transit into any of his bridges, expressways, or parkways. In 1947 he predicted that with an adequate program of parkway and expressway construction, much of which was under way as he wrote, New York would have solved its traffic problem, except for an area in midtown Manhattan, by 1960.[43] When that year came, the disillusion with continued highway construction and the renewed interest in mass transit was just beginning.

CHAPTER SIX

BENEATH THE WONDER CITY

A young poet in Elmer Rice's play *The Subway* (1924) rhapsodizes about the New York City of the 1920s: "The city . . . the city . . . steel and concrete . . . industrialism, rearing its towers arrogantly to the skies. . . . Higher and higher . . . deeper and deeper. . . . Up and up . . . fists of steel shaking defiance at the skies." But if the skyline inspires ecstatic visions, its transportation system only provokes alarm: "Under the steel towers that scrape the skies. . . a subway train . . . roaring . . . roaring . . . the beast of the new Apocalypse."[1] Many New York writers and artists turned to the skyscraper and the subway in order to portray what one writer called the new New York. They portrayed them not just as physical monuments but as emblems of the city's moral condition.

Ecologists speak of a climax forest. After World War I New York appeared as a climax city. All the trends which had been developing since the eighteen-thirties burst forth in a city of massive apartment buildings and huge office towers, glamorous theater marquees, and Times Square advertising signs.

But the new metropolis was more than glamorous. It was also profoundly worrying. Americans in quieter, more sensible towns devoured such articles as "Why I Wouldn't Trade Des Moines for New York" (*American Magazine*, 1919), "Greenwich Village Virus" (*Saturday Evening Post*, 1921), "What's the Matter With New York?" (*Atlantic*, 1921), "But Home Was Never Like This" (*Collier's*, 1923), "Pace That Kills" (*Saturday Evening Post*, 1923), "Pied Pipers of Manhattan" (*Ladies Home Journal*, 1924), "All Right for a Visit Maybe" (*Outlook*, 1927), "Is New York Society as Slack as it's Painted?" (*Pictorial Review*, 1925), and "Trying to Learn New York" (*Saturday Evening Post*, 1930). "Where did all these New York-ers come from?" the editors of *Scribner's* asked in 1931. "This city which is the object of hatred or the goal of desire for many people, is it foreign or is it the most American in the United States?"[2]

Artists and writers no doubt watched this hand-wringing in the popular journals with superior amusement but in fact they conducted a similar debate among themselves. In doing so they focused on the same physical elements of the new city that already preoccupied Daniel Turner, Henry Curran, and Lewis Mumford. They too saw that the skyscraper and the subway existed in symbiotic relation. But the artists and writers went further than the engineer, the politician, and the urban critic. They saw that the engineering polarities of the city also expressed the emotional dynamics of the men and women caught up in it. They interpreted the relation between skyscraper and subway as a complex opposition between upward and downward, aspiration and confinement, freedom and compulsion, and, ultimately, life and death. Some or all of these polarities appear in the films of Harold Lloyd, King Vidor, and Rouben Mamoulian, in the Futurist art of Fortunato Depero, in Elmer Rice's play *The Subway*, in John Dos Passos's novel *Manhattan Transfer* (1925), and in Hart Crane's poem "The Tunnel" (1926).

SYMBOLS FOR THE NEW NEW YORK

The archetypal first encounter with Manhattan was by water. Booth Tarkington recalled himself as a young man standing on the forward deck of a steamer in the early years of the century: "Before him the immense castellated sky line that amazed the world swam to meet him as the steamer rushed toward it over the flat water; and, stirred by the wonder of this great sight, he exultantly whispered to himself: 'New York! New York! New York!'"[3]

For years architectural historians seemed mildly embarrassed by the emotional power of this spectacle. They produced an account of skyscraper history that focused on either its Chicago origins or the creative daring of the continental architects who stripped away the excretions of historical ornament to produce the International Style. In this context the gothic revivalism of the Woolworth Building and the art deco of the Chrysler Building represented an exaltation of mere style at the expense of the perfect marriage of form to function.

In recent decades, however, such writers as the architect Rem Koolhaas, in *Delirious New York* (1978), and the architectural historian A. P. van Leeuwen, in *The Skyward Trend of Thought* (1988), have shifted attention from the march toward modernism to the skyscraper's roots in popular fantasy and its place in social semiotics. Koolhaas traces the skyscraper back to its fantasy prototypes in Coney Island. Van Leeuwen goes back much further to show how architects consciously sought to utilize the ancient connotations of the tower. Both treat the skyscraper as a form of cultural assertion.

Certainly that was how every New Yorker of the early twentieth century regarded it. The skyscraper was a symbol of the new city before it was anything else. That was so whether it was regarded with appalled horror or awestruck fascination.

The cultural case against it received early, vehement expression in Henry James's *The American Scene* (1904). To James, skyscrapers represented a modernism which had abandoned tradition to identify itself wholeheartedly with the profit motive. "Crowned not only with no history, but with no credible possibility of time for history, and consecrated by no uses save the commercial at any cost, they are simply the most piercing notes in that concert of the expensively provisional into which your supreme sense of New York resolves itself."[4]

Architects tried to counter such charges by designing in styles which asserted the historical roots and the cultural stability of the new city. Their towers rose up out of Greek temples or were covered with Classical or Gothic ornament. Yet little of this seems to have affected the viewer's perception of them. The skyscrapers represented a society in motion and in the representations of John Marin and Abraham Walkowitz they seemed to soar and writhe and dance.

Observers compared these buildings to the archetype of moral giddiness—the Tower of Babel. In 1893 Paul Bourget, standing at the corner of Broadway and Wall Street, declared that the surrounding buildings gave him an "impression of Babylon."[5] A 1907 article in *Harper's Weekly* described the "Modern Towers of Babel in New York." This quickly became one of the dominant clichés of the age. In 1932 the Singer Building could still be extolled as a "modern 'Tower of Babel'" in W. Parker Chase's *New York—The Wonder City*.[6]

Before World War I the Babylonian metaphor was imposed by journalistic observers. After the zoning law of 1916 it was embraced by architects themselves. By requiring that skyscrapers be designed in a series of setbacks, the law encouraged a ziggurat-like shape. An article in the *New York Times Magazine* (illustrated, inevitably, by Hugh Ferriss) predicted that "the Hanging Gardens of Babylon" would be re-created in modern New York.[7]

For many celebrants this was an appropriate result of the miraculous dynamism of the capitalist economy. Fiske Kimball declared that the skyscraper was the physical expression of the "American system"—one which required not the grinding down of the masses but rather "the development of their own capacity to buy more and more material luxuries—cars, phonographs, radio." Consumer demand, he told his readers, stimulated by the new advertising industry, ensured that "quantity production could be developed on an unexampled scale."[8]

Although Lewis Mumford complained about a culture of gadgets, the participants in this boom were giddy with excitement. Squire Vickers, who was responsible for much of the ornament in the Dual Contract subway stations, declared in 1927 that "there are signs that the architecture of these huge towers of Babel will more and more symbolize the energy responsible for their existence, and for the growth, prosperity, and enterprise of the time in which we live."[9]

Although the subway opened in 1904, artists, playwrights, novelists, and poets were largely content to leave it to politicians and journalists for the first two decades of its existence. O. Henry called New York Baghdad on the Subway but his stories remain in the age of the el. The subway provided the subject for minor but still significant poems by Ruth Comfort Mitchell in 1916, Maxwell Bodenheim in 1921, and Claude McKay in 1922, but it was only in the mid-twenties that subway scenes began to appear in great numbers. John Sloan's two subway etchings date from 1926 and Anatol Shulkin exhibited what appears to have been the first oil painting of the subway in 1927. His *Half Past Five*, according the *New York Times*, showed "shopgirls, businessmen and workmen attempting to cram into one subway door as a brutish-looking guard does his best to close the entrance."[10]

The subway became an important subject when it was treated not for its own inherent interest but as part of a strategy to subvert the myth of the skyscraper. The Polish anthropologist Bronislaw Malinowski recalled that on his first visit to New York he was struck by the contrast between the exotic beauty of the towers and the "microscopic bacteria called man, sneaking in and out of the subway."[11] Waldo Frank accepted the white towers of Manhattan as arrows of will but pointed out that the office workers who crammed into the subway were a drab, shuffling mob: "In the fetid stations, men and women stand packed as no western rancher packs his cattle. Masses of them, mute, unangry, wait for the next train to glide in beside them and slough off its loadful. The doors slide open, the brackish human flow pours through, the doors cut like knives the mass within from the discarded mass without."[12]

Poets described the subway in similarly doleful terms. In *Harlem Shadows* Claude McKay described how "In the packed cars the fans the crowd's breath cut, / Leaving the sick and heavy air behind."[13] Maxwell Bodenheim, in a poem published in the *Dial*, compared a subway train to "soiled caskets joined together."[14]

Credit for the first extended poetic treatment of the subway belongs to Ruth Comfort Mitchell. Author of twenty-five books, Mitchell is now quite unknown. Her 103-line poem "The Subway" is sometimes blatant in its effects but at its best it is a forceful portrayal of the subway ride as an unrelenting assault on the reader's sensibilities. She describes the crowds pouring down from the street onto the platforms, the noisy commands of the guards, and the barrage of stimuli from the ever-present advertising placards:

> They scream of somebody's soup and soap and garters,
> Somebody's pajamas and tea and cigarettes,
> And somebody's gloves and gum and flour and tonic,
> Somebody's whisky and collars and breakfast food.
> The eyes that read must run from color to color,
> Stabbed and prodded with yellow and rasping red
> Until with the jolt and jar of the frantic gong
> Is mingled the crash of unrelated tones.
> There are reds and blues and yellows that are noises
> And noises that are yellow and blue and red;
> The senses of sight and sound are nagged and goaded,
> Noise in the eyes as harsh as noise in the ears.[15]

These denunciations are forceful but they lack a context that would extend their meaning. The poets try to juxtapose the subway world to that of nature. Thus Ruth Comfort Mitchell interrupts her account of the noise and uproar inside a packed car to remind us that "Over hill and plane/There is sanctuary/Inviolate and still." Claude McKay's "Subway Wind" contrasts the heavy air underground with Caribbean breezes. This contrast has biographical resonance for McKay, who came to Harlem from his native Jamaica, but it is otherwise too obvious to be interesting. Subway riders already know that they are not riding through a sanctuary, inviolate and still; they don't have to be told.

To extend the significance of the subway, it was necessary to treat it in explicit opposition to the skyscraper, making the one represent the city's aspirations and the other its daily ordeal. This happens in three popular films of the twenties: Harold Lloyd's *Speedy*

49 ▪ Harold Lloyd in *Speedy*.
The Museum of Modern Art/Film Stills Archive.

(1928), King Vidor's *The Crowd* (1928), and Rouben Mamoulian's early sound picture *Applause* (1929).

All three films celebrate the skyline and all three include notable subway scenes. Much of *Speedy* is a delighted tour of the modern city. Speedy, the Harold Lloyd character, meets its challenges with deadpan humor. He takes us to Coney Island and Yankee Stadium and introduces us to the great Babe Ruth himself. Skillfully using a dollar bill dropped on the floor (but retrieved by a hidden string), he even gets a seat on the packed subway (Ill. 49).

The Crowd takes a more skeptical view. The film introduces its protagonist, Johnny Sims, to New York in a remarkable sequence filmed in the downtown streets that starts by showing the glories of the skyscraper and ends by reminding us of the crowding and regimentation it imposes. Johnny's ambitions are as big as the city itself but he is a very average young man, one who works in an impersonal office, proposes marriage in a crowded subway car, and settles into an apartment with an elevated train rattling outside the window.

Applause is a tearjerker and a very good one. It deals with a young girl who finishes her sheltered, convent education in the Midwest and comes to New York to discover that her mother is the fading star of a shabby theatrical company. The choice she has to make is between stardom on Broadway and a happy marriage in a small town.

One of the film's most important sequences shows the young lady exploring the city with a handsome young sailor on leave. Their most romantic moment occurs on Brooklyn Bridge as they survey the skyline and share their dreams. Their tour ends as they part, seemingly forever, in the Times Square subway stop. The sailor leaves on the train and the girl, weeping, walks after him down the platform. A portly, middle-aged New Yorker walks down the stairs just after the train disappears into the tunnel. He sees the girl's tear-stained face as she walks back toward him, solicitously holds out his hand, and assures her "That's all right, dearie—there'll be another."

All three films acknowledge the power of the Wonder City, then resolve their plot conflicts by reaching outside it. *Speedy* assures us that there is a traditional American small town surviving in modern New York and the Harold Lloyd character defeats the efforts of the Traction Trust to take over the last horsecar line in the city by summoning a lovable troop of aging Civil War veterans to one last ride-to-the-rescue. At the end of *The Crowd* it is clear that while Johnny may find a job in the city, he is sustained by the adoration of his son and the loving support of his stay-at-home wife. The heroine of *Applause* rejects Broadway to embrace the bedrock virtues of a happy marriage amid tree-lined streets.[16]

Fortunato Depero, Elmer Rice, John Dos Passos, and Hart Crane refused to follow this strategy. Each of them felt an initial enthusiasm for the city that gave way to disillusion. Each turned to the subway in order to test the rhetoric of the skyscraper. But none of the four was willing to retreat into the heartwarming domesticity of the small town. They gave themselves a more desperate choice—the big city or nothing.

THE FUTURIST SUBWAY

Fortunato Depero came to New York from his native Italy in 1928. Twelve years earlier, in a youthful burst of enthusiasm, he had published a leaflet projecting his urbanism of the future. It would be a city composed in three layers. The first would consist of the necessary practical and utility elements—factories and warehouses. The second would consist of the mechanical and electrical parts which would provide the skeleton of the new town. The third layer would support the intellectual and emotional life with promenades high in space, revolving bars, stations for airplanes, coffee shops one thousand meters above ground level. There was no vision of what would lie beneath the streets.

When he arrived in New York, Depero stepped into his myth of the future. He quickly established a promising career before the Depression cut it short. His gallery exhibitions received admiring reviews and he did stage designs for the Roxy Theater, interior decoration for Zucca's Restaurant, ad campaigns for Venus Pencils and Campari, and covers for publications as diverse as *Vanity Fair*, *Movie Makers*, and the *New Automobile Atlas*.

At first he was totally entranced by the sheer spectacle of the city. New York was *The New Babel*—he designed sets for a show with that name to be produced at the Roxy by Leon Leonidoff with choreography by Léonide Massine. But the boundlessly ambitious artist soon learned how much disappointment the city could offer. When Depero is optimistic about his future in the city, his thoughts move upward to the summits of the skyscrapers. When he despairs he sees himself lost in the city's elevators, its elevateds, and its subways.

In some moods Depero could see the city as a series of endless conduits. "I must tell you," Depero wrote a friend back home, "that tubes and pipes are one of the characteristics of this super-metropolis. Visible or invisible, they make up its tentacular bowels, roots and veins, from its deep foundations to its highest pinnacles. Tubes for the Subway. Tubes for the heating. Tubes for the currents of water, or air, or light. Tubes of every diameter and in every direction." [17]

Depero's new sense of the opposition between aspiration and restriction in the modern city appears in *Broadway—Shop windows—Crowd—Cars—Paramaunt* [sic] (Ill. 50). Its composition recalls the stage designs that he did for *The New Babylon*. The viewer is seated in an orchestra seat, with the skyscrapers shooting up over the heads of the dancers. The composition dramatizes the tension between the energy of the city, expressed in the great

50 ▪ Fortunato Depero. *Broadway—Shop Windows—Crowds—Cars—Paramaunt.* 1930. 60 × 71 cm. © 1994 Estate of Fortunato Depero/VAGA, New York.

51 ▪ Fortunato Depero. *Subway.*

1929. 44.3 × 30.2 cm. © 1994 Estate of Fortunato Depero/VAGA, New York.

diagonals of the skyscrapers in the top third of the design, and the regimentation it forces on the pedestrians who jerk along the street like mechanical dolls. The face of the woman confined within the subway car at lower left expresses a sudden eruption of pain. The effect is as if a German expressionist had suddenly painted one corner of a Futurist painting.

Depero portrayed the world beneath the skyscraper in two astonishing works. One is his oil painting *Subway, Crowd to the Underground Trains*, now in a private collection but illustrated in Maurizio Scudiero and David Leiber's *Depero, Futurista & New York*.[18] It shows the midtown crowds caught in a totally enclosed world. There are stairways and passageways which appear to lead out of the scene but they are all empty; the rhythm of the crowd is entirely circular and shows no escape into a world of light and air.

The other portrayal appears in what Depero called a free wordist plate. In 1930 he called for a Futurist poetry which would find expression through typography as much as through words and which would consist of torn words, dismembered words, repeated words, elongated words, words in spirals like the smoke of a cigar, words in motion like a train, words that explode like a revolver shot.[19] He made two major attempts to portray the subway using the arrangement of words on the page as well as their contents.

Illustration 51 shows the more elaborate of the two. The forms of words as well as their meaning unite to capture the confinement, the smells, and the movement of the 23rd Street BMT stop. The word *travi* (beams) actually holds up the street and a tunnel is filled with the repeated word *teste* (heads). The *estrattore di puzze solide* (extractor of solid stinks) can be felt through the *surrogati d'aria* or substitute air. The train appears as a *serpenti di luce sulla pelle* (snakes of light on the skin of the city) and as a *serpenti di buio nell-animo* (serpent of darkness in the soul).

Depero expresses an ambivalent vision of the city but, unlike Rice, Dos Passos, and Hart Crane, he never had to ask whether the regimentation of the subway canceled the glory of the skyscraper. The Depression saved him from having to make a choice. When he returned to his native Italy in 1930, he remained a Futurist, still celebrating the dynamism of the mechanical city.

THE SUBWAY ON STAGE

Elmer Rice is today best remembered for *The Adding Machine*, an Expressionist satire on modern business culture produced by the Theatre Guild in 1923, and for *Street Scene*, a naturalist portrait of life on Ninth Avenue which received the Pulitzer prize in 1929. *The Subway* is not one of his best works; he didn't reprint it in his *Seven Plays* (1950). It is nonetheless notable for its sharp, satiric analysis of the city of the twenties.

Rice was a native New Yorker who had, by 1925, experienced the subway in three distinct phases. At first, it had been a civic miracle. As a thirteen-year-old living at 114th Street and St. Nicholas Avenue, he had anticipated the opening of the new subway in 1904 as if it were a national holiday. His autobiography, *Minority Report* (1963), describes the tooting of whistles, the reverberations of cannon, and the tolling of church bells and then, a few days later, the family's first, excited trip down to the City Hall station. "The dimly lighted interior, with its tile mosaics and steel pillars, was magical and awesome, the train a splendid chariot."[20]

Later, after Rice entered the High School of Commerce, the subway became a daily routine. He recalled the trick of getting six rides for a quarter by tearing his strip of five tickets into six pieces and he remembered waiting with his fellow students to rush the ticket-chopper as a group so that they could avoid paying the fare at all.

Finally, as construction of new lines lagged far behind growing ridership, Rice's daily journey became an ordeal of physical discomfort and a nagging reminder of the city's political failures. By 1923 the subway had a acquired a semantic weight for both Rice and the public at large. It represented the memory of civic hopes and the daily reality of their disappointment. It was an attractive subject for a writer who wanted to anatomize the inhumanity of the new city.

Sophie Smith, Rice's heroine, lives in a world of bureaucratized work and mechanized leisure. Her days are spent filling out quadruplicate forms in the offices of the Subway Construction Company, which builds both skyscrapers and subways. Her evenings are passed in her family's cramped uptown apartment where she pours over *Pictureland* and *The Silver Sheet* in preparation for visits to the neighborhood movie theater. She exists in a world of clichés. Her boss sounds like a Chamber of Commerce press release; one of her coworkers spouts slogans from correspondence school advertisements; her father's conversation at home consists entirely of newspaper headlines. Sophie's agony is her daily subway ride. Her dream is a suburban bungalow with climbing roses.

The social satire is challenging but the plot is depressingly familiar. Sophie attracts the attention of Eugene, a young, handsome, but callow artist who is creating a new epic of industrialism titled *The Subway*. He tells her that she is its inspiration—the vision of beauty that is born in the age of the skyscraper, survives the apocalyptic destruction of the subway, and endures forever. As a strategy for seduction this succeeds admirably. Sophie is soon pregnant and abandoned. She ends her life by flinging herself in front of—what else, a subway train.

However we judge his plot, Rice's stagecraft is consistently inventive. The play's most daring piece of theater is its presentation of Sophie's daily subway ride. The movement of the train is simulated by the rapid alternation of light and darkness and by such grating sounds as the grinding of a flat wheel and the whistle of air brakes. We see Sophie pressed against the window by the largely male crowd. She is pale, gasping in the stale air. As the scene progresses the sexual overtones grow stronger. Sophie is pressed between a fat man with heavy jowls and thick lips and a thin man with a sharp nose and beady eyes. After one instant of darkness marking the alternation between platform and tunnel the men have been transformed by masks into a dog, a pig, a monkey, a wolf, a rat.

Though it took *The Subway* four years to find a producer, the semi-amateur production that opened at the Cherry Lane Theater in 1929 proved to be an effective piece of theater.[21] The set for Sophie's ride collapsed on opening night and the scene had to be aborted but in subsequent performances the subway ride was the high point of the evening. The production moved to Broadway for a short run and the play was later produced at the Garrick Theatre in London. In the sixties the English composer and lyricist Beatrix Thomson worked on plans for a musical version.[22]

DOS PASSOS'S BURTHEN OF NINEVEH

John Dos Passos rejects the claims of the Wonder City but, like Elmer Rice and Hart Crane, he does not do so without having felt its power. He was widely traveled as a young man—his letters after Harvard bore such postmarks as London, Paris, Barcelona, and Baghdad—and, having seen so many ancient cities, he easily slipped into an intellectual's snooty disdain for the raw newness of American life and culture. "Our books are like our cities," he wrote in 1916. "They are all the same."[23]

Several months in Manhattan in late 1920 and early 1921 convinced him otherwise. He measured the city with the eye of a seasoned travel writer and saw it as noisy, crowded, exotic, and glamorous. When he next went to Europe Venice seemed only "a sort of high-falutin Coney Island" and he passed his time there writing a poem about garment workers in Madison Square.[24] He was soon at work on a novel that would present the city whole—its sounds, its smells, its advertising signs, its sensational newspapers, its booming real estate, and its scandalous politics.

In *Manhattan Transfer* (1925) Dos Passos took up New York's proud claim to be the New Babylon and restored its original prophetic meaning. His New York is not only Babylon but also Sodom and Nineveh—the latest in a series of proud cities marked for destruction. The skyscraper is its Tower of Babel, uniting overbearing assertiveness, sexual sterility, and linguistic confusion.

The opposition of subway to skyscraper is not as central to *Manhattan Transfer* as it is to Rice's *The Subway* or Crane's "The Tunnel." None of Dos Passos's three principal characters is ever shown riding it. Jimmy Herf, Ellen Thatcher, and Stan Emery are each defined in relation to the skyscraper alone. Nevertheless, subway references appear constantly in the novel conveying a sense of the city's physical expansion, giving a taste of its daily life, and suggesting its political corruption. Dos Passos uses one minor but important character, the architect Phil Sandbourne, to make the symbolic relation of subway and skyscraper explicit.

References to New York's expanding transportation system are historically precise. "A whiff of coal smoke"[25] from a passing el train and "a funny little train with a green engine" (70), for example, tell the reader that a scene is set before 1902, when the little green steam engines were replaced by electric power.

Subway references begin when young Jimmy Herf hears his alcoholic uncle, the failed broker Joe Harland, assure his wealthy relatives that Interborough Rapid Transit bonds are "worth a snifter" (104). Gus McNiel, the hapless delivery man who becomes a Tammany regular, will later get into trouble when he can't explain how he acquired a sizable number of those same bonds. James Marivale, hurrying to his publicity job at Famous Players, will rush down the steps of the 72nd Street IRT station "to the jammed soursmelling platform" (310). Anna Cohen, depressed by her dull job at a sandwich counter, will see an image of futility in "the endless files of people jostling in and out of the subway" (313).

The three appearances of architect Phil Sandbourne invoke both the skyscraper and the subway in order to dramatize the gap between what New York might have been and what it actually becomes. Since Phil is as eager for romance as he is for architecture, Dos Passos is able to connect the aesthetic failures of the Wonder City with its emotional cost. This in turn allows him to echo and underline the skyscraper symbolism that explains the varied fates of Jimmy Herf, Ellen Thatcher, and Stan Emery.

In Phil's initial appearance, which can be dated to around 1904 by a reference to Judge Alton Parker's presidential candidacy, the Wonder City is still a vision. Sandbourne is working for an older architect named Specker and enthusiastically praising the old man's projects for the city of the future. Although in 1904 New York buildings were still clothed in Roman and Gothic decoration, Specker sees a totally rebuilt city of steel, glass, and vitreous tile. "It's some pipedream," Phil says admiringly (76). Phil's own pipedreams require him to invest his meager salary on restaurants and theater tickets in futile pursuit of a young stenographer.

Phil's second appearance juxtaposes architectural and sexual failure. He opens it by alluding to the murder of architect Stanford White by Harry K. Thaw over Evelyn Nesbit—Thaw's wife and White's mistress. A nearby reference to the Woolworth Building, erected in 1913, suggests that the year is 1915, just after Thaw's release from a mental institution. By this time Specker is dead. Sandbourne sees a vulgarized commercial city growing up all around him and recalls the older man's visionary plans for seventy-five-story buildings stepped back in terraces with hanging gardens on every floor. In distinction to the specialized office structures of the twenties, these would have been true communal buildings containing hotels, theaters, Turkish baths, swimming pools, department stores, and market spaces all in the same structure. Specker wanted the kind of visionary city that such architects as Harvey Wiley Corbett were advocating at just about the time that *Manhattan Transfer* was published. Dos Passos connects architectural failure to romantic disaster by having Sandbourne run down by a car because he is staring at a pretty girl instead of oncoming traffic. "She might have stayed to see if I was killed," he comments forlornly as he is lifted into the ambulance (171).

Sandbourne's last appearance in the novel both recalls the promise of the technological city and reinforces our sense of its failure. Sandbourne is riding the subway with the rising politician George Baldwin. "Faces, hats, hands, newspapers," Dos Passos reports, "jiggled in the fetid roaring subway car like corn in a popper" (256). Alluding to the continuing delays in subway construction, Sandbourne hopes that George and his playmates down at Tammany Hall will stop squabbling and give the wage slaves a little transportation. His own solution to the subway crush is a series of endless moving platforms under Fifth Avenue.

Phil Sandbourne remains the novel's most enthusiastic advocate for the technological marvels of the new city. He even exclaims in excited delight as he sees a downtown express pass his own car, with "window telescoping window till they overlapped like scales" (256). He excitedly tries to explain to George Baldwin that "you can see Fitzgerald's contraction." He is referring to the hypothesis of the physicist George Francis Fitzgerald, which marked an important step toward Einstein's theory of relativity, that a moving body is foreshortened in the direction of travel by a ratio that increases with increasing speed. A subway train would be flattened completely if it reached the speed of light. This enthusiasm awakens no echo in his companion. "I'll be seeing the inside of an undertaking parlor," Baldwin replies, "if I don't get out of this subway soon" (256).

Sandbourne hasn't lost his enthusiasm for a rebuilt city of vitreous and superenameled tile. Moreover, he is sure that such architectural glories would encourage emotional liberation: "If there was a little color in the town all this hardshell inhibited life'd break down. . . . There'd be more love an' less divorce" (257). But these hopes that New York might build a kind of skyscraper that would be an emotional revivifying force are expressed by a character on the decline. As Sandbourne walks to the subway at the end of the scene, the brownstone buildings drag past monotonously like the days of his life.

Sandbourne's presence in the novel reminds us that the skyscraper might have been a symbol of liberation. No such hopes are held out for the subway—it is only associated with sexual frustration and death. For a petty thief pressed against a tall blond woman in a packed car, the subway ride produces a fantasy that he will never have the nerve to act out: "If I could have a dame like dat, a dame like dat'd be wort havin de train stalled, de lights go out, de train wreck, I could have her if I had de noive an de jack" (148).

For Ruth Prynne, riding home from her doctor's office after hearing a diagnosis of cancer, the insistently cheerful advertisements mingle grotesquely with her terrors: "Cancer he said. She looked up and down the car at the joggling faces opposite her. Of all those people one of them must have it. FOUR OUT OF EVERY FIVE GET . . . Silly, that's not cancer. EX-LAX, NUJOL, O'SULLIVAN'S. . . . She put her hand to her throat" (293). Her fellow riders are transformed into a trainload of jiggling corpses as she gets out at 96th Street to change for the local.

THE REDEMPTIVE SUBWAY

Dos Passos denies any symbolic difference between the subway and the skyscraper—they are both places of sexual frustration and spiritual death. It is a measure of Hart Crane's tough optimism that in elaborating the darkest symbolic meanings of the subway he still presents it as purgatorial, not hellish. Where Rice and Dos Passos try to resolve their ambivalence about the Wonder City with rejection, Crane works hard to end with an affirmation.

Born in Cleveland, Ohio on July 21, 1899, Hart left home for New York City when he was only seventeen. He went back to Cleveland late in 1919, returning to New York in 1923. Malcolm Cowley helped him get a job writing copy for *Sweet's Architectural Catalogue*—a guide to building products which was (and still is) to be found in most architectural and engineering offices. It seems likely that the precise knowledge of the physical city that Crane shows in *The Bridge* owes something to his experience at *Sweet's*.

In April 1924 Crane rented an apartment at 110 Columbia Street in Brooklyn Heights—the same building in which the engineer of the Brooklyn Bridge, George Washington Roebling, had lived during its construction. The move to Columbia Street increased Crane's daily experience of the subway.

His first response was enthusiastic. "I can ride to Times Square," he wrote his mother, "under the river and all and without changing cars on the subway in twenty minutes."[26] Crane's friend Sam Loveman recalled that "riding on the subway was just one holocaust of laughter because he saw double meanings in all the ads, and usually obscene meanings. He claimed that most of them had some sexual or phallic undercurrent of meaning."[27]

But what kind of art could be based on this experience? McKay, Mitchell, Bodenheim, Frank, Rice, and Dos Passos had all made startlingly negative use of the subway ride. To this group we may add Crane's close friend the poet and critic Allen Tate, whose first response to underground travel was, like Crane's, quite positive. "The subway is simply marvelous," he wrote Donald Davidson; "Fancy going under a huge river at 40 miles an hour!"[28] Three years later his sonnet "The Subway" takes a dramatically different view.

Tate's poem resembles Rice's *The Subway* in viewing mechanism as a deranging, destructive force. It opens as an apostrophe to the train:

> Dark accurate plunger down the successive knell
> Of arch on arch, where ogives burst a red
> Reverberance of hail upon the dead
> Thunder like an exploding crucible![29]

The harshness of these sounds and the crabbed intensity of these metaphors reflect the deranging impact of the ride. The movement of the train—its bursts, its thunders, its plunges—generates sounds that are muffled, harsh, and explosive. The underground landscape is unnatural, the forest having been transformed into the iron columns of the subway. The only human emotion that enters the octet is an repellent one—the false humility of the train's angry worship as it proceeds down the church-like sequence of ogive arches.

But what are these arches? The subway is almost entirely post and lintel construction which is, in any account of engineering science, the opposite of arched construction. If there were arches, they would certainly not be ogives, which are decorative but structurally weak. Ogive arches have a great deal to do with the pattern of connotation Tate develops— they are used in churches and so connect with the "angry worship" he ascribes to the train later in the poem—but they have very little to do with any actual experience of the subway.

Crane does not make such mistakes. As Gianfranca Balestra observes in an article on the "Poetry of the Subway," Crane uses the plain facts of a subway journey to achieve a perfect equivalence of the literal and the symbolic.[30] The poem deserves a commentary that gives as much attention to the actual ride as it does to the symbolic journey.

Within the larger context of *The Bridge*, "The Tunnel" forms part of an intricate structure of echoes and oppositions. Its opening reference to Columbus Circle recalls Columbus's prayer in "Ave Maria"; the sudden glimpse of Edgar Allen Poe parallels the encounter with Walt Whitman in "Cape Hatteras"; the Italian washerwoman extends a series of female figures who have appeared throughout the poem. It is nevertheless possible to discuss "The Tunnel" with only minimal reference to the larger work. It was first published as a separate poem, it is frequently anthologized by itself, and it provides a very useful point of entrance into the larger complexities of *The Bridge*.

The ride begins in the section of Broadway that runs from Times Square to Columbus Circle. Times Square had become the theater district in the first decade of the century but it was after World War I that Broadway, now lined with giant movie theaters and huge, illuminated advertising signs, became The Great White Way. It was an eye-popping sight. The year before Crane's poem was written, a visiting Englishman described himself turning out of a dark side street and standing amazed "before an enormous face, with a hand and tooth-brush cleaning his teeth, and behind it a giant in a motor-car smoking a cigarette, and further away four giant gnomes in a reindeer carriage, all drawn in moving light against dark buildings."[31]

Although this is what many called the liveliest part of town, the poet is in a state of mental torpor. It is not easy in the opening lines to decide whether he is walking down the street or attending the performance of a play—some lines imply one, some the other. The confusion is deliberate. The entire street is a performance—even the frequent views into first-floor apartments recall the naturalistic settings of what were called kitchen-sink dramas.

Like most spectacles, it eventually palls. The city dweller cannot remain in a continual state of excitement. The poet has searched all the faces, seen each famous sight, and now finds the drama stale and boring. Fingering his knees, he wishes himself home in bed with a tabloid propped in front of him. He reaches for his hat and leaves.

The topical reference to "subscription praise" in line 16 suggests that the poet had been attending the Theatre Guild, then Broadway's only subscription theater, on West 52nd Street. He enters the subway at the 50th Street IRT station. Since that is a local stop and only the expresses go under the river to Brooklyn, he will have to change trains later in the poem. He thinks briefly of walking "a brisk / ten blocks or so" to the express stop at 42nd Street but weariness dictates an immediate descent into the subway:

> As usual you will meet the scuttle yawn:
> The subway yawns the quickest promise home.

The use of "scuttle" and "yawn" exemplifies Crane's ability to make single words compress many meanings. "Scuttle" is either a metal pail for carrying coal, a small door in a ship's deck, or a narrow hatchway in a watercourse for fish to pass through. All three of these senses can apply to the metal kiosk through which the poet enters the subway. (The word has already been used this way in *The Bridge*'s first section.) The poet's yawn of boredom is transferred first to the gaping opening of the kiosk's stairwell, then to the wider passage of the subway beneath.

So the poet submerges himself in the crowd. This requires another step in his psychological descent as he becomes "minimum," withdrawing into himself. The poet glances nervously to his right at the revolving door opening into the subway from a skyscraper basement arcade. Like the scuttle, the turnstile, and the gongs that will mark the closing of the platform to further passengers as the train arrives, the revolving door is a mechanical way of channeling crowds. But it is also a danger to the mind that has adjusted to the crowd because it imposes, during the brief enclosure at the midpoint of its revolution, an unwelcome moment of isolation. Better to be submerged in the crowd in a comfortable state of suspended animation.

The rhythm of the rider's thoughts merges with that of the train:

> . . . . In the car
> the overtone of motion
> underground, the monotone
> of motion is the sound
> of other faces, also underground—

The motion of the car is metaphorically identical with the monotone—that is, the blankness, the monotonousness—of the deadpan faces within it.

In "The River" Crane had re-created the experience of a train journey by blurring the signs that flash past the windows. In lines 39 to 65 he accomplishes a similar effect for the subway with fragments of overheard conversation. Crane told Waldo Frank that "The Tunnel" consisted largely of "notes and stitches I have written while swinging on the strap at late midnights going home."[32] These stitches are hard to interpret, as fragments devoid of context should be. A few of them simply ask or give directions. Most of them, however, make oblique, slangy references to a debased sexuality. Placed among them are two passages in a different tone which comment on the futility of our casual desires.

The first, in lines 46–49, places our idle chatter in the long chronological perspective; our words are simply the dead outward covering for our sexual drives, like verdigris that appears on copper or like hair that grows even though the body is dead.

The second, in lines 58–60, uses machine imagery to express the degradation of sexual desire. The tortured sequences of our subconscious fears are conflated with the maddening hum of the moving trains and the endlessly reiterated sounds of a gramophone that rewinds itself. Love itself becomes only "a burnt match skating in a urinal."

Prompted by the presentments of pain that he has been overhearing and perhaps struck by a chance resemblance in some straphanger's face, the poet suddenly visualizes Edgar Allen Poe. The association is unexpected but not really surprising. Poe was a New Yorker during a significant part of his career, his face, in surviving images of it, implies suffering, and he has been interpreted as the archetype of the rejected, ignored American poet.

The vision of Poe—a lynched Poe, with the "swollen strap" doubling as the lyncher's rope and the subway rider's strap—is a startling expression of the poet's own anxieties for himself and his poem. It ends with the hope that even at the moment of death, when (according to legend) a drunken Poe was dragged by machine politicians from voting place to voting place to cast corrupt ballots, Poe might have redeemed himself by, at least in his own mind, denying the mindless optimism of his time.

Lines 83–99 return us to the sensations of the subway as Crane keeps his literal and symbolic rides closely related to one another.

The section begins with route directions:

For Gravesend Manor change at Chambers Street.

Since the Poet has boarded a local which stops at South Ferry, he will have to transfer to the express to go under the river to Brooklyn. Gravesend was one of Brooklyn's original villages. Real estate atlases of the period do not reveal a Gravesend Manor but there was a Gravesend (now McDonald) Avenue and many apartment houses in the area had similarly pretentious names.

But of course Crane is really interested in capturing the connotations of death that the place name holds. The same concern informs the next line:

The platform hurries along to a dead stop.

Once again, Crane accurately records the sensory world of mechanized travel. To an observer standing still on a train that is coming to a stop, it does indeed appear to be the platform rather than the train which is moving.

The descent under the river begins in the next line. Park Place is a deep station because the tracks of the West Side IRT had to descend beneath those of both the 1904 subway and the BMT. An escalator was therefore installed in 1919. Crane uses this escalator to juxtapose two worlds. Those leaving the train and ascending the escalator are escaping the underground world toward someplace freer; the "escalator" lifts a serenade, the riders, after their confinement in narrow spaces, bolt outright into streets that are suddenly washed by rain.

Those still on the train, by contrast, are confined in a narrow world where their ears are assaulted by platform gongs, hissing electro-pneumatic doors, electrical (i.e., galvanic) thunder, and the screaming sound of the metal wheels on curving metal tracks.[33] These hideous sounds provide a counterpoint to the music of the next and final section of *The Bridge*, "Atlantis," where, according to the epigraph from Plato, music is "the knowledge of that which relates to love in harmony and system."

At this point the train enters the tunnel. The entire subway is sometimes carelessly referred to as a tunnel but Crane, who was scrupulous about the meaning of words, would have known that while most of the subway was built by opening the street from above, a tunnel has to be driven horizontally beneath the surface. He had originally planned to call this section of *The Bridge* "The Subway." The shift in title to "The Tunnel" focuses attention on lines 100–122 where the train actually passes through the tunnel under the river.

Once again we have a face picked out of the crowd: a "wop washerwoman" bringing "mother eyes and hands/Back home to children and to golden hair." That she is Genoese connects her with Columbus and his faith in the Virgin in the second section of the poem. That she is a washerwoman who has been cleaning Manhattan offices before returning in love to her children shows that the Daemon that carries her home is ultimately beneficent, that it brings those it devours from "gaunt sky barracks" to a golden land.

Ironically, it is only now, after the saving vision of the washerwoman, that Crane turns to his most harshly negative portrayal of the subway. Its reverberating noise becomes "the muffled slaughter of a day in birth" and the images of these clotted lines, though not easily disentangled, all return to the theme of death. They lead, however, to Lazarus in line 119 feeling "the sod and billow breaking" as both water and earth part to reveal "some Word that will not die."

The ending is a controlled recession from the intensity of lines 115–122. The poet is walking by the East River, hearing the echoes of a tugboat's blare, watching the lights of Manhattan's skyscrapers reflected on "the oily tympanum of waters" and seeing the "ticking towers" across the river. Thoughts of death again come into his mind but only briefly as he begins ascending toward the ecstatic vision of "Atlantis."

Yet if "The Tunnel" is one of *The Bridge*'s most lucid and successful parts, "Atlantis" has been universally and rightly judged a clotted failure. It was nevertheless a brave attempt to move beyond the duality of skyscraper and subway. Crane wants to show that the city of the imagination can transcend its material origins.

The skyscraper was available as a symbol of transcendence. Claude Bragdon, architect and translator of one of Crane's favorite books, Ouspensky's *Tertium Organum*, acclaims it in precisely this way: "These campanili of the New Feudalism, however base-born and aesthetically uninspired, are nonetheless the planet's most august and significant symbol of proud-spirit man flashing unquenched defiance to the stars."[34] Similarly the French art historian Elie Faure proclaimed that America's gigantic cities possessed "an element of un-reality, a poetry, almost a music; a play of spiritual energy challenging space."[35] One might expect, then, that Crane's poem would end with a subway ride underground leading to a heavenward ascent into the skyscraper.

Crane's decision to swerve from the skyscraper to the bridge was a brave attempt. Juxtaposing the subway to the skyscraper is really, as we have seen in the work of Depero, Rice, and Dos Passos, a strategy of exposure: it reveals the hidden truth that, for all its magnificent rhetoric, the skyscraper is as brutally inhuman as the subway. Crane therefore seeks to move beyond this apparent dualism by focusing on a third object, the bridge, which he hopes will reconcile the commercial and the aesthetic, the horizontal and the vertical, and the earthbound and the soaring.

Crane's most successful treatment of the Brooklyn Bridge as a transcendent symbol occurs not in the poem's final section but in its opening invocation which describes a madman who emerges from the subway to throw himself from the parapet. The implication is that although the bridge may represent some mystic unity, it is one far beyond anything the human mind can comprehend. That apparently remains true at the end of the sequence. The conclusion to *The Bridge* suggests that the city of the skyscraper and subway inspired an ambivalence too profound to be resolved.

CHAPTER SEVEN

ART, REVOLUTION, AND THE SUBWAY

E V E N before the Depression some writers and artists had begun using the subway to portray the contradictions of the capitalist city. In the January 1927 issue of *New Masses* James (Slim) Martin re-created the thoughts of a worker building the new Eighth Avenue line:

> Eighty cents an hour, for carfare, insurance, books, theatre tickets, a pack of Camels, laundry bills, payment on an electric sweeper, a graduation dress for the oldest girl, doctor bills for

the last case of measles. . . .

Eighty cents an hour! and a few blocks to the east great crowds milling in and out of great department stores. Fur coats and silken wraps on display in street windows. Spats, canes, tuxedos. Bags, steamers rugs. Shining, purring motor cars. . .[1]

But for all the muck and labor of its construction, no one doubted that building a municipally owned subway was a progressive step.

Artists of the thirties did not think of themselves as heirs to the capitalist city-builders of the nineteenth century but they did in fact preserve an awareness that a wonderful city could still be built and that efficient transportation was vital to the building of it. They shared both the nineteenth century's optimism about the subway and the twentieth century's disillusion. This put them in a position to treat the subway either as an example of capitalist failure or as an emblem of socialist hope.

During the thirties artists returned to the theme of subway building again and again.

140   SUBWAY CITY

Some, like Don Freeman (Ill. 52), showed it as part of the city's entertaining spectacle. Others were fascinated by subway construction because they saw it as a step in the process of social reconstruction. Some artists sought the work of decorating the new IND lines, offering their proposals in the 1938 Subway Art exhibit. Meanwhile writers organized by the Works Progress Administration (WPA) described the subway in a proposed book to be titled *Underground New York*. Both projects were assailed for Communist influence and neither was completed. Their unrealized condition is perhaps appropriately symbolic of the Left's urban agenda.

LOUIS LOZOWICK, HARRY STERNBERG, AND CHARLES KELLER

Artists interested in subway construction had a great deal of it to observe between the late twenties and the eve of World War II. The excavation of the Eighth Avenue–Washington Heights line began in 1925; the Sixth Avenue–Queens line was not completed until 1940. Although subway construction involved thousands of men, complicated underpinning of existing buildings, and extensive tunneling, journalists describing this work comment on how little attention the public paid. "Of all this [activity]," said the *New York Times* in 1927, "New York is blissfully unconscious. It passes in and out of the doors of a skyscraper, rides up and down its elevators, transacts its business in its offices unaware that deep down men are transferring the entire weight of the building from one foundation to another. It rushes uptown and downtown in the old subways and never suspects that it is being held up here and there by temporary stilts of steel and coverts."[2]

Although the public treated it as just another inconvenience, some artists found subway building an important subject. Harry Sternberg and Charles Keller drew construction laborers as part of their interest in the nature of industrial work. Louis Lozowick used subway construction to show that the present city contains the promise of an improved social order.

Lozowick united the machine aesthetic of the twenties with the social radicalism of the thirties. A participant in the 1927 Machine Age Exposition, he was well acquainted with the work of Fernand Léger, Laszlo Moholy-Nagy, and El Lissitzky. He was also a contributing editor to *New Masses* and a constant participant in left-wing and Popular Front organizations, once saying that he had never joined the Communist Party because it was unnecessary.[3]

The Left praised the Machine Age Exposition not so much for its aesthetic program as for its social content. Genevieve Taggard made this clear in her July 1927 *New Masses* review of Jane Heap's catalogue. She was entranced by the exhibits, which ranged from a proposed all-glass skyscraper drawn by Hugh Ferriss to a nearly noiseless meat slicer from Dayton, Ohio, and called them an effective rebuke to presumed radicals who could not accept the modern age. "Our Ruskinian boys and girls," she proclaimed scornfully, "keep talking about the evils of present day standardization, and the robot crowds in the subways, and the horrors of cleanliness and order. They make me sick, they make me tired."[4]

This anger was presumably aimed at Lewis Mumford, who replied in the September issue by drawing a Ruskinian distinction between machines that enhance life and those that

Sixth Avenue Excavation

Don Freeman

52 ▪ Don Freeman. *Sixth Avenue Excavation.*
1937. Lithograph, 9⅝ × 13½ in. Bayley Art Museum of the University of Virginia, Charlottesville. Gift of Lydia Cooley Freeman.

degrade it. He repeated his view that the skyscraper and subway resulted from nothing more than a cycle of congestion aimed at inflating real estate values. "Our weaker brothers and sisters, who started by worshipping the machine," said Mumford, "end by swallowing it whole—bonds, Babbitts, installment buying, speculation in necessities of life, and the bourgeois comforts generally—including slices of very thin ham cut by exquisite machinery in delicatessen stores."[5]

Lozowick had only limited sympathy with Mumford's assaults on the skyscraper and praise of decentralization. While he agreed that the capitalist city encouraged a vicious cycle of congestion, rising land values, higher skyscrapers, and greater congestion he thought regionalization only satisfied a middle-class desire for return to "a semi-patriarchal, semi-parochial individualism."[6] He had no doubt that the good society would be a big city.

He also thought that the machine was bringing an underlying rationality to American life. "Beneath the apparent chaos and confusion," he declared in 1927, America was moving toward "order and organization which find their outward sign and symbol in the rigid geometry of the American city: in the verticals of its smoke stacks, in the parallels of its car tracks, the squares of its streets, the cables of its factories, the arcs of its bridges, the cylinders of its gas tanks."[7]

These tendencies toward order, however, were hamstrung by the contradictions of capitalism. Lozowick believed that by revealing the order that had been created thus far in technology, he could encourage social engineering as well. His art abstracts the underlying rationality of the city and portrays it freed from the accidents of daily use. He knew that the Third Avenue el and the Astor Place subway kiosk were rusting hulks but in his representation of them the tensile strength of el girders frames the clean, monumental dignity of the kiosk (Ill. 53). He shows what might have been and still could be.

This approach could lead to misunderstanding. Lozowick's New York does not look like a city in crisis. Hugo Gellert, art editor of the *New Masses*, once complained that there was no class struggle in Lozowick's art and urged him to clarify his views by showing oil tanks, skyscrapers, and crumbling power plants to symbolize the collapse of American capitalism. Lozowick sensibly rejected this advice. He also scorned "the unsolicited heroization of the

53 ▪ Louis Lozowick, *Subway Station.*
1936. Lithograph, 11½ × 14¹⁵⁄₁₆ in. Print Collection, Miriam and Ira D. Wallach Division of Art, Prints and Photographs, The New York Public Library, Astor, Lenox and Tilden Foundations.

worker" as a "petty bourgeois legacy."[8] His fixed purposes were to reveal the underlying order of technology and to encourage the objective, dispassionate, and ultimately humane state of mind that would lead to efficient social engineering.

Lozowick's lithograph *Subway Construction* shows the building of a portion of the Independent system's Eighth Avenue line where it turns to run east-west under Houston Street (Ill. 54). (These tracks are now used by the Sixth Avenue line's B, D, F, and Q trains.) In making space for four tracks, the city seized an opportunity for slum clearance by tearing down some two hundred old stores and tenements. It promised new housing and moved pushcart vendors into new city-owned markets along Essex Street.

When Lozowick drew this lithograph, then, he was showing a progressive building project—a city-owned subway that would bring efficient transportation to the Lower East Side for the first time and let in light and air to a neighborhood of rickety tenements. The print shows an expanse of girders across Houston Street. At upper left we are able to look into the back courtyards of tenements because the buildings that would have blocked our view have been torn down. At the top right we see a temporary gas main above the street that is being demolished now that the underground work nears completion. Our view is toward the Second Avenue el, an example of the old technology that the new subway will replace.

Where Lozowick shows the subway being built, Harry Sternberg and Charles Keller show the men who built it. Many observers thought that progress had made grinding physical labor a thing of the past. "New York's first subway was dug with pick and shovel," an article in the *New York Times Magazine* declared on July 17, 1927. "The new subway is machine-built." A 1931 article ignored the workers but described the "almost human" steam shovels swinging their mouths from side to side, nibbling at broken stone, snuffing aside indigestible boulders, and gulping down mouthfuls of miscellaneous debris.[9] A 1936 article on the

54 ▪ Louis Lozowick. *Subway Construction.*

1931. Lithograph, 16^{11}/$_{16}$ × 13¼ in. Print Collection, Miriam and Ira D. Wallach Division of Art, Prints and Photographs, The New York Public Library, Astor, Lenox and Tilden Foundations.

Sixth Avenue IND insisted that while earlier subways had been built by "moles," this one was constructed by "subway surgeons."[10]

Sternberg and Keller reacted against this rhetoric, insisting that it was still human brawn, not machines, that built subways. The glorification of the worker was a common thirties theme. Dan Rico's wood engraving *Subway Drillers*, done for the WPA's Federal Art Project and published in the October 5, 1937, *New Masses*, provides an example (Ill. 55). It shows a brawny figure with a sunburst of light emanating from him and the city rising around its edge as a result of his labors.[11] Sternberg and Keller take a different approach, stressing the grit and strain of underground labor.

Sternberg's *Subway Construction* shows work proceeding under a temporary roadway (Ill. 56). We are positioned below the street, looking up at the wooden deck, a sewer pipe, and a row of pedestrians lining the wooden railing. Sternberg said of this etching: "I was fascinated by the complex timbered supports of the street overhead, the maze of pipes and cables that wormed everywhere, and the activities of the workers."[12]

The emphasis is on physical labor. The pneumatic drill, the most sophisticated technology in sight, is almost hidden by the broad, muscular bodies of two workmen who stand with their backs to us. The design is held together by the strong vertical of the workmen's

56 ▪ Harry Sternberg, *Subway Construction.*
1927. Etching, 8 × 9⅞ in. Edwin A. Ulrich Museum of Art, Wichita State University, Endowment Association
Art Collection.

bodies—the laborer with the upraised arm at left, the central group of muscular figures
around the pneumatic drill, and the Negro workman wielding the shovel at right.

Under Columbus Circle dates from the same year (Ill. 57). The building of the first Interborough had required complex work to prop up the huge Columbus monument.
Work on the Eighth Avenue line was even more difficult. Since the new line had to
cross under the Broadway line at this point it was necessary not only to prop up the
monument once again but also to support the IRT line so that it could function as
usual while the IND was built under it. The result was the creation of a huge, multi-
level excavation. Here we are positioned on an intermediate level; we can look to the roadway and suspended sewer pipe above, while we see the curving tracks of the new subway
below.

Charles Keller shared both Sternberg's politics and his concern for a socially committed art. For a time he and Sternberg shared a studio near Union Square.[13] Between 1937 and 1941 Keller produced a suite of six lithographs showing the construction of the Sixth Avenue portion of the IND.

Sternberg had won acceptance on the construction site by handing out quick pencil sketches to the workmen. Keller had more difficulty because he wanted to show the tunneling beneath the rivers. He received a clearance to go into the tunnel, signed a waiver, got a medical checkup to show that he had no respiratory ailments, and wore heavy shoes and a hard hat.

Sternberg vividly conveys the uproar of the construction site and the strain of physical labor but he is not as concerned to make us understand the precise part of the construction process that we are observing. Keller's approach is more specific. We always see exactly what his workmen are doing, whether they are pouring concrete from a Transit-Mix truck or assembling the metal lining of the tunnel.

Three of Keller's prints show the process of building under the rivers. Beneath the East

57 ▪ Harry Sternberg,
Under Columbus Circle.
1927. Etching, 7⅜ × 4½ in.
Edwin A. Ulrich Museum of
Art, Wichita State University,
Endowment Association Art
Collection.

and Harlem rivers and at several points on land it was necessary to tunnel horizontally with a drilling shield. The shield is a giant drill. Behind the drill is a two-level chamber. On the upper level an operator controlled the valves that used as much as 125 tons of hydraulic pressure to move the shield forward. On the bottom level men loaded the earth into muck carts for removal. Behind the drilling shield workmen bolted and caulked the cast-iron lining of the tunnel. All of this had to be done in a compressed air chamber that prevented water from seeping into the unfinished tunnel head.

Keller produced three images showing the work that goes on in the tunnel head. *Muck Removers* shows men filling the carts in semi-darkness. *Tunnel Heading* shows three men using an air-driven mechanical arm to move a metal ring segment into place for bolting (Ill. 58). *High Air to Low* (1941) shows the men after their work, sitting in a decompression chamber before they are allowed to escape to the world above (Ill. 59).

The "sand hogs" had to adjust to the lower air pressure of the outside world before they could leave the tunneling area. They needed only a brief time to adjust when pressure was increased as they entered but required a longer period at the end of the work day. If they left without a long period of decompression nitrogen would release into their bloodstreams causing the extremely painful, often fatal cramps called the bends.

The men in *From High Air to Low* have been doing physically arduous work near the shield drill and are now passing time in the air chamber before they can leave. The man sitting with

58 ▪ Charles Keller.
Tunnel Heading.
1939. Lithograph. Courtesy of the artist. Photograph courtesy of the Susan Teller Gallery.

High Air to Low. (Tunnel Workers Series)   20 proofs   Charles Keller '41

59 ▪ Charles Keller. *From High Air to Low.*
1941. Lithograph. Courtesy of the artist.

his hand on the lever controls the pressure. When it decreases to the same level as the air outside, the door will spring open. An accurate observer, Keller avoids the heroic-worker syndrome. For all the importance of their work, the men are simply weary and bored and exhausted.

ART UNDERGROUND

The drive to create subway art should be seen as part of an effort to redefine the nature of artistic work and to create new relations between artists and the public. Louis Lozowick expressed the new artistic class consciousness when he said of Daumier's famous statement "*Je suis de mon temps*": "We ought to revise this to read: *Je suis de ma classe*, and make clear that *la classe ouvrière* is implied."[14] If the artist was a "cultural worker," then he or she should form organizations to defend his or her economic interests and should seek to break out of the old capitalist system of artistic patronage by the rich.

The political and aesthetic aims of the thirties found an ideal medium in printmaking and a valuable subject matter in the subway. Harry Sternberg spoke for many thirties artists when he bitterly denounced the "false, unhealthy, unnatural precocity" that based an artwork's value on its rarity: "Society has forced the artist into playing this game, into trying

60 ■ Albert Potter. *"I Am All Right," Says The President.*
Woodcut, 12½ × 9 in. Courtesy of the artist's daughter, Alberta Potter Levitan, and the Susan Teller Gallery.

to catch with special tricks, special techniques and especially limited editions, the eye of
the few who can pay. Such perversions have resulted in the spiritual death of many artists
and almost in the death of graphic art." [15] Now artists, frequently working through the
WPA, explored lithography, woodcuts, and color silk screens which could be produced at
small cost in great numbers.

A significant number of the artists who explored printmaking chose the subway as their subject. Their images typically dramatize social crisis. Albert Potter's woodcut *"I Am All Right," Says The President* shows a family of beggars in an IND train crossing the Manhattan Bridge (Ill. 60). The artist juxtaposes the placard for emergency unemployment relief with a headline on the President's health to comment ironically on the relation between the beggars and the prosperous riders who ignore them.

In Nan Lurie's WPA prints of the subway the advertisements become much more menacing. The leering face on the poster in *Subway Bootblack* is almost as threatening as the shadows in the station (Ill. 61). Her lithograph *Riding Home* shows a Negro woman straphanging wearily while a juxtaposed ad offers a painkiller that will never alleviate her oppression.

The subway art movement was an extension of this effort to communicate with ordinary men and women. The subway is obviously a place where people are looking for something to look at. In 1936 a group of artists realized that subway stations offered what their exhibition catalogue would later call "436 potential underground art galleries." [16]

The drive for subway art was born in the discussions following a lecture at the Artists Union by the art historian Meyer Schapiro. He urged artists, in their quest for government funding, to form closer alliances with working-class groups. This would be difficult, he said, so long as they were merely producing pictures to decorate the offices of city or state officials. It was necessary to turn toward an art that would have a more direct relation to the lives of the working class.

The subway art project was designed to answer Schapiro's call. Although it is a fascinating example of the aesthetic idealism of the thirties, it was essentially forgotten until it was described by Helen A. Harrison in the *Archives of American Art*.[17] Her article shows three aspects of the new artistic climate. First, artists organized collectively to demand public patronage. Second, they sought themes that would interest a broad public. Finally, they determined to put their work where the public would see it.

Their first efforts were made in 1936 under the auspices of the WPA. Elizabeth Olds of the Artists Union told the press that discussions had been held with the city about the possibility of decorating the subway platforms with "polychrome sculpture of the type shown recently by Isamu Noguchi."[18] Another possibility was to replace the strips of advertising panels in subway cars with mosaics.

The organizational drive for subway art soon passed from the Artists Union to a new group called the Public Use of Art Committee. The core group included Doris Kravis,

61 ▪ Nan Lurie. *Subway Bootblack.*

Print Collection, Miriam and Ira D. Wallach Division of Art, Prints and Photographs, The New York Public Library, Astor, Lenox and Tilden Foundations.

Robert Cronbach, Ruth Chaney, Ida Abelman, and Paul Block, who later died in Spain while serving in the Abraham Lincoln Brigade. They proposed a plan in which artists would be paid by the WPA and the city would be required only to meet the cost of materials.

Of course there was already art in the subway. The decorative work of Heinz and LaFarge in the first subway had been continued by Squire Vickers, Jay Van Everen, and Herbert Dole in the Dual Contract lines. They simplified LaFarge's work and introduced a modern element of Synchronist color theory. Vickers expressed the view that each colorful plaque on a subway wall would give a "joyous note like a banner flung from the frowning window of a castle."[19]

To the socially conscious artists of the thirties, however, these efforts were pitifully inappropriate to the modern world. Doris Kravis, chairman of the Public Use of Art Committee of the Mural Painters and Sculptors Section of the New York Artists Union, complained that these works used only a single medium, colored terra-cotta, that they were ludicrously small in proportion to the stations, and that their subject matter deserved severe criticism. "Subways are a swift, fantastic and marvelous means of transportation," she said in a May 1937 statement to the *New York Times*. "Without them a city the size of New York would be an impossibility. Yet here, in the largest, richest, most complex and interesting city in the world, the subjects of the decorative plaques are a beaver, a ferry boat and the cupola of City Hall!"

A decorative scheme for the subway, Kravis continued, should be concerned with "vital ideas, with activities of contemporary society." If the subway entrance was surrounded by considerable open space, as in a park or a square, there should be freestanding sculpture of stone, bronze, or concrete. The station platforms would be excellent settings for a few large decorations in fresco, colored tile, or mosaic. It was time to move ahead with subway art, she argued. The artists were ready and "the necessary administrative machinery has already been set up in the WPA Federal Art Project." To further show what could be done, the New York Artists Union planned to hold an exhibition the following autumn on "Art for Parks and Subways."[20]

The Public Use of Art Committee realized that an exhibit would both encourage artists and arouse widespread interest. A committee to organize the project was set up with Ruth Chaney as chairman. Ralph Mayer, a conservation expert at Columbia University, helped work out new techniques for porcelain enamel and silicon ester paint that would withstand the humidity and constant vibration of the underground environment. Artists were invited to submit proposals and the designs were exhibited from February 8 to March 5, 1938, at the Museum of Modern Art, then in temporary quarters at the Time-Life Building in Rockefeller Center.

Most of the works exhibited have disappeared. We can guess something of their nature from other subway images created by the exhibit organizers and from newspaper reviews. Ida Abelman's 1937 lithograph *Wonders of Our Time* uses subway crowding for a sardonic social commentary (Ill. 62). A contemporary reviewer credits Ruth Chaney with showing that "subways were built with brawn." Her contribution was presumably in the same spirit as her WPA lithograph *Subway Excavation* (Ill. 63). Claire Mahl is said to have shown the "anguished morning rush of workers to beat the time clock and their dogging homeward pace."[21]

Elizabeth Olds juxtaposed the heroic workers who build and operate the subways with the conformist businessmen who take advantage of them.[22] The satiric portion of her design went into the lithograph "Brokers," reprinted in the July 7, 1936, *New Masses*, showing a group of Wall Street capitalists dashing through the subway to their offices. The proposed works were not limited to social criticism and the celebration of labor. The exhibit also included abstractions and semi-abstract compositions by Eugene Morley, Balcomb Greene, and Hanani Harari.

Members of the WPA's Federal Art Project contributed a plan of a typical station and a model of a subway train showing where art could be incorporated within them. Both plan and model were based on the IND because, as committee chairman Ruth Chaney put it, the IRT was "too dark, too dirty, and has too much commercial advertising."[23]

The *Daily Worker*'s Louise Mitchell was enthusiastic. She pointed out that the new Moscow subway led the way in adornment. Subways in capitalist New York, by contrast, had been designed "to pack in as much tonnage of human flesh per square inch as possible at the greatest possible speed." But the city-owned subways promised a new day, with larger entrances, roomier stations, and a general atmosphere of comfort. Mitchell quoted with approval Ruth Chaney's declaration that "the idea of subway art is to bring art to the people who never go to the museums." [24]

City officials, however, were hostile to both the proposed artworks and the politics they seemed to preach. Henry Curran, then deputy mayor in the La Guardia administration, responded with horror: "Never have I seen such uncanny, uncouth and unkempt men and women as these pictures portray, in the agony of their horrible huddle under the ground." [25]

The committee made a deliberate attempt to appeal to the public by handing out a questionnaire asking each of the exhibit's 35,000 visitors to indicate the subjects he or she wanted to see on subway walls. On February 21 the *New York Times* reported the first week's results:

New York City Scenes	274
Industrial scenes (including subway construction)	178
Landscapes and Country Scenes	153
Abstract decoration	147
Historical episodes	127
Science	105
Fantasy	91
Sports	73[26]

62 ▪ Ida Abelman. *Wonders of Our Time.*
1937. Lithograph, 15⅛ × 11⅛ in. Author's collection.

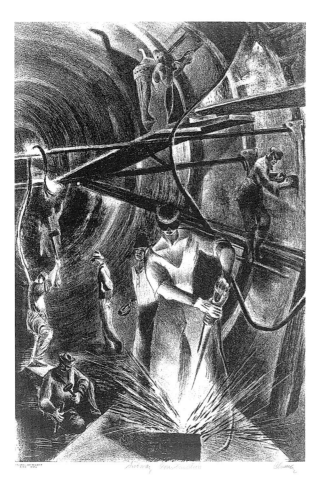

63 ▪ Ruth Chaney.
Subway Excavation.
1938. Lithograph, 45.5 × 32.2 cm.
University of Michigan Museum of
Art, Gift of the U.S. Government,
WPA Federal Art Project.

These categories are not easy to interpret but it appeared that only a minority of subway riders wanted to see the socially relevant art that the artists wanted to produce. Many wanted pleasant landscapes. Subway workers, who were polled separately, wanted romantic scenes and pictures of far-off places—"something that'll get you away."[27]

The organizers pressed ahead building support. Once the show at the Modern closed, they transferred their exhibit to the headquarters of the Transport Workers Union, whose leader, Mike Quill, supported their efforts. They persuaded a councilman, Albert D. Schanzer, to introduce a resolution calling for murals, sculptures, and other decorative features to be installed in the city's Independent line.

For a brief time subway art became a topic of widespread discussion. A cleaning man in Owen Dodson's one-act play *The Shining Town*, set in the 167th Street subway station, warns a man selling flowers that he is about to have competition. "Cause I read where the government's thinkin' 'bout bakin' flowers into the walls. Murals! That's it—murals'll put ya out of business."[28]

In June and July 1938 supporters made a broader appeal to the public with four fifteen-minute broadcasts on "Art for the Subways" on station WBNX. In the first of these Dr.

Thomas Cusack, a well-known psychiatrist, argued that subway art would improve the city's mental health.

"Do you arrive at your office impatient and irritable?" he asked. "Are you cranky and disgruntled in your dealings with those who work with you? Do you return to your home at night in a quarrelsome mood?" The New Yorkers who answered yes to these questions were suffering from "Subway Personality."[29] Dr. Cusack explained that a subway neurosis comparable to claustrophobia was developing in the city. He said it was no accident that the subway was the scene of so many suicides.

Art in the subway would have a therapeutic effect. It "would certainly cause a stability of our emotions, alter our feeling tones and condition us for our daily tasks."[30] New Yorkers would have healthier minds and healthier bodies.

The Public Use of Arts Committee generated wide publicity for subway art and presented over 100,000 signatures to Mayor La Guardia supporting Councilman Schanzer's bill. On February 7, 1939, Councilman Schanzer's bill supporting subway art passed the city council by a vote of 19 to 6.

Now lobbying began in earnest. The city council had been won over but the support of the Board of Transportation was still needed. Subway art advocates sponsored a new round of public forums with such prominent artists as George Biddle, Rockwell Kent, and Philip Evergood.

Unfortunately, the Board of Transportation was unswervingly hostile. John H. Delany, its chairman, declared that "I'd hate to come home from a good dinner at 10 o'clock and have to face some of those pictures. I think they might make some people fall on the tracks. God knows we have deaths enough in the subway."[31]

The city did gain one example of subway art but it was created independently of the Public Use of Art Committee. Just as one group of artists had organized to promote their employment in the subway, so another formed an Architects, Painters, and Sculptors Collaborative to attract patronage from exhibitors at the forthcoming World's Fair. The group, which included sculptors such as William Zorach and Isamu Noguchi as well as many mural painters, exhibited projects at the Museum of Modern Art in the summer of 1937. One was an animated mural with electric lights and synchronized sound by the painter Louis Ferstadt.

As it happened Ferstadt was the only one of the group to get a job—but it wasn't actually at the Fair. He was hired to paint two murals for the entrance to the IND subway station nearest the Flushing Meadow's fairgrounds. It was not a permanent part of the station and was destroyed after the Fair closed, but it showed one version of what subway art might be. As subway riders left the station they saw a mural titled *Security—Work* and as they returned they saw *Democracy—Peace*.

Ferstadt told an interviewer from the *Daily Worker* that he had purposely avoided the expected portraits of haggard workers. Instead, he conveyed social messages with humor. He considered the Fair a standard bearer for consumerism, one that played up such products as canned fish and breakfast food instead of "housing, relief, the important social projects of the government." Accordingly his murals present the Fair as an allegorical figure made up of "a hodgepodge of chewing gum, breakfast food, toothpaste, cheap cosmetics, canned fish, a burlesque strip-girl togged in such clothes as advertising glorifies."

Ferstadt's humor reinforced his straightforward didacticism. *Security—Work* included a porter opening the way to the world of tomorrow modeled after A. Philip Randolph, the militant civil rights leader who was president of the Brotherhood of Sleeping Car Porters. *Democracy—Peace* featured a figure of Paul Robeson symbolizing culture.

Ferstadt also managed to include references to the division between the craft-based AFL and the industrial CIO. Ferstadt himself was a organizer of the AFL Mural Painters' Guild but he took pains to include an appeal for unity in the labor movement. One mural featured a worker with an AFL button; the other included a miner with a CIO button.

The *Daily Worker* quoted Ferstadt responding to a disgruntled AFL worker demanding to know why a CIO man was shown. "The idea," Ferstadt explained, "is that we of the rank and file, regardless of the leadership, want trade-union unity. The men in there who will drive the subway are C.I.O. Transport Workers. You who build it are A. F. of L. It's half and half, so the murals represent you both, and the public, too, is made up of people in both unions."[32]

Meanwhile, the spirit of artistic cooperation animated one last thirties subway project: the WPA's Federal Writers Project's proposed book for young adults to be titled *Underneath New York*.[33] Although it was never completed, surviving drafts in the New York City Municipal Archives show that it would have dealt not only with the subway but also with "the vast and intricate system of water mains, sewers, steam conduits, gas pipes, telephone and telegraph cables, electricity ducts, underpasses for pedestrians, tunnels for cars and trucks, signal system wires for fire and police alarms and for traffic guidance, and pneumatic mail chutes—all of which thread below the streets and sidewalks to make New York's subsurface an unbelievably complicated warren of tunnels."[34]

There are many reasons why the *Underneath New York* project was never completed under WPA auspices. One was a simple shortage of funds. Another was that World War II ended the Depression and absorbed all available energies. But surely the strangest reason of all is that the project was the target of red-baiting.

The Right hated the WPA and Martin Dies's House Un-American Activities Committee kept it under constant assault. On July 19, 1940, the Committee, meeting in Beaumont, Texas, heard an "Un-Named Witness" testify on *Underneath New York*.[35] He said that while the writers claimed to be producing a children's book, they were actually producing a work that could be "of value to saboteurs"[36]

It is an remarkable accusation, one that could be lodged with the same justice against any road map. What makes it especially astonishing is that *Underneath New York* was shaping up as an eloquent expression of faith in the machine, in the city, in America. Most of the troubled history of the subway—its fare battles, the struggle against private ownership, the crowding—was blithely ignored. Instead the authors focused on the mechanical intricacy of the system, the vision of those who designed it, and the skill of those who kept it running. In an age when one scarcely ever encounters the noun "infrastructure" without the adjective "crumbling," it is slightly astonishing to see the subway used to exemplify a city that works. After enduring nearly a decade of the nation's longest Depression, the authors were still able to recover at least some of the optimism that had greeted the first subway in 1904.

CHAPTER EIGHT

THE SUBWAY CROWD

A simple request for subway directions at the beginning of Thomas Wolfe's short story "Only the Dead Know Brooklyn" develops into an extended metaphor in which the complexity of the borough's transit system represents the vast unknowableness of the human experience it contains. To Eugene Gant in Wolfe's *Of Time and the River* the essential mysteriousness of the city is situated above all in the figure of the crowd: "The people, common, dull, cruel, and familiar-looking as they were, seemed to be a part, to comprise, to be fixed in something classic, and eternal, in the everlasting variousness and fixity of time, in all the fabulous reality of the city's life: they formed it, they were part of it, and they could have belonged to nothing else on earth."[1]

Many artists, photographers, and painters—including men and women as diverse as Reginald Marsh and Saul Bellow, Walker Evans and James Baldwin, Isabel Bishop and Ann Petry—chose the subway for the study of the urban crowd. They were not—though Reginald Marsh is a partial exception—primarily interested in the opposition between subway and skyscraper or the building of the physical city. Instead, they focused on the men and women who populated it.

Their common subject was the crowd and it filled them with complex, ambivalent emotions. As writers and artists, as sensitive intellectuals, they had some reason for feeling superior to the masses of ordinary people around them. As democrats, however, they hoped to find a certain solidarity with the common people. They recognized that the challenge the crowd poses was ultimately political. At a time when democracy was threatened from within by a vapid consumerism and from without by the rise of dictatorships, they sought to vindicate the crowd, to assert its essential dignity.

158   SUBWAY CITY

All of these writers and artists conceived the crowd as possessing a certain cohesion. For all their careful attention to individuals, they shared a conviction that the crowd could be thought of in the singular. It was ultimately one crowd, not two indifferent or hostile ones colliding in a common space. But even the unified crowd contained divisions of class, race, ethnicity, and gender that could not be ignored.

Of these, class and ethnicity were least threatening in portrayals of the subway. The very rich were elsewhere in their limousines and most of the others could be united under the rubric of the common people. Their varying ethnicities could be celebrated as evidence of the crowd's variety even as they were assumed to be disappearing in the melting pot.

Distinctions of gender and race were more troublesome. Although they hoped to show its unity, observers of the subway crowd could not help seeing that the distinct historical experiences of women and African-Americans in the city as a whole were reflected in their experience underground.

IMAGINING THE CROWD

All observers of the subway crowd face a common set of problems. First, it has to be seen. Then it has to be conceptualized. Finally, it has to be evaluated.

Seeing it begins with an anxious glance. The sociologist Georg Simmel thought that modern city was characterized by "a great preponderance of occasions to *see* rather than to *hear* people." In the village, he argued, social relations between men had been founded on relatively intimate oral communication. The social life of the big city depended on visual contacts: "Before the appearance of omnibuses, railroads and streetcars in the nineteenth century, men were not in a situation where for periods of minutes or hours they could or must look at each other without talking to one another." Simmel thought this produced lonesomeness and estrangement, a "feeling that the individual is surrounded on all sides by closed doors." [2]

The situation is even more problematic than Simmel imagines. He writes as if streetcar riders engaged in prolonged steady gazes but in fact such an activity borders on the illicit. Sit in the subway, gaze at your fellow riders, and you will be surprised at how few eyes meet yours. An individual, forced into uncomfortable proximity to strangers, responds by creating a private space of his or her own. Sometimes this is done by posture, sometimes by reading a newspaper or retreating into a world of thought. Eye contact shatters this sanctuary.

Those who wanted to understand the subway crowd had to violate this decorum. "Go out into the street," Reginald Marsh commanded his students, "stare at the people. Go into the subway, stare at the people. Stare, stare, keep on staring." [3] Drafting a preface for his subway photographs, Walker Evans recalled that one of his mother's commandments was "Don't Stare" and insisted that this was one rule his viewers should ignore: "Stare. It is the way to educate your eye, and more. Stare, pry, listen, eavesdrop. Die knowing something." [4]

But what will we know? Richard Aldington, writing a poem on his experience in the London tube, describes himself glancing across the aisle at a row of eyes—"Eyes of greed, of pitiful blankness, of plethoric complacency"—and realizing to his discomfort that they are glaring at him with the same contempt with which he glares at them.[5] But it is striking that nothing quite like Aldington's poem is ever created in New York City. New York writers and artists, even when society tells them that they are superior to those around them by class and education, seek to come to terms with their fellow riders and to define a common humanity.

Once the crowd had been carefully observed, it had to be conceptualized. As Thomas Wolfe's barrage of adjectives suggests, it was much easier to proclaim the mysteriousness and omnipresence of the crowd than to define its nature with any precision. A New Yorker between 1920 and 1950 was likely to hold, perhaps simultaneously, three distinct but overlapping conceptions.

The first was that of the subversive mob, easily swayed by demagogues and out for blood. This nightmare vision was powerfully expressed in Gustave Le Bon's *The Crowd*, which was reprinted many times after its first American appearance in 1896 and which strongly influenced the new discipline of social psychology. Le Bon was what the French call a man of the Right and his book was written out of fear that the bloodthirsty mobs of the French Revolution and the Paris Commune would reappear in the new century. His great lesson was that in a crowd the individual is submerged into a new collective mentality. The crowd had its own personality—it was excitable, irrational, violent, and easily led, the enemy of all order and all culture.

In the twenties and thirties, as images of vast crowds cheering dictators filled the newsreel screens, Le Bon's revulsion against the nineteenth-century mob easily evolved into an elitist fear of the masses. Ortega y Gasset gave this view sophisticated expression in his book *The Revolt of the Masses*. Others were less subtle. Many must have sympathized with Albert Jay Nock when he declared in the April 1935 *Atlantic Monthly* that "official Hitlerism, Bolshevism, Fascism, and the New Deal" were collectivist forces marshaling the mass-mind to bring western civilization to an appalling end.[6]

But most New York writers and artists were liberals or radicals. They needed a contrary vision, one that appreciated the vitality of the crowd and recognized its ability to pursue positive goals. They could have found such a vision in many novels of New York life. The middle-class narrator of Ernest Poole's immensely popular novel *The Harbor* (1915) exclaims: "When you see the crowd in a strike like this loosen up and show all it could be if it had the chance—that sight is so big it blots you out—you sink—you melt into the crowd."[7] The idealistic young radical in Daniel Fuchs's *Summer in Williamsburg* (1934) expresses a similar enthusiasm after getting caught in the surge on the 14th Street–Canarsie BMT. "Did you see them squeeze me against the door?" he asks. "How vital, how living, these people are. What force, what—how dynamic—the surge of the crowd. Essentially it is a poetic thing . . . Believe me."[8]

It was not entirely easy to believe him. Most New York writers and artists wanted to reject Le Bon's antagonistic view of the crowd and endorse the Left's vision of the oppressed coming together to reclaim their birthright. But neither the fears of the Right nor the hopes of the Left quite explained the ordinary men and women who packed into New York City subway cars to spend a day at their jobs in one of the city's new office towers or an evening in one of its new centers of commercialized amusement.

The crowds of the Right and of the Left have a certain symmetry—they are nearly mirror opposites of one another. There was a third way of conceiving the crowd which disrupted traditional ways of thinking about society. It was described by Gerald Stanley Lee (Ivy Lee's second cousin) in his best-selling book *Crowds; A Moving Picture of Democracy* (1912), dramatized in King Vidor's silent film *The Crowd* (1927), and discussed by a host of popular writers in books and magazine articles.

Lee's crowd was created by the giant business organizations of the modern city. It consisted of all those who worked in skyscrapers, shopped in department stores, read mass-circulation newspapers, and went to the movies. "Everywhere the individual finds himself surrounded by crowds," said an article in the 1924 *Literary Digest*. "A crowd surrounds him as he goes to work, and a crowd surrounds him as he returns from work. Often he does his work as part of a crowd."[9]

The new crowd, as many commentators observed, did not even have to be gathered in one place. Its essence lay in its mass-mind and this could characterize the reader of a tabloid newspaper or the member of a book club as much as it did an angry worker at a union rally. Abram Lipsky argued in *Man the Puppet* (1925) that "crowds may be crowds just as truly though they be invisible and dispersed, especially under the conditions of modern rapid communication."[10]

Many observers found it easy to condemn the modern crowd. Charlie Chaplin began *Modern Times* by juxtaposing images of commuters leaving a subway with sheep rushing up the same stairs. A writer in 1923 deplored "the potency of the herd instinct" in the city's subway terminals.[11] Everett Dean Martin declared in *The Behavior of Crowds* (1920) that he knew of nothing which so menaced "the values of civilization" as "the growing habit of behaving as crowds."[12]

Others, however, looked at the crowd with a kind of awe. The essayist Christopher Morley claimed to find a terrific and savage beauty in the men and women he saw each day in the subway: "As one watches each of those passengers, riding with some inscrutable purpose of his own (or an even more inscrutable lack of purpose) toward duty or liberation, he may be touched with anger and contempt toward individuals; but he must admit the majesty of the spectacle in the mass."[13] That is a judgment which many New York writers and artists struggled to affirm.

FROM THE SPECTACLE TO THE LONELY CROWD

Reginald Marsh, Walker Evans, and Saul Bellow all use the subway as a crucial site in which to examine and evaluate the urban crowd. Their work shows a certain progression. Marsh sees the crowd as a continually unrolling spectacle, then focuses on individuals within it. Evans reverses this procedure. His photographs show hauntingly mysterious individuals with only the sheer volume of them reminding us that they belong to a crowd. This inward movement continues in the fiction of Saul Bellow, who shows prickly, socially estranged protagonists glancing uneasily at the men and women in the subway.

Reginald Marsh was fundamentally a celebrant of New York life. He told a reporter from the *Brooklyn Eagle* in 1929. "I love this city. There is no end of meat here. And I notice that it is just beginning to be exploited by artists. New York is a gold mine for color. Some time ago the city had a depressing effect upon me. Constantly I felt downhearted in the great place, but times have changed and now I hesitate to leave it. When I go out into the country and look upon the green leaves I am bored. I would rather be here than anywhere else."[14]

By the end of his life Marsh had documented the city in approximately 800 paintings, 650 watercolors, and many engravings and lithographs. His vision is selective. He had little interest in the precincts of the wealthy or the blander portions of the middle class. He rarely shows domestic scenes or even, as John Sloan did, scenes of private intimacy enacted in a public space. Instead, he was drawn to the culturally raucous and the blatantly commercial. He portrays a city of cheap, small-scale leisure activities—Coney Island, taxi dance halls, and movie theater entrances—places where patrons were in constant movement against a backdrop of advertising posters, neon signs, and display windows.

Marsh's work was created amidst widespread anxiety about the the crowd's appetite for sensationalism. "There is something in the presence of huge numbers of people," the social reformer Mary Simkovitch warned the First National Conference on City Planning in 1908, "which makes people desire more and more excitement to satisfy the jaded senses."[15] Concerned citizens and enlightened intellectuals were appalled by the ways in which commercial media were now shaping the consciousness of millions. When the spectacle is commercialized, George Elliott Howard insisted in the *American Journal of Sociology*, it always moves toward the lowest standard.[16]

When Marsh graduated from Yale the most recent example of this alleged mass degra-

The Melting Pot

64 ▪ Reginald Marsh. *The Melting Pot.*
New York Daily News, June 26, 1923.
Courtesy: Library of Congress.

SUBWAY SUNBEAMS

Taking the Chambers Street Curve.

65 ▪ Reginald Marsh. *Taking the Chambers Street Curve.*
New York Daily News, March 14, 1923.
Courtesy: Library of Congress.

dation was the tabloid newspaper. The first of these, the *Daily News*, was founded in 1919. It quickly achieved a circulation of over a million and by 1924 had two imitators—Hearst's *Mirror* and Bernarr MacFadden's *Graphic*. Screaming headlines were the most visible features of the new papers, followed by sensational photographs of bathing beauties and dead gangsters. "The better-educated, the intelligent, the mature-minded adults do not read tabloids," warned a writer in the *Forum*. "The regular addicts are shop-girls, stenographers, housewives, lower theatrical folk, laborers, and,—what is most serious,—school children." [17]

In this context it is of some importance that Marsh's first steady work was with the *Daily News*. He is often too easily viewed as an unrelenting critic of the crowd's cultural banality. A reviewer in 1932 said that he displays the "mental underworld of people whose brains have been shot to hell by the radio, the moving pictures and the press." [18] A more recent critic suggests that he emphasizes "distance and alienation—a breakdown in the solidarity of 'we, the people.'" [19] But if Marsh's purpose is to show the cultural collapse of city life and the vacuousness of the crowd, the editorial page of the *Daily News* is a very odd place to begin doing it.

And he didn't just draw a few cartoons. Between November 1922 and October 1923 he contributed 111 drawings to the *Daily News* editorial page (Ills. 64 & 65).[20] Bearing such headlines as "The Frantic City Life," "At The Zoo," and "People We'd Like to Kill, But Don't," these sketches constitute a remarkable survey of New York life and introduce many of the themes and specific compositions which would appear years later in Marsh's paintings and prints.

The subway quickly became one of Marsh's favorite settings. On December 27, 1922, a small boy, struggling to penetrate "The Subway Crush" at the entrance to a Seventh Avenue express, asks himself, "I wonder if I'll be able to get in there any easier when I grow up." "People We'd Like to Kill But Don't" include "The Man Who Sticks His Feet Out in the Subway Car" (February 15, 1923), and "The Anxious Subway Guard Who Guillotines His Passengers between the Closing Doors" (February 24). In March of 1923 Marsh began using the recurring title "Subway Sunbeams."

All of these cartoons mix satire with affectionate celebration—a combination that is not part of the classical theory of genres but appears on the funny pages of any newspaper. The problem is to identify what is being satirized and what is being celebrated. One of the best guides to Marsh's world is an article by the journalist and social critic Benjamin De Casseres in the October 1927 issue of the *American Mercury*. It attempts to characterize what was felt to be a new phenomenon of New York in the twenties—"The Broadway Mind."

This mental state, which was actually far-flung over the five boroughs, depended on knowing the news and, if possible, being in the news: "Broadway Man," said De Casseres, "believes everybody should be Somebody. Democracy's aspiration to aristocracy is embodied in being Somebody. This Somebody should appear somewhere, somehow, some time in the daily prints. If Somebody's photograph has appeared once or twice, this person passes into the Pantheon of the Broadway Mind." And the tabloid mind, for De Casseres, was simply a reflex of the Broadway Mind among the vulgar: "The girls and boys who devour these sewer-rags in the subway by the million will be the Broadway wisecrackers of another year." [21]

Broadway Man, with his energy, his cocky knowingness, his full participation in the life the city, is one of Marsh's most frequent subjects. He is often shown reading the newspaper, the essential instrument of his up-to-dateness. We see an unusually scrawny member of the species in the workman who pauses on the mezzanine of the Times Square station, transfixed by the *Evening Graphic*, while his fellow subway riders rush past. We see another, since Broadway man is often a woman, in the lady immersed in her newspaper in the etching *BMT #2*.

Marsh often uses tabloid headlines to point the contrast between the dull outward demeanor of his subway riders and the riotous adventure of their fantasies. The director of sales and publicity for a New York department store explained the popularity of the *Daily News*, the *Mirror*, and the *Graphic* by pointing to the opportunity they offered for vicarious adventure. "[These readers] tread their daily grind in the home, the office, the workshop; but they are potential adventurers,—we all are. And the tabloids dish up to them, every day, food which keeps alive an unexpressed part of their nature, makes them feel they belong in the human chorus, though not in the spotlight." [22]

This precisely describes many of Marsh's riders. They sit passively but the headlines they read betray their longing for lives of daring and sexual escapade. The *Daily Graphic's* "MCMANUS SLAYER" in the etching *Two Girls in Subway* (1928) refers to George A. McManus, a gambler who had witnessed (and some said actually committed) the murder of crime boss Arnold Rothstein. The *Daily News* headline "VANDERBILT ELOPES" in the etching *Second Ave. El* (Ill. 66) refers to Cornelius Vanderbilt Jr., who had scandalized his wealthy family by formalizing his second marriage to Mary Weir Logan only thirty minutes after her Reno

66 ■ Reginald Marsh. *2nd Ave. El.*

1929. Etching, 7 × 9 in. Print Collection, Miriam and Ira D. Wallach Division of Art, Prints and Photographs, The New York Public Library, Astor, Lenox and Tilden Foundations.

divorce. "SINCLAIR" in *BMT (#3)* (1929) refers to Harry F. Sinclair, a wealthy oil magnate and central figure in the Teapot Dome scandal whose struggles against prosecution kept him in the headlines for more than a decade. In each case, these headlines hint at a world of money, sex, and daring that is far beyond the reach—though not beyond the longings—of the subdued figures who fill the cars.

Taken individually, Marsh's subway riders are a little absurd and yet it is very difficult to condemn them with any easy cultural superiority. They are restrained in their manners and awkward in their poses. Their heads are probably stuffed with the latest trivia, but they have life and hope and ambition. Reginald Marsh's subway riders are part of a surprisingly vital mass whose ceaseless motion makes it a terrific spectacle. Marsh satirizes individuals but enjoys the crowd.

Walker Evans's attitude is more hesitant. By the late thirties he was best known for studies of southern sharecroppers and carefully composed scenes of small industrial towns. He had published three photographs to accompany Hart Crane's *The Bridge* in 1930 but they

67 ▪ Walker Evans. *Subway Portrait (Man in a Leather Jacket)*. 1938/41. Gelatin Silver Print, 5¹³/₁₆ × 3½ in. Gift of Kent and Marcia Minichiello, © 1996 Board of Trustees, National Gallery of Art, Washington, D.C. © Walker Evans Archive, The Metropolitan Museum of Art.

show the physical structure rather than the people. There was no subway photograph to accompany "The Tunnel." Later in the decade, Evans's interests turned to documenting urban life. Between 1938 and 1941 he took a series of photographs in the IRT.

Photography was (and is) illegal in the subway so Evans worked surreptitiously, riding with a 35 mm. camera concealed in his coat. He could fix the lens on the individuals across from him but could not look through the viewfinder before pressing his cable release. In 1966 he published eighty-nine of his photographs in the book *Many Are Called*—one of the masterpieces of urban portraiture.

Evans's people sit quietly, drawn into themselves, their fragility emphasized by the fact that their faces fill so comparatively little of the frame relative to the hard metal and glass surfaces of the wall (Ill. 67). In one sense, they are people who have not yet put on a mask—only a few seem to guess that they are being observed. In another sense, however, they have drawn into themselves against the uproar of their surroundings. They are at once open and on their guard. They are both ordinary and mysterious. They are totally fascinating.

Marsh conceived his subway project as a true exploration—one that would be conducted with a minimum of preconceptions. Not long before turning to the subway he had completed his collaboration with James Agee on the portrait of southern sharecropping families in *Let Us Now Praise Famous Men*. At the end of that book Agee, no doubt with Evans's agreement, includes four contemptuous pages on the photographer Margaret Bourke-White who had, with the writer Erskine Caldwell, produced a volume of text and photographs entitled *You Have Seen Their Faces.* The burden of his assault is that Bourke-White had by her choice of faces, by her composition, by her selection of the particular moment at which to take the photograph, made her subjects conform to a preestablished image of noble poverty.[23]

Evans wanted to avoid preconceiving his subject. "I would like," he said, "to be able to state flatly that sixty-two people came unconsciously into range before an impersonal fixed recording machine during a certain time period, and that *all* these individuals who came into the film frame were photographed, and photographed without any human selection for the moment of lens exposure."[24]

The photograph of a woman holding a folded copy of the *Daily News* in her lap is characteristic of the photographs that resulted (Ill. 68). The newspaper headline reads: " KEN-NEDY FIGHTS AID BRITAIN BILL." Marsh would have used the headline to lead us straight into the mind of his character. Thus the headline "DOES THE SEX URGE EXPLAIN JUDGE CRATER'S STRANGE DISAPPEARANCE" in Marsh's 1930 tempera *"Why Not Use the 'L'"* clearly comments ironically on relation between the sleeping Negro laborer and the alarmed, repressed female beside him. No such necessary relation exists within Evans's photograph. She may not have chosen the *Daily News* for that day's headline and it reveals nothing about her psychology.

But of course it is not finally possible to work without any element of preconception. Evans's shaping of his images begins with his decision to photograph on the IRT. If he had photographed on the BMT, where the seating arrangement was different, many of his subjects would have been seated on cross benches. He would have been unable to both keep

68 ▪ Walker Evans. *Subway Portrait (Woman Holding a Newspaper: 'Kennedy Fights Aid Britain Bill').*
1941. Gelatin silver print, 5³⁄₁₆ × 4⁵⁄₁₆ in. Gift of Kent and Marcia Minichiello, in Honor of the 50th Anniversary of the National Gallery of Art, © 1996 Board of Trustees, National Gallery of Art, Washington, 1941. © Walker Evans Archive, The Metropolitan Museum of Art.

a sharp focus with his slow film and isolate his subjects. By restricting himself to the IRT, where riders sat across the aisle against the wall, he was able to get the particular frontal view, combining the dignity of traditional portraiture with the anonymity of the mug shot, which contributes so powerfully to his photographs' fascination.

Moreover, Evans expected that though he wouldn't impose an interpretation in advance, one would emerge in the course of his work and would be communicated to his viewers by the sequencing of his photographs and by his title. The woman with the *Daily News* comes early in the sequence. If the headline doesn't tell us anything certain about her attitude toward Ambassador Joseph Kennedy or Lend Lease, it certainly reminds us that these subway riders are being photographed at a time when democracy is under international assault. That Evans's true subject is the crowd is suggested by the sheer number of individuals he presents in sequence and is confirmed by the sudden, unexpected view of the crowded car which brings the sequence to a close.

But it is above all the title which shapes our attitude toward these photographs. Evans's editor suggested the Biblical quotation "Many are called but few are chosen," which Evans shortened to *Many Are Called*. The eighty-nine photographs definitely show the many; it is

69 ▪ O. Louis Guglielmi. *Subway Exit.*
1946. Oil on canvas, 29⅞ × 28 in. Collection of Auburn University, Auburn, Alabama.

possible that they are also, as in the Biblical citation, the excluded, the damned. But by truncating the quotation, Evans leaves us free, almost invites us, to consider the opposite possibility—that they are, if not the saved, then souls of considerably greater worth than might appear at first glance.

These photographs are startlingly tough-minded examples of a constant thirties theme— the praise of the common man. The phrase sounds more oratorical than Evans would have liked, but he was always clear about his ambition to portray "the general run of the social mill: those anonymous people who come and go in the cities and who move on the land."[25]

The only surprise is that Evans was able to find this greatness in the subway crowd made up, as Ayn Rand said scornfully in *The Fountainhead* (1943), of "the anonymous, the un-selected."[26] At a time of growing Fascist power in Europe, Evans explores the decency of ordinary citizens. "These," he said, invoking the quintessential democratic institution, "are the ladies and gentlemen of the jury."[27]

The progress from Marsh's subway images to Evans's is partly a movement from outward bustle to inward experience. This shift in emphasis is even more striking in several paintings of the forties that tend to show the crowd only by implication while dramatizing the personal or existential anguish of individuals.

Painting the subway before he turned to abstract color compositions, Mark Rothko reduced the crowd to a few elongated figures in an empty space. O. Louis Guglielmi, in *Subway Exit* (1943), presents the subway stairs in the shape of an open grave from which mother and child are struggling to escape (Ill. 69). Bernard Perlin's *Orthodox Boys* (1948) shows two yeshiva students who are menaced not so much by the crowd as by the graffiti which covers every millimeter of the subway wall (Ill. 70).

George Tooker brings the trend to a climax in his tempera painting *The Subway* (1950), which offers a nightmare inversion of an annunciation scene (Ill. 71). The corridors of the station recall the vanishing point perspectives of a Quattrocento courtyard, the pale reds and blues echo the traditional symbols of passion and sanctity, and the woman uses her hand to protect her womb against the threatening messages of the men around her. Tooker said that he chose the subway as the setting for this painting because it represented "a denial of the senses and a negation of life itself. Its being underground with great weight overhead was important."[28]

Like Tooker's woman, Saul Bellow's protagonists feel a weight pressing in on them from the city overhead and from the presence of the subway crowd. In *The Victim* (1947), "A Father-to-Be" (1955), and *Seize the Day* (1956) he employs the subway as a setting in which his narcissistic protagonist's sense of oppression builds to a crisis and, in the two novels, to a transformation. At their best, his characters break out of isolation to achieve a sympathetic identification with their fellow riders and, by extension, with suffering humanity.

Rogin, the protagonist of "A Father-to-Be," fails to achieve this transformation. Much of the story is a record of his subway ride to his fiancée's apartment. "Thoughts very often grow fertile in the subway," Bellow's narrator observes, "because of the motion, the great company, the subtlety of the rider's state as he rattles under streets and rivers, under the foundations of great buildings."[29]

He is an emotional child cringing at the prospect of adulthood, marriage, and parenthood,

70 ▪ Bernard Perlin. *Orthodox Boys.*

1948. Tempera on board. The Tate Gallery, London/Art Resource, New York. By permission of the artist.

whose wide-ranging thoughts in the subway center on his fear of being caught in the great chain of human reproduction. These fears focus on the rider opposite him. The man looks disturbingly like Rogin's fiancée, Joan. Then, worse, he looks like Joan's father. Finally, much, much worse, he looks like the son that he and Joan will someday have. Rogin is looking at his biological destiny. "Yes, think forty years ahead, and a man like this, who sat by him, knee to knee in the hurtling car among their fellow creatures, unconscious participants in a sort of great carnival of transit—such a man would carry forward what had been Rogin." [30]

Rogin's situation is a nightmare reversal of Walt Whitman's in "Crossing Brooklyn Ferry." Where the poet had reveled in his intimacy with riders and readers to come, Bellow's character feels his kinship with crowds past, present, and future as the ultimate constriction. Infantile himself, he is appalled at the thought of producing an infant. "Rogin," he tells himself as he approaches Joan's apartment, "don't be a damned instrument. Get out of the way."[31] But Joan knows her man. "Oh my baby," she exclaims and draws him into her web.

The subway provides the setting for more positive insights in *The Victim* and *Seize the Day*. *The Victim* centers on the relation between the nonobservant Jew Asa Leventhal and the unreligious Christian Kirby Allbee. Asa is a man who has seen some bad times. During the worst of them he worked in a hotel near the Bowery and memories of the derelicts recur to him throughout the novel. He still fears a fall into the part of humanity "that did not get away with it—the lost, the outcast, the overcome, the effaced, the ruined."[32]

Bellow treats the subway as a symbol that Asa longs to escape. It is both the past he fears and the present he finds unendurable. It is where the lost are on display. When Allbee, torturing him, wants to illustrate the futility of human effort, he exclaims, "Is there anything you want? There are a hundred million others who want that very same damn thing. I don't care whether it's a sandwich or a seat in the subway or what."[33] When he wants to tell Asa how people play it safe when they ought to break the rules, he uses the example of a policeman who fails to help a subway rider who has fallen onto the tracks. Throughout the novel the subway, with its muggy air, its yellow light, its slowly revolving fans, and the distant concussion of its cars, becomes the physical representation for Asa's psychological burdens.

Appropriately, the subway also provides a setting for two scenes in which the re-

71 ▪ George Tooker. *The Subway.*
1950. Egg tempera on composition board, 18 × 36 in. Collection of Whitney Museum of American Art, Purchase, with funds from the Juliana Force Purchase Award, 50.22.

pressed Asa is finally able to wholeheartedly love those closest to him. Asa's conflict with Allbee takes place within the context of his two other troubled relationships—one with his brother, Max, and the other with his wife, Mary. Both these troubled relationships are transformed at the end of the novel and in each case the transformation is associated with the subway.

When Asa catches his last glimpse of his brother on a departing subway car, gripping a strap and peering out over the heads of passengers, he discovers that he can finally love Max's frailty and decency. His love for his wife is expressed in a dream in which the reverberating subway merges with the train on which Mary will return: "Over and over gain he saw the station platform, the cars in the tunnel, and made out Mary's face in the crowd of passengers—her hat, her light hair, and last of all her face." [34]

Tommy Wilhelm's situation in *Seize the Day* (1956) is even more desperate than Asa's, but it follows the same curve from isolation to identification with suffering humanity. This happens twice—once, tentatively, in the subway and then, more definitively, in a funeral home. In the first of these scenes, set in the Times Square station, Tommy is both repelled by the urban crowd and eager to achieve some communion with it. Then, like an urban Ancient Mariner, he finds himself transformed: "All of a sudden, unsought, a general love for all these imperfect and lurid-looking people burst out in Wilhelm's breast. He loved them. One and all, he passionately loved them." [35] The mood fades but it prepares Tommy for the darker epiphany with which the novel ends.

THE FEMININE SUBWAY

If the male study of the subway crowd begins with an anxious glance at fellow passengers, there are reasons to believe that women saw differently—and, just as important, were seen differently—than men. "The Gaze" has a achieved a certain status as a subject of theoretical inquiry among feminist scholars in recent years. In an influential essay on "Visual Pleasure and Narrative Cinema" Laura Mulvey argued that popular films used women as passive raw material for a controlling male gaze. Since the publication of Mulvey's essay, the male gaze, the ability of women to inhabit the male gaze, and possibility of a female gaze have been extensively discussed. [36]

Ever since Baudelaire's great essay on "The Painter of Modern Life" (1869) cultural critics have been fascinated by the figure of the *flâneur*—the passionate spectator, the lover of crowds, who melts incognito into the street life of the metropolis. A number of feminist critics—notably Janet Wolff [37] and Griselda Pollock [38]—point out that there is no corresponding *flâneuse* and argue that the modern city remains hostile to full female participation. Griselda Pollack puts the case as strongly as possible: "Modernity is still with us, ever more acutely as our cities become in the exacerbated world of postmodernity more and more a place of strangers and spectacle, while women are ever more vulnerable to violent assault while out in public and are denied the right to move around our cities safely. The spaces of femininity still regulate women's life—from running the gauntlet of intrusive looks by men on the streets to surviving deadly sexual assaults." [39]

But another argument can be made. Much of it is presented in Elizabeth Wilson's *The*

Sphinx in the City (1991). She sees that while the modern city is often inimical to women, it is just as often a place of exploration and, potentially, of liberation. Blanche Gelfant points out that the woman who leaves home is a recurring figure in the urban novel.[40] She appears in works as diverse as Anzia Yezierska's *Hungry Hearts*, Mary Antin's *The Promised Land*, Betty Smith's *A Tree Grows in Brooklyn*, Gail Godwin's *The Odd Woman*, Lisa Alther's *Kinflicks*, and Louise Meriwether's *Daddy Was a Numbers Runner*. In the city she encounters both restriction and the promise of fulfillment.

Against this background, we can see that the representation of women in the subway, whether by women or by men, involves complex psychological and cultural forces. At the very least, images of sexual and social power are involved. Male gazers were strongly aware of the female presence. Some felt challenged by it. Others felt sexual vibrations in what were, after all, conditions of astonishing physical closeness. Women inevitably saw the subway as an ordeal—one that sometimes went beyond discomfort to involve physical harassment. But it was an ordeal that had to be faced because it led to the dream of a good job and an independent life.

Two incidents from subway history, both occurring before passage of the Equal Suffrage Amendment in 1920, suggest not only how women's relation to the subway mirrored the crusades and compromises that defined their participation in the larger city but also how women were themselves divided about the terms on which they would enter the urban public space. These incidents also suggest that women were not so much welcomed into the modern city as channeled into particular parts of it.

In 1907 Julia L. D. Longfellow, wife of a member of a prominent law firm and member of the Morrisania branch of the Woman's Municipal League, proposed that the last car of each IRT train should be reserved for women who were traveling alone and unprotected. Women would be able to ride in any car if they wished, but the last car would always be a refuge from "inconveniences" and "insults."

This was by no means a foolish suggestion but its premise was alarming. It smacked of Victorian womanhood. "The last thing in the world women want is to be segregated," said Florence Kelly, secretary of the Consumer's League. "The subway belongs to all alike," said Ida Husted Harper. "The women who can go home before the rush hour and don't do it are not entitled to special consideration. The women whose legitimate work keeps them until the last hour, just as it does men, of course, must take their chances."[41] Mrs. H. S. Blatch, president of the Equality League of Self-Supporting Women, said that women often behaved as badly in the crowds as men.[42]

In fact the proposal was highly impractical. The IRT management had discovered that the time it took to transfer from local to express trains was a major cause of subway delays and strongly opposed anything that would complicate patterns of movement on the platforms. Moreover, if women were 25 percent of the riders on express cars, then one car out of seven would hardly meet their needs.[43]

The place of women in the subway became an issue in a quite different way at the end of World War I. During the wartime labor shortage the companies had turned to women as cashiers, ticket choppers, and guards. The women were paid the same as men. Perhaps worried about public relations, the Brooklyn Rapid Transit Company hired a medical expert to assure the public that the women's health didn't suffer. Dr. Alice Bowman reported that not only was their physical condition good but that she had observed "a remarkable improvement in the spirits of girls who have entered the service, a marked change for the better in the mental attitude, a broadening of their outlook on life."[44]

It seems likely that the most important behind-the-scenes opponents of women's employment were the male-dominated unions eager to provide jobs to returning veterans, but the loudest voices in public were those of women themselves—club women and social reformers. They wanted better conditions for workers as a group and special consideration for the weaker sex. In March 1919 the New York State legislature considered bills limiting the hours that women transportation workers and elevator operators could work and preventing them from working at night. About six hundred women went to Albany by special train to support the legislation. To their astonishment, they were greeted by an equally determined band of women wearing purple badges with the word "Opposed."

The opponents argued then, and for months to come, that the bills were paternalistic and would drive women out of employment. The women demanded a meeting with Governor Al Smith. They wanted a law that applied to men as well as to women. They were extremely angry that proponents of the new bills had whispered that women working at night had engaged in immoral conduct. "I have brought up five children," Mary Murray told the governor, "and I have kept my morals." The women were also annoyed that so many spokespersons for women's organizations had lobbied for the bills. "The sooner the society women understand that they must keep their hands off the working women," said ticket taker Mary Donnelly, "the sooner the working women will be better off."[45]

Nevertheless, the BRT terminated 1,531 women from its surface and subway lines.[46] The IRT had hired fewer women but it too let them go. By the time the Equal Suffrage Amendement passed in 1920 it was clear that the subway offered equal opportunity crowding to both sexes but employment only to men.

During these same years, young ladies were eagerly welcomed into the white-collar workforce. The number of women working in the new skyscrapers as typists, stenographers, and salespeople grew from 171,000 to 2,000,000 between 1890 and 1920.[47] The popular assumption was that they would go from high school to a sleek Art Deco office, work with brisk efficiency, dress stylishly, attract the admiring attention of an upwardly mobile young man, and end at home happily married with a loving family.

A certain kind of culturally sophisticated gentleman looked on these young ladies with some condescension but also with an admiring conviction that they signified something hopeful for the future. "These girls," said James Huneker, in *The New Cosmopolis* (1915), "all dress above their station, wear clothes that are manifestly cheap, in imitation of prevailing fashionable modes." He saw that their dress dramatized their ambition. "No self-respecting woman will dress according to her 'class'—or her means, either—for she is ever hopeful that her 'class' will be a better one, or that her daughters will marry 'above' them."[48] "They are so young, so slender, so untutored, such unconscious vessels of amazing life," said Christopher Morley of the young ladies he saw flashing past in a subway train. "Surely they are a new generation of their sex, cool, assured, even capable."[49]

The subway was one of the most important public spaces that these ambitious young woman had to pass through and it plays a recurring role in works dealing with their careers and marriage choices. In 1912 the popular illustrator James Montgomery Flagg (today best known for his World War I recruiting poster "Uncle Sam Wants You") began publishing a serial novel in pictures in the *Sunday World*. Entitled *The Adventures of Kitty Cobb*, it followed Kitty's adventures from her arrival in New York through her first job in the handkerchief department of a big department store to her eventual happy marriage in the upper reaches of New York society.

In Episode Seven, Kitty has just been taken to the Broadway theater by Mr. Theobald Tripper, the not-too-young, not-too-handsome floorwalker at her store. Kitty sits in the balcony with him, but, in what Flagg insists is her sweet, innocent, and unassuming way, she has already set her sights on the tonier society down in the orchestra seats. Tripper proposes marriage to Kitty in the subway on the ride home. "She Says No Without Looking at Him," Flagg's lengthy caption tells us. "In Fact She Hardly Hears Him, So Interested Is She In The Appearance and Personality of a Young Gentleman a Seat or Two to Her Left. Luckily For Her Modesty, the Swagger Youngster Does Not Notice the Gaze of Our Heroine. He Is Thinking Over a Successful Little Deal He had Managed in 'the Street.'"[50] The handsome young stockbroker will reappear five episodes later as young Bob Caldicott and he will soon be Kitty's husband.

Why does this first encounter take place in the subway? If a young woman's rise in life was to be accomplished through marriage, she required a place where she could meet an eligible young man from a higher station. The department store was a possible location and the office was an even better one. The subway, with its noise and impersonal public manners, would not seem very promising and in fact Kitty's eventual introduction to Bob will take place in a drawing room. But it is not just accidental that he is seen in the train. The subway functions as a sign that though he is upper class, he is not a snob. He rides with the regular people and is one of them at heart.

The subway functioned in this way in a great many movies of the period—both a sign of the ordinariness that a heroine would want to escape and a guarantee of the regular guy that she would want to attract. In *Subway Sadie* (1926) a young saleslady has to choose between a glamorous career in the effete world of Parisian fashions and marriage to Herb McCarthy, a sturdily masculine subway guard. She makes the nobler choice and is instantly rewarded as her love reveals himself to be the son of the subway company's president. In *Love Over Night* (1928) Jeannette Stewart is saved from a loveless marriage to a Long Island millionaire by a subway ticket chopper who turns out, happily, to be the son of a well-to-do hotel owner.

These films do not invariably deposit their heroines in the upper classes. In *The Girl from Woolworth's* (1929), Daisy King, a clerk at the five and dime, passes up a singing job in a glamorous nightclub to marry subway guard Bill Harrigan. But the dominant pattern is to give the heroine a choice between romance and fortune and then let her have both. In Samuel Goldwyn's *This Is Heaven* (1929), Eva Petrie, a poor Hungarian girl being sponsored in America by her uncle, a humble subway motorman, tries to invade high society by pretending to be an exiled Russian princess. When the chauffeur she accidentally falls in love with at last reveals himself to be a millionaire in disguise, Eva exclaims "These ees Heaven!"[51]

The presence of so many ambitious, attractively dressed young ladies in the subway could pose a challenge to the male imagination. In this context, it is appropriate to return to Reginald Marsh for a moment. Marilyn Cohen points out that his work is populated by

The Subway is fast~ *Cert.*
But the *Open Air Elev.*
gets you there quickly,
~ *and with more con.*

Why not use the '

72 ▪ Reginald Marsh. *Why Not Use the "L"?*
1930. Egg tempera on canvas, 36 × 48 in. Collection of Whitney Museum of American Art, Purchase.

powerful female figures and weak males.[52] (His Coney Island muscle men can be regarded, subversively, as overcompensating.) The contrast of male weakness and female strength is especially clear in Marsh's Bowery scenes where he violates his customary realism to introduce a confident, striding woman into the almost exclusively male world of the flophouses. He needed a prosperous female because only her confident presence could dramatize the

thoroughness of male defeat.

This contrast is not so overt in his subway images but once we are alerted to the pattern we can see that the women in them are nearly always bright and confident while the men are drab and recessive. Marsh's most famous subway image, *Why Not Use the "L"?* (Ill. 72), with its timid female next to a sleeping, but, in the woman's mind, intimidating male, is an inversion of his usual pattern. But his other subway paintings, such as *BMT* and *HITLER ESCAPES* (the title is from the *Daily News* headline) show women who easily eclipse the men around them.

Like Huneker, Marsh tries to condescend to the young women he shows. Several of his etchings—notably *Subway— Three Girls* (1928), *Three Girls on Subway Platform* (1930), and *Schoolgirls in Subway—Union Square* (1930)—are studies in shrieking schoolgirl vulgarity. In each case the point of view seems to be satiric, with the raucous vigor of the modern young ladies seen from the superior viewpoint of the gentleman artist. The vitality of the young women, however, challenges the social distance. Whether prim and dainty in *Subway—Three Girls* (Ill. 73) or loud and raucous in *Schoolgirls in Subway—Union Square*, they communicate strength. In part this is because the low vantage point increases their physical presence. It is also because behind these trios the viewer can sense a long tradition of representations of the Three Graces or the trio of goddesses who tempted Paris. Marsh's young ladies in the subway, though they are modern, gum-chewing goddesses, still command respect.

Sometimes the sexual vibration that men could feel in the subway took more sinister forms. In 1980 Sanford Garelik, head of the Transit Police (and later president of the city council), and Anne Beller and Sydney Cooper, both of the Juvenile Diversion Project, published an article on "Sex Crimes in the Subway" which identified a category of crime which was both gender and place specific. Most subway offenses simply reflected crime patterns elsewhere in the city. Reports of muggings rose and fell with those in the city at large. Certain types of sexual harassment, by contrast, occured predominantly in the subway. Exhibitionism and frottage (or genital rubbing) constituted "a virtually indigenous and perhaps unique problem of urban underground 'ecology.'"[53] Julia L. D. Longfellow was not mistaken in her diagnosis. Women really did face special insults in the subway.

Their dilemma is very effectively described in Betty Smith's *A Tree Grows in Brooklyn* (1943). One of the great turning points in the life of its protagonist, Francie Nolan, oc-

73 ▪ Reginald Marsh, *Subway—Three Girls.*
1928. Etching, 5 × 4 in. Print Collection, Miriam and Ira D. Wallach Division of Art, Prints and Photographs, The New York Public Library, Astor, Lenox and Tilden Foundations.

curs when she crosses the Williamsburg Bridge to her first Manhattan office job. After becoming a regular subway rider she soon learns that it has a routine: as the train leaves the Marcy Avenue elevated station and comes onto the bridge, many of those seated rise as if in one accord and then sit down again. "There's a bank with a big clock," her experienced brother explains. "People stand up to look at the time so's they know whether they're early or late for work." [54] Like the others, Francie develops a split-second rhythm, pushing to the car door before it grinds to a stop so she can be one of the first out and up the stairs.

If the subway has skills that must be learned, it also has ordeals that must be faced. Francie never gets used to the swarming crowds and a single repeated incident causes her to dread each ride:

There had been that time in the train when, hanging from a strap and so tightly wedged in the crowd that she couldn't so much as lower her arm, she had felt a man's hand. No matter how she twisted and squirmed, she couldn't get away from that hand. When she swayed with the crowd as the cars swerved, the hand tightened. She was unable to twist her head to see whose hand it was. She stood in desperate futility, helplessly enduring the indignity. She could have called out and protested but she was too ashamed to call public attention to her predicament.

When Francie complains to her mother and her Aunt Sissy, the two women react quite differently. Aunt Sissie treats the incident as a great joke: "It means you're getting in good shape and there are some men who can't resist a woman's shape. Say! I must be getting old! It's been years since anybody pinched me on the El." Francie's mother is more practical: "Learn to stand in the train without holding on to a strap. Keep your hands down and keep a long sharp pin in your pocket. If you feel a man's hand on you, stick it good with the pin."[55] Francie takes her mother's advice rather than her aunt's.

The artist Minna Citron treats the same situation.[56] Her 1933 lithograph *Subway Technique* shows a group of riders clustered around a central pole (Ill. 74). The focus is on the

74 ■ Minna Citron. *Subway Manners.*
1930. Lithograph, 11¼ × 16 in. Courtesy: Sragow Gallery, NYC. © Estate Minna Citron, 1996.

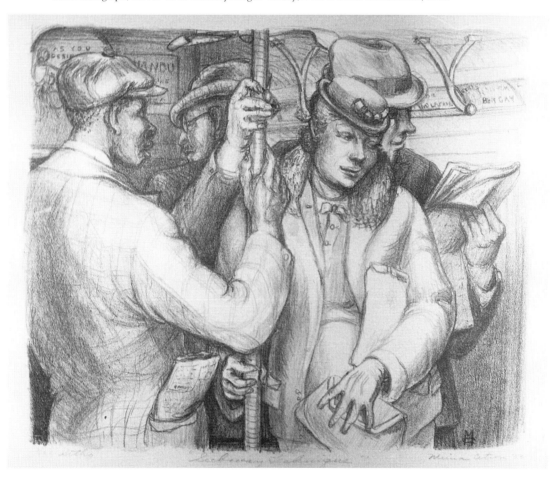

75 ▪ Isabel Bishop. *Virgil and Dante in Union Square.*
1932. Oil on canvas, 27 × 52 in. Delaware Art Museum, Gift of Helen Farr Sloan.

rather tentative facial expression of the woman in the center. She is being pinched. She is wondering what to do about it. Is she to maintain her dignity and pretend that nothing has happened? Is she to cry out in public against a culprit whom she cannot identify? Like Francie Nolan, she can't quite attach the hand to a person. It would be comfortable for the viewer to think that it is the nasty-looking gentleman on the right but it might also be the pleasant-looking one on the left. The arm movements are ambiguous and the artist always refused to say who was guilty. It is the ambiguity that matters.

The subway emerges as a much more benign place in the postwar paintings of Isabel Bishop, who uses it as a setting to explore the efforts of individual women to create private spaces of intimacy within the larger pressures of urban life.

Bishop's career dramatizes a conflict between an awareness of social distance and a wish to bridge it. Her family had been genteel but not prosperous. Unable to afford a home in a suitably upper-class neighborhood of Detroit, where Bishop's father taught Latin in a private school, the Bishops tried to preserve their status by keeping themselves—and especially their daughter—at one remove from their lower-class neighbors. This had a dual effect. One was to confirm the daughter in a lady-like deportment that lasted throughout her life. The other was to implant a kind of longing for what seemed the richer lives of the people below her on the social ladder. "I wasn't supposed to play with the children on my block," she told an in-

terviewer in 1976, "but I wanted to. I thought, they have a warmer life than we do—they all see each other, and we are isolated."[57]

The contrast between her own life and that of ordinary people was repeated when, every working day, she took a subway ride from the gracious Riverdale section of the Bronx to the commercial blocks around Union Square. Although it has entered American mythology as the site of Communist rallies, the Square was really bordered by banks, insurance companies, and small offices. Its workers were accountants, bookkeepers, secretaries, and stenographers. At the south end there was a vigorous shopping district anchored by the bargain department stores Hearns, Ohrbach's, and Klein's. Seeing its crowds, Bishop admired "the incredible richness of this coming and going of these multitudes of people. I can't fully explain, but it was like eating, looking out of my window on the people walking below, it was nourishment."[58]

Bishops's earliest portrayal of the urban crowd appears in the 1932 painting *Virgil and Dante in Union Square* (Ill. 75). It shows the two poets standing at the west side of the square gazing at the urban throng. (They are located, appropriately, near the section of trolley track known as Dead Man's Curve because of the frequent accidents there.) Dante and Virgil are looking at neither Gustave Le Bon's crowd of angry violence nor Ernest Poole's crowd of awakening solidarity. They see the same well-dressed, well-mannered, almost anonymous men and women that Gerard Stanley Lee had described and that King Vidor had filmed. Bishop implies that they are in limbo, but expresses no condemnation. Like Walker Evans, Bishop concedes that the urban crowd lacks grandeur but gives it her allegiance nonetheless.

In later years, Bishop's focus shifted from the crowd as a unit to its individual members. She typically selected individuals from the mixed crowd of office workers and derelicts who inhabited the square. She studied them in their most ordinary activities—sitting at a lunch counter, putting on a coat, eating an ice cream cone. *Virgil and Dante in Union Square* shows a crowd that is equally divided between men and women but Bishop focused increasingly on women in the thirties and they are the exclusive subject of her subway paintings.

She turned to the subway in the early fifties after an unpleasant incident in the Square in which a group of down-and-out men objected in a threatening way to her sketching them. A policeman, appealed to for help, simply suggested that she go someplace else. She was, she told an interviewer with a certain dry humor, "driven underground." On the platforms she could sketch undisturbed. "I find no one watches me at all. I draw down there and nobody notices me."[59]

Bishop was one of the few artists to find the subway a kind of refuge. In this respect, as in so many, it mirrored the city at large. The impersonality of urban relations was often treated by sociologists in the Durkheim tradition as a source of *anomie* but it also conferred a certain freedom.

At first Bishop found it difficult to portray the subway without echoing George Tooker's claustrophobic anguish. In an interview she said of the painting *Homeward* (1951) that when she tried to paint the figures "and nail them down," she found, "the whole subject froze and none of the meaning that I wanted was present." The same thing happened when she drew the setting—as she worked on the iron columns the scene became a prison.

She got the effect she wanted by focusing on the moment of intimacy between the two women and by suggesting the surrounding environment rather than precisely delineating it. She shows her people to be good and decent in a setting that is crowded but not confining. Its flowing movement reflected the larger opportunities of city life.

The subway fascinates Bishop because it is a place of transition. Her work is informed by an implicit metaphor between physical movement and social mobility. She saw her subjects as young women on the move—literally so, because they came to the Square by subway and were usually seen walking down the street or catching a quick bite at lunch. They were also figuratively on the move, hoping to move up the ladder or working at an office job for a few years until they married. She frequently painted them at moments of rest, eating an ice cream cone or reading a book, but the pose suggests that it is only a momentary pause amid the fundamental mobility of these young ladies' lives.

76 ▪ Isabel Bishop.
Subway Scene.
1957–1958. Egg tempera and oil on composition board, 41 × 28 in. Collection of Whitney Museum of American Art.

The humanism of Bishop's work is exemplified by *Subway Scene* (Ill. 76). It shows one of art's classic subjects: a woman reflected in a mirror. She is not, as in Marsh's *BMT*, a fashion plate checking her lipstick. Bishop deliberately avoided showing fashionable dress because she thought that confirmed the condescending assumption that the women she studied were somehow light and non-serious. "There is a great discrepancy in American women," Bishop said. "Their hats and clothes make them look like flibbertigibbets, light as air, when they are not."[60]

In Bishop the subway ceases to be an ordeal or a menace. It becomes a place where contradictions are reconciled. In her paintings we see figures enjoying moments of privacy, though their postures suggest the pressure of the crowd around them. We see people at rest in a place of movement. It's "the appearing and disappearing in this situation that makes the charm of it for me," she said. It constitutes, she said, "a kind of map of life."[61]

A SEPARATE SUBWAY?

The subway served as a map of the city's racial life as well, but one that was treacherously difficult to read. It is a place where the races mingle easily but also one where the separations and tensions of the larger society are often reproduced in covert, unacknowledged forms. The subway became a place of repressed resentments and when they erupted in the mid-sixties they shattered the unity of the subway crowd.

Segregation had been spotty but persistent in the earliest years of New York's transit system. No law required it but African Americans on several of the city's routes had to let horsecars go past until they found one bearing a placard declaring "Colored People Allowed in This Car." This was a serious handicap in a New York which was growing from a walking to a riding city and black ministers argued passionately against it.[62] As late as 1864 the *Tribune* could still complain that some horsecars excluded Negroes with impunity.[63]

Discrimination in New York transit faded in the years after the Civil War. Visitors later in the century frequently observed that Negroes traveled freely on horsecars and elevateds. In 1904, after southern states had passed laws requiring racial segregation on transit, an English tourist would report that when he boarded an el train with a southern companion, "Mr. Simes looked with such horror at the presence of Etheopians in any but a Jim Crow car that almost involuntarily his hand went to his hip-pocket."[64]

The subway companies, including the city-owned Independent line, discriminated against blacks in employment. African Americans didn't become bus drivers in New York until a boycott led by Adam Clayton Powell forced the hiring of ten on the 125th Street route in 1942. It was only in the 1950s that they broke into subway employment. So far as riding was concerned, however, the trains were open to all and this was a crucial fact for white public opinion. When Rosa Parks launched the Montgomery Bus Boycott in 1955, most New Yorkers complacently regarded discrimination in transit as an example of southern perversity.

The paradox of the subway was that it was a relatively unsegregated place in a society characterized by a high degree of racial separation. This created an interesting challenge for those writers and artists who used the subway as a way of representing aspects of the larger city.

One strategy was to point to the subway as a space that millions shared every day with more important things to think about than the race of the person next to them. Reginald Marsh carefully included a Negro in his subway melting pot for the *Daily News* editorial page in 1921 and three decades later Langston Hughes expressed the same message in his poem "Subway Rush Hour" when he pointed out that black and white were mingled so closely together in the subway that they had no room for fear. His working-class narrator in *The Sweet Flypaper of Life* (1955) points out that black and white, Gentile and Jew had learned to get along in the subway long before the Supreme Court outlawed segregated schools.

Yet even those who portrayed a relaxed equality had to acknowledge that African Americans occupied a special position in the subway crowd. That is the secret message of Fritz Eichenberg's woodcut *Sleep* (Ill. 77). The artist's intent was no doubt the same as Marsh's. He shows a cross-section of weary New Yorkers riding home late at night on the West Side IRT. Two African Americans are part of the crowd, a man nodding wearily in the fore-

77 ▪ Fritz Eichenberg.
Subway.
1934. Woodcut. Museum of the City of New York. Gift of Constance Veit Sherwin.

ground, a woman on the long bench opposite. Eichenberg shows a subway crowd united in sleepy equality, then wittily goes a step further. The woman's broad-brimmed hat becomes a halo. Even in a crowd marked by ragtag equality, the African American is the victim of particular oppression and therefore the object of special solicitude.

We see similar complexities and cross-currents in representations of the subway ride by African American writers and artists. First, while they tend to see the subway as a symbol of the city, they are also keenly aware that it has a special relation to their own city of Harlem. Second, they use it to almost simultaneously assert and deny the importance of racial difference.

James Weldon Johnson argued in *Black Manhattan* (1930) that the subway helped create Harlem as an Afro-American enclave. In 1900, when construction of the Interborough began, African Americans had lived in a few crowded districts in midtown. Apartments uptown in Harlem had been overbuilt in anticipation of the Lenox Avenue branch of the Interborough. When its opening was delayed, landlords who were starved for tenants began accepting African Americans and the black population grew.

Whites, remembering their first encounter with New York, describe skyscrapers rising out of the water or recall the great concourses of Penn Station or Grand Central. African Americans, by contrast, remember their arrival as a contrast between the noisy confinement of the subway and the sudden release of climbing the stairs into a Harlem where they could feel free. "I can never put on paper," Langston Hughes said, "the thrill of that underground ride to Harlem." He came from the north and as he rode downtown on the Eighth Avenue line he kept watching for the sign 135TH STREET. When he finally arrived he felt like shaking the hand of every person he saw.[65]

Rudolph Fisher's classic short story "The City of Refuge" puts this contrast in its most dramatic form. Fleeing the law in North Carolina, his protagonist arrives in New York and is immediately plunged into the subway to endure the "shuffle of a thousand soles, clatter of a thousand heels, innumerable echoes," the "heat, oppression, suffocation," and the "screeching onslaught of the fiery hosts of hell."[66] At last, however, he steps out into the streets of Harlem and feels a sudden rush of joy at arriving in a land of plenty where he sees Negroes everywhere and has rights protected by law.

Once African Americans had reached the promised land, they found much that was bitterly disappointing. Owen Vincent Dodson's ironically titled one-act play *The Shining Town* (1938) uses the subway to dramatize their new experience.[67] Set in the 167th Street IRT on the Jerome Avenue line, where blacks riding northward from Harlem could meet housewives coming down from the Bronx, it dramatizes a scene that unfolded each morning as Harlem women gathered to auction off their services as day workers.

The subway could have provided many more such studies in desperation but most African-American writers use it to explore subtler manifestations of racial tension. Ann Petry, Ralph Ellison, and James Baldwin use subway rides to explore situations where racial separation is overtly absent but psychologically present.

The subway ride in Chapter Seven of Ralph Ellison's *Invisible Man* (1952) presents the young, unnamed protagonist's introduction to the city and his first ride to Harlem. The car is so crowded, the young man notes, that "everyone seemed to stand with his head back and his eyes bulging, like chickens frozen at the sound of danger."[68] The observation is a shrewd one. The anthropologist Edward T. Hall points out that this posture is a technique that subway riders have developed to guard against intimacy in the shared space of public conveyances: "The basic tactic is to be as immobile as possible and, when part of the trunk or extremities touches another person, withdraw if possible. If this is not possible, the muscles in the affected areas are kept tense."[69] The young man, however, interprets impersonality as hostility. He fears hidden dangers in the "salt-and-pepper mob."

In this state of mind he finds himself pressed against a huge white woman. He is instantly fearful, recalling an earlier incident in which southern businessmen had taunted him with a white striptease dancer. But a situation that might have led to a lynching in his old life means nothing here. The woman is smiling blandly, not in response to any covert stimulation but simply as an impersonal way of fending off any personal interaction with the crowd. She hasn't noticed the young man's race. But then she hasn't really noticed him as an individual at all. The young man's position in the racially segregated south had been comparatively simple, he begins to realize, in comparison with the new forms of invisibility that he is beginning to experience in the urban north.

Ellison treats the subway ride as an introduction to the anonymity of New York life. By contrast, Ann Petry's Lutie Johnson is an experienced New Yorker and her subway ride in Chapter Two of *The Street* (1946) is simply part of her daily routine. It provides the author with a chance to look at crowd behavior, introduce a long flashback, and suggest some of the racial complexities of daily life.

Lutie is taking the A train to her home on 116th Street in Harlem. As the ride begins, the passengers, white and black alike, push and heave their way into the car. All of them settle down "into small private worlds, thus creating the illusion of space between them and their fellow passengers."[70]

Within her private world Lutie is free to explore her recent experiences working as the maid in an affluent suburban home, largely a story of unconscious slights and deliberate humiliations from her white employers. At the beginning of her ride Lutie doesn't register any awareness of difference between herself and the whites in the subway car but after she has recalled the conditions of her work the racial tensions in society as a whole are transferred by association to the subway setting. By the time Lutie gets off at 125th Street she reflects that "she never felt really human until she reached Harlem and thus got away from the hostility in the eyes of the white women who stared at her on the downtown streets and in the subway."[71]

James Baldwin uses subway rides to explore his characters' relation to white America in both *Another Country* (1962) and *If Beale Street Could Talk* (1974). Both rides takes place under desperate circumstances. In *Another Country* Rufus rides the Eighth Avenue IND to the George Washington Bridge to commit suicide. In *If Beale Street Could Talk* Tish steps into the train at a moment when her lover has just been falsely imprisoned and she is alone, pregnant, and frightened.

Rufus's subway ride is the more desperate of the two. His city is crashing down about him and as he stands on the platform he images the beams collapsing, the motorman gone mad, and "the people screaming at the windows and doors and turning on each other with all the accumulated fury of their blasphemed lives, everything gone out of them but murder." But that is the apocalyptic subway of his imagination. As soon as he gets on the train the discipline of a public space takes hold and each rider sits or stands "in the isolation cell into which they transformed every inch of space they held." [72]

Both novels portray the subway ride with a double awareness, using it to represent an oppression which burdens white and black alike and, at the same time, to show blacks at a particular disadvantage even in this shared environment. Rufus, gazing out the car window at the 59th Street platform, sees "many white people and many black people, chained together in time and in space, and by history, and all of them in a hurry." This sounds like a grim sort of equality, but the next paragraph describes the train lurching "as though protesting the proximity of white buttock to black knee."

Tish, awakening to the realities around her, tries to read the faces in the subway as a guide to the racial and sexual complexities of her world. She knows that the heavy man pressing against her in the crowded, stifling car isn't thinking of rape. She is as invisible to him as Ellison's young man was to the blonde lady. "He was probably wondering only— and that, dimly—how he was going to get through another day on his job." [73] The subway car, Tish reflects, looks like the pictures she has seen of slave ships—except that the riders have newspapers. The analogy describes an oppression that applies to all but does so with an image drawn from the bitter historical experience of blacks.

If the subway ride can be used to dramatize the relations between races, it can also provide the setting for a rediscovery of the African-American community itself. This happened for the young artist Palmer C. Hayden who returned from academic training in France to paint the newly opened A train in his painting *The Subway*—a work which marked the beginning of a career devoted to African-American subjects.

In a crucial scene in Ellison's *Invisible Man*, Ellison, like Hayden, finds worth, in fact potential heroism, in an aspect of black life that many cultural spokesmen found undignified. From the beginning of the novel the Invisible Man has been tempted by the idea that he might be a leader of his people. The form this leadership might take and the precise definition of his people keep shifting. By this point in the novel he has been groomed as a potential leader by the Brotherhood—a white-dominated organization modeled after the Communist party. By Chapter Twenty the young man has come to his moment of disillusion. He realizes that the intellectual members of the Brotherhood had analyzed the Harlem "masses" entirely within a white, European framework. As Leninists, a small body of advanced theoreticians working through the "natural" leaders of the people, they had manipulated him as if he were a Sambo doll on a string. Now the young man needs a new image of history and a renewed understanding of his own African-American community.

He finds both as he steps into the Times Square subway station and finds his attention arrested by three zoot-suited teenagers, with carefully conked hair, swinging their shoulders down the platform. [74] Nobody thought of the zoot-suiters in political terms. They were simply teenagers following a dance hall craze. In the Brotherhood's terms these boys are scarcely even members of the lumpenproletariat. They are outside the laws of history.

Ellison, however, saw another possibility, writing at the time in the *Negro Quarterly* that however much it was scorned by white intellectuals and black leaders the zoot suit was nevertheless "one of the myths and symbols which abound among the Negro masses." [75] Though no one knew it then, Cesar Chavez and Malcolm X were both members of the zoot-suited crowds. Seeing the young men in the subway, an appropriate setting for the unheroic and the ordinary, Ellison's invisible man begins to realize that history is not the Brotherhood's dialectical lawgiver. It is a gambler, playing one hand but keeping these three unheroic boys as an ace in the hole. His encounter in the subway has persuaded the invisible man that he should look again for the hidden genius of his own people. By the time he reaches 125th Street he is ready to begin discovering Harlem all over again.

In the early sixties perceptions of race relations in the city changed dramatically. Some of the reasons will be explored in Chapter Nine. Here it is only necessary to recall that the vision of racial harmony that had inspired the civil rights movement gave way to angry division at the same time that protests against the Vietnam War gained momentum. Martin Luther King's leadership was challenged by Malcolm X, groups such as the integrationist Congress of Racial Equality began removing whites from positions of leadership, and Frantz Fanon's *The Wretched of the Earth*, with its controversial analysis of the culturally therapeutic effects of violence, became required reading among intellectuals. The subway, which had seemed a home of peaceful integration, became a natural setting in which to explore the eruption of long-suppressed tensions. We can see that happening in Chester Himes's innovative detective novel *Blind Man With a Pistol* (1969), where a senseless shooting in the subway represents the political disunion both in Harlem and in the nation at large. The most dramatic example, however, was LeRoi Jones's play *Dutchman*.

LeRoi Jones had been an active figure in New York's literary world—a poet, a jazz critic, and editor of the important avant-garde magazine *Kulchur*. He and his white wife exemplified the free racial equality that existed in artistic and Bohemian New York. Suddenly, to the hurt and dismay of his white friends, he took an entirely new direction.

The painter Larry Rivers said that before *Dutchman* Jones had been his friend and his connection to significant aspects of modern culture. "Then after 1964, after his play *Dutchman* was produced, suddenly it all changed. . . . he decided to come out of some kind of closet with the most intense hatred of every white person he knew. It was the beginning of those very aggressive situations. I couldn't believe it. I was shocked and upset, and that began the deterioration of our friendship."[76] LeRoi Jones returned to his native Newark, New Jersey, changed his named to Imamu Amiri Baraka, and became a leader of the emerging black arts movement as well as a force in Newark politics.

The stage directions for *Dutchman* explain that its setting is "the subway steeped in modern myth."[77] One of the myths the subway in the play exemplifies is that of a non-segregated social realm. After opening with a seemingly race-neutral setting, *Dutchman* reveals its irreconcilable racial conflict.

The action, which combines surface naturalism with underlying ritual, involves the temptation and destruction of an outwardly conformist African-American man by a provocatively teasing white woman. The man's name is Clay, suggesting the Hebrew Adam who is born from clay. The woman's name is Lula, which suggests Lilith, Adam's rebellious first wife—though Lula also suggests Eve, since she enters eating an apple. The conflict between Clay and Lula resonates with recollections of other legends in which an upright man is tempted by a woman, from Tannhäuser in the Venusberg to Strindberg's *Miss Julie*, Wedekind's *Lulu*, Somerset Maugham's *Rain*, and Von Sternberg's *The Blue Angel*.

Clay seems the pattern of well-behaved, upwardly mobile gentility. He is in fact a potential murderer, one who doesn't even realize his own violent impulses until Lula forces him to scream out his suppressed rage. His clean-cut exterior is an act, an entertainment, a kind of madness. Lula is an undercover policeman for white civilization ferreting out the murderousness in the black man's heart, forcing him to reveal it, and then punishing him. As Clay's body is dragged away she turns to the next seemingly mild-mannered black man who enters the car.

Dutchman provoked consternation among white, liberal-minded theatergoers. As a shocked reviewer for the *New York Times* put it: "If this is the way the Negroes really feel about the white world around them, there's more rancor buried in the breasts of colored conformists than anyone can imagine."[78] The expression of once buried rage was about to become a central fact of cultural life.

Dutchman gave New Yorkers dramatic proof that the unity of the subway crowd had been shattered. That same year Bellow's *Herzog* used the subway to show a new, more despairing vision of the city. Where Asa Leventhal and Tommy Wilhelm had discovered their kinship with humanity in the subway, Moses Herzog, passing through a subway turnstile and noticing that innumerable millions of hips had polished its wood, concludes that such an object creates only "a feeling of communion—brotherhood in one of its cheapest forms."[79] Responding to the changed New York of the sixties, Bellow becomes our most biting analyst of cultural disorder.

The subway art of an earlier period seemed to show a world before the flood. "You won't believe it," Walker Evans said in a draft text for his subway photographs written sometime after 1956, "but there was a time, quite recent, when the New York subway was almost a peaceful, restful place."[80] The critic John Russell struck the same note in his comments on Isabel Bishop: "As recently as 1966, she had portrayed the subway station underneath Grand Central Station as a place in which people stood tall and walked free and had room to swing their arms, rather than as a place to get out of as fast as possible."[81] The subway continued to serve as a microcosm of the city but both it and the city it reflected were changing dramatically.

CHAPTER NINE

A SHOOTING ON THE SUBWAY

T some point in the nineteen-fifties New Yorkers began to regard their subway with fear. For the first half-century of the system's existence people had complained vociferously about its crowding but it had rarely occurred to them that it might be dangerous. The fear of crime that began in the late fifties grew in intensity over the next decades until finally, in 1984, it produced one of the most remarkable dramas that has ever held a city in its grip—the shooting of four black teenagers by a frail, bespectacled young white man named Bernhard Goetz.

The facts of the case are comparatively simple. A few days before Christmas in 1984 Bernhard Goetz boarded a southbound Seventh Avenue express near his home at 14th Street. There were four teenage boys in the car—Barry Allen, Troy Canty, James Ramseur, and Darrell Cabey. They were sprawling across the seats and generally behaving in a rowdy manner. Goetz may not have noticed it as he entered, but the other passengers had moved to the far end of the car. One of the boys, lying stretched out on the bench opposite, asked casually, "How are ya?" Then either one or two of the boys approached Goetz and asked for five dollars. Goetz, interpreting this behavior as the prelude to a mugging, took a gun from his pocket and fired five bullets. He may have fired all five in rapid succession or he may have paused after the fourth and said "You seem to be all right; here's another." He then went to the platform between the subway cars, unfastened the safety chain, and escaped into the tunnel. On December 31 he surrendered to the police in Concord, New Hampshire.

The "subway vigilante" immediately monopolized newspaper headlines and talk shows. Telephone switchboards of newspapers and television stations were lit up by calls of support. Interest did not fade as time went on. The Goetz case remained a major news story for over two years. It spawned three books: Lillian B. Rubin's *Quiet Rage: Bernie Goetz in a Time of Madness*, Mark Lesly's *Subway Gunman; A Juror's Account of the Bernhard Goetz Trial*, and George P. Fletcher's incisive account of the legal issues raised by the trial, *A Crime of Self-Defense*. An edited version of Goetz's videotaped confession was offered for sale and public television dramatized the trial. There was even a song, "Subway Vigilante," recorded by Ronny and the Urban Watchdogs.

Bernhard Goetz has not faded from public memory. George P. Fletcher comments that when people noticed what he was writing about they invariably wanted to discuss the case. I have had the same experience. Passions remain both intense and bitterly divided. Some of Goetz's admirers were potential vigilantes—I could almost see their trigger fingers moving as they talked. Some of his detractors were passionately hostile. I am not likely to forget the mild and friendly bookstore clerk who burst out with passionate delight when I mentioned that Goetz was suffering from testicular cancer.

The Goetz case fascinated so many New Yorkers because it expressed their deep-seated emotions. The trial in Judge Stephen Crane's courtroom dealt with very specific questions: Did Goetz reasonably interpret the youths' approach as a threat? Did he pause after the fourth shot and fire the fifth with cold-blooded intent? Was Darrell Caby standing and menacing Goetz when he was shot or was he cowering in his seat? But these questions were tangential to the public drama. The story that monopolized newspaper headlines and talk shows in the days after the shooting, by contrast, was a symbolic drama, one that utilized the subway as a setting to crystallize the feelings of New Yorkers about their city.

BERNHARD GOETZ AND THE URBAN CRISIS

To understand this drama, we need follow a path which leads from the social reality of New York City into the realm of private fantasy. Goetz's New York differed dramatically from the optimistic metropolis of earlier decades. It was a city in which the crime-victim narrative could become a recognized category of urban folklore. Eleanor Wachs's study of these tales does not list "revenge" in its index and it does not figure as a motive in any of her tales.[1] Nevertheless, newspapers, films, and novels show fantasies of revenge gaining power during the sixties and seventies. The Goetz story was waiting to erupt. But it did not achieve its final shape spontaneously. Elements already present in the urban unconscious were skillfully manipulated by one newspaper—the *New York Post*.

The late forties and fifties have recently come to be seen as New York's golden age, the time "when the city was livable." The subway system had gained riders during the war and its managers, dreaming that the good years would continue forever, made ambitious plans to redesign the trains. Schoolchildren were proudly taught how many decades the system had gone without a serious accident.

In retrospect, the subway presented in song and story during these years seems an oddly welcoming place. In *On the Town* (musical 1944, film 1949), three zestful sailors set out to explore a city where "the people ride in a hole in the ground" and find themselves competing for the affections of Miss Turnstiles. In Vincente Minnelli's *Bandwagon* (1953) Fred

Astaire woos Cyd Charisse with a dance in the Times Square subway station. Although the dance spoofs Mickey Spillane novels, the characters are Runyonesque and the violence is entirely make-believe.

Grimmer images of New York's transit system were available but even they seem innocent compared with what came later. The constant offscreen noise of the el in Alfred Hitchcock's film *The Wrong Man* (1956) symbolizes the urban pressures that afflict its protagonist but the subway that we see is clean and the crowd is well behaved. The down-and-outers in Edmund G. Love's fine account of his years as an alcoholic, *Subways Are for Sleeping* (1957), get a night's rest in the warm trains; they don't fear for their safety and no one fears them. A few years later the Broadway musical version of Love's book (1961) showed middle-class dropouts singing and dancing through the stations with no sense of incongruity.

The 1960s saw both a renewal of urban hopes and increasing premonition of disasters ahead. Jane Jacob's *The Death and Life of Great American Cities* (1961) opened the decade with a powerful defense of the hidden order of city neighborhoods. But four years later Kenneth B. Clark published his *Dark Ghetto* (1965) in which he described a pathology of the racial slum that included emotional illness, delinquency, drug addiction, suicide, and homicide. The next year, Edward T. Hall's *The Hidden Dimension* (1966) publicized experiments with rats which seem to show that high population densities led to forms of aggressive, self-destructive behavior that he termed a behavioral sink. Hall worried, very discreetly, that "the American Negroes and people of Spanish culture who are flocking to our cities are being very seriously stressed."[2]

This mixture of hope and apprehension grew more anguished during the mayoralty of John V. Lindsay from 1965 to 1973. Elected promising a revitalization of the city, Lindsay understood that this meant improving the condition of the urban poor and focusing on the subway rather than the automobile as the basis of city transportation.

In 1969 the Lindsay administration announced a ten-year strategy to raise the city's three million poor into the middle class.[3] At the same time, it promised to improve subway schedules, air-condition the trains, and build a new line under Second Avenue, a crosstown route under 48th Street, a new line in Queens, a new line along Utica Avenue in Brooklyn, and a new underground route in the Bronx to replace the demolished Third Avenue el.

But if the subway was the subject of promises, it was also the site of some of the administration's most obvious failures. Lindsay began his first term by provoking an eleven-day subway strike. Three years later, eager to avoid a repetition, he signed a contract with such generous retirement provisions for subway workers that the system experienced a major shortage of skilled maintenance workers. He improved the financing of the system, gaining state and federal aid and tapping the revenues of the Triborough Bridge and Tunnel Authority. He could claim credit for air-conditioning the cars but any New Yorker who expected city renewal to start in the subways was bitterly disappointed.

From the sixties on we see a growing literature which insists that despite the vast amounts of money being made there, New York was in decline. The city's traditional rhetoric of booming optimism is increasingly replaced by a language of impotence: the city is "not livable," it is a "hassle," it is "not working," its only hope is in "planned shrinkage." In 1965 the *Herald Tribune* ran a five-month series of articles under the standing head "City In Crisis."

The same year Richard Whalen published his angry polemic *A City Destroying Itself*. In 1971 Miles Donis published *The Fall of New York*, a futuristic novel set in the late nineteen-seventies which portrayed a world where gangs of thirteen-year-olds roamed the streets shooting adults for sport. Jules Feiffer's play (1967) and film (1971) *Little Murders* showed the city as a place where the besieged middle class could save itself only by joining gleefully in the violence of the streets.

Not only were the poor not raised and the subways not transformed in the seventies but the gap between the rich and the increasingly numerous poor grew dramatically. The city that produced the Goetz shooting was beginning to appear. Much of the garment industry had migrated to the South or to other countries. The port had declined dramatically. New York retained and extended its power in communications and finance, but it had lost the industries which had traditionally absorbed large numbers of unskilled or semi-skilled immigrants. By the 1980s economists could write of two New Yorks: one core, the other periphery; one consisting of "money providers" to the city treasury, the other of "service demanders."[4]

The two New Yorks were adjacent but scarcely ever touched. One was what city planners now called either the World City or the Central Business District. The spatial ambiguity implied in these names is significant. The bankers and bond brokers—the Masters of the Universe, as Tom Wolfe called them—were in daily touch with Paris and Tokyo but their social and business lives were centered in a small portion of Manhattan island. Their New York saw an economic boom in the years just before the Goetz shooting. The number of stockbrokers and bond dealers in the city, for example, grew from 56,000 to 99,000 between 1977 and 1984.[5] The central business district saw a major real estate boom.

The other New York was epitomized in the popular imagination by the South Bronx—where Barry Allen, Troy Canty, James Ramseur, and Darrell Cabey all lived. A study published by the Community Service Society a few weeks before the Goetz shooting reported that almost a quarter of the city's population was trapped below the poverty line.[6] The rate was 43 percent among Hispanics and 32 percent among blacks. The study showed a rise in joblessness among the young and an increase in households headed by single women. Fifty thousand families were below the poverty line, even with their main wage earner working full-time. This was so despite an economic boom in the central business district that was actually lowering the city's overall unemployment rate.

The two cities were largely irrelevant to one another. If the World City was largely white, the South Bronx was black and Hispanic. If the World City was immensely prosperous, the South Bronx was on welfare. If part of Manhattan approximated to what Hugh Ferriss had predicted in *The Metropolis of Tomorrow*, large areas of the South Bronx looked, as stunned visitors kept saying, like Dresden after the war.

People like Bernhard Goetz felt caught between the two cities. They hoped for renewal and saw disorder. Their situation was exacerbated by a fear of crime.

It was only in the late fifties that the subway began to be regarded as a dangerous place. Crime appeared as the proportion of teenagers in the population rose. In several well-publicized incidents gangs of high school students rioted on the cars, breaking windows, pulling up seat cushions, bending fan blades, and terrifying passengers.

Newspapers fanned public alarm. "HIGH SCHOOL GANGS ARE TURNING TRAINS INTO HELL ON WHEELS" read a 1958 headline in the *Daily News*.[7] Other aspects of subway crime began to command attention. In 1963 the *Journal-American* sent reporter Joan Hanauer into the trains to experience the danger to women. She reported back under such headlines as "TERROR LURKS IN THE DARK, LONELY HOURS."[8] In 1964 the *World-Telegram and Sun* told readers that "TERROR RIDES ALONG WITH YOU WHEN YOU TRAVEL AT NIGHT."[9] The next year the *Post* ran a series on "TERROR IN THE SUBWAYS."[10]

It was in 1965 that subway crime stories became a major factor in the annual index to the *New York Times*. The key event in transforming public awareness was the stabbing death that year of seventeen-year-old Andrew Mormile on an IND train in Brooklyn. Two other teenagers, apparently drunk, came on board the train in East New York. They began harassing two girls and generally behaving in a way that indicated danger. Some passengers moved to the next car, others buried themselves in their newspapers. When Mormile tried to walk to the next car, one of the boys shoved him. He shoved back. The boy drew a knife. Two of the stabs were strong enough to fracture his skull and a third entered his left ear and penetrated four inches.

Since crime had not been a major threat in the system, no one had designed an effective means of calling for help. The year of the Mormile killing the Transit Authority experimented with a pathetic system in which a tollbooth attendant, aware of a crime in progress, would press a pedal with his or her foot, thus setting an amber light blinking on the street level which, it was hoped, would be noticed by a passing pedestrian "who, it is expected, will then call the police."[11] Lacking even this Rube Goldberg device, the motorman of the train on which Mormile lay dying had to blow loud whistle blasts at each station he passed in an effort to summon aid.

Crime continued to increase. The Mormile stabbing had been the first subway murder in over a year. In 1981 there were fourteen murders in the system. Crime stories appeared almost daily in the newspapers while anecdotes of small indignities became a normal feature of New York conversation.

The Transit Authority insisted, with absolute accuracy, that crime was growing more slowly in the subways that it was in the streets above. "The perception of crime is much greater than actual crime," said a TA spokesperson in 1978. "Of 3,000 rapes in the city, on the subway system there are eight. Of 1,500 homicides, there are six in our system."[12]

That, however, was no comfort to anyone. The subway stands for the city. To most New Yorkers a murder at the corner of Westchester Avenue and Castle Hill Avenue happens in a far distant place but one on the Pelham Bay line is next door. Even articles minimizing subway crime do not avoid the mythology of danger. In 1985 and 1987 the *New York Times* published two reports under the headlines "STATISTICALLY, AT LEAST, IT IS RATHER SAFE DOWN THERE"[13] and "THE NUMBERS SAY SUBWAYS ARE SAFER THAN THEY SEEM."[14] Each article was accompanied by a photo—a policeman peering nervously out of a graffiti-marked car, a dark subway entrance yawning like an open grave—which dramatically undercut the content of the text.

The new equation of a violent city with a menacing subway found expression in Larry Peerce's 1967 film *The Incident*. Adapted from a 1963 *DuPont Hour* television show titled "Ride with Terror," it featured an impressive number of the city's best actors and actresses—

Martin Sheen, Tony Musante, Jack Gilford, Thelma Ritter, Ed McMahon, Donna Mills, Brock Peters, Ruby Dee, Robert Bannard, Diana Van Der Viis, Jan Sterling, and Beau Bridges among others. Nicholas Baehr's script shows a selection of middle-class New Yorkers terrorized by two giggling, knife-wielding punks on a late-night train.

Worried by the possibility that the film would provoke copycat incidents, the Transit Authority refused permission to film *The Incident* in actual stations. Instead, the crew worked with a very convincing replica of an IRT train in the old Biograph studios and used stock footage. Gerald Hirschfeld's camerawork fills the screen with menacing shots of the Lexington Avenue–Woodlawn train roaring above garbage-strewn streets and through narrow tunnels.

The Incident ought to have been better than it was. Its situation spoke directly to the fears of its audience and its middle-class passengers were efficiently sketched. Its major weakness was a complete failure to explore the psychology of the two young men terrorizing the passengers—they were demented degenerates and that, apparently, explained everything about them. In its first half, the film settled for an easy sensationalism.

But the second half of Nicholas H. Baehr's script moves toward a conclusion that while it may be too easily ironic is disturbing nonetheless. By the end all the riders have been humiliated by the two delinquents. None have stood up against them. At last one, a newly discharged soldier with his broken arm in a plaster cast, rises, struggles, and manages to stop the criminals even though he is mortally stabbed in the process. Significantly, he is the only non-New Yorker in the car. "Where were you, buddy?" he asks as he lies stabbed and dying on the floor. None of the passengers has an answer as they file silently out of the car.

The punks in *The Incident*, like most of those involved in early subway rampages, were white. But increasingly, as New York's demographics changed, middle-class subway riders were confronted with black teenagers whose swagger seemed to violate the decorum of a public place. As the novelist Wesley Brown put it, "a display of bravado by a young, indigo-skinned black male, moving through a crowded subway car like a point guard bringing the ball up the court, sporting a haircut that makes the shape of his head resemble a cone of ice-cream, and wearing barge-size sneakers with untied laces thick as egg noddles, is immediately considered a dangerous presence whether he is or not."[15]

The trains in *The Incident* are also not marked by graffiti. That did not appear until the early seventies. When it did, it added a powerful new element to many New Yorkers' feelings of anger and frustration. It was almost inevitable that middle-class New Yorkers would interpret the outburst of graffiti in terms of a power struggle between them and us. "Them" was a young male, probably Puerto Rican or black. "Us" was the average, productive, law-abiding citizen, the person who ought to be served and protected by the city authorities.

But the spread of graffiti showed how little protection law-abiding citizens could expect. Riders quickly linked the tags and air-sprayed patterns on the train walls to the damaged doors, the delayed arrivals, and all the other signs of breakdown that they encountered daily. Mayors Lindsay and Koch called for attack dogs to protect the train yards and long jail terms for offenders but their rhetoric swelled in exact proportion to their helplessness. Graffiti became a symbol of the city's inability to solve even the most visible of its problems.

The emotional response to the Goetz shooting grew out of a double experience of hope and anguish. New Yorkers looked for a dramatic improvement in their city and instead saw spreading poverty, rising crime, and growing racial tension. The subway, which had been offered as a starting point for renewal, became both a daily irritant and a vivid symbol of failure. Five months before Bernhard Goetz boarded that southbound IRT, the *New York Times* published a survey of the prospects for the subway system under the headlines "GREATER WOES LIE AHEAD FOR CITY'S TRANSIT RIDERS" (July 30), "INEFFICIENT WAYS OF THE PAST STILL HAMPER TRANSIT SYSTEM" (July 31), and "TRANSIT SYSTEM IS FACING A TROUBLED FUTURE" (August 1). The subway, which had been offered as a starting point for the city's renewal, became instead its preeminent symbol of urban collapse.

STRIKING BACK

Feelings of helplessness bred fantasies of resistance to which the following digression may be relevant. In 1983 I was mugged, not in the subway but in a far more dangerous place—the entrance vestibule of a New York City apartment building. The door to the inner lobby was locked while I waited from someone to buzz me in. Three young men approached rapidly from behind. One caught me in a chokehold. When I regained consciousness I had lost the usual items—a watch, a wallet, some money, various credit cards.

When I told people this story over the ensuing weeks their response was invariable: "You should have had a gun." It was clear from my telling that I was approached from behind, taken by surprise, and that my gun would have fallen into very bad hands. It didn't matter. "You should have had a gun." The implication was not simply that I was entitled to protect myself. The implication was that I was entitled to inflict justice.

During the eighties this fantasy of striking back became widespread among New Yorkers. One of its oddest and most striking forms was found not in the movies but on the subways themselves.

In February 1979 a young man named Curtis Sliwa, night manager of the McDonald's on East Fordham Road in the Bronx, organized a group of friends into an informal and completely unauthorized anti-crime patrol. First calling themselves "The Magnificent Thirteen Subway Safety Patrol," they soon became the Guardian Angels.

Sliwa had a genius for publicity. Guardian Angel patrols were in fact few and infrequent but many a subway rider felt a thrill when a well-muscled young man, wearing a white T-shirt and sporting a red beret, stepped into a subway car and took up his position near the door. Newspapers and televisions stations carried frequent reports on Guardian Angel patrols. The fact that the police so obviously resented the Angels' presence only added to their glamour. A careful study reported in Dennis Jay Kenney's *Crime, Fear, and the New York City Subways* (1987) failed to substantiate any Guardian Angel impact on actual crime rates but they had a major presence in the consciousness of ordinary New Yorkers.

In November 1992 Sliwa, by this time a radio talk-show host, admitted that several of the group's earliest exploits had been faked. Soon other Angels joined in with more stories of manufactured bravery.[16] In the early eighties public appetite for resistance to crime had been so great that Sliwa could depend on a credulous press.

In this environment Bernhard Goetz–like incidents began to occur. In October 1971 a fifty-eight-year-old real estate salesman, faced with two young men attempting to rob him in the Astor Square station, drew a licensed .38 caliber revolver and shot them. The *Times* called this unexpected turn of events "implausible" and "improbable."[17] On October 31, 1979, a passenger shot an assailant dead on the Lexington Avenue IRT and disappeared into the crowd. In February 1984 seventy-one-year-old Lop B. Lee drew a licensed revolver in the East Broadway station and shot seventeen-year-old Darrius Cox. These incidents received little press attention, though the 1979 Lexington IRT shooting inspired Jerry Oster's detective novel *Sweet Justice* (1985), begun before the Goetz shooting though published after, in which the police search for a man acclaimed in the tabloids as "Subway Samaritan."

The fantasy of striking back received vivid expression in Bradley J. Steiner's self-defense manual *Subway Survival!* (1980). Its author selects the best moves from British and Canadian Commando Systems, Kenpo-Ju-Jitsu, Karate, Combat Judo, Box, and Street-Fighting in order to show the ordinary transit rider how he or she may use chin-jab attacks, hand-axe chops, knee attacks, elbow blows, concussion blows, front kicks, side kicks, and back-stamp kicks against the punks, the scum, the low-lifes, the savages, and the street rats who terrorize the subways "thanks to liberal, scum-sympathizing laws, gun control, and a corrupt juridical and police establishment."[18]

Setting out to portray the quirks and tensions of New York life in *The Bonfire of the Vanities*, Tom Wolfe very nearly gave this revenge fantasy the mocking it deserves. As he explains in his essay "Stalking the Billion-footed Beast," he began his novel with the knowledge that any big book on New York City required a subway scene. An assiduous researcher, he began riding the subways looking for material and quickly struck gold. He found a distinguished-looking broker commuting through the South Bronx to Manhattan in a dirty raincoat and moldy orthotic running shoes. He had been mugged once and feared being mugged again. Once safely arrived at his Wall Street office, he would exchange his shabby coat and shoes for properly distinguished equivalents. Then, when the day was finished, he would revert to protective shabbiness for the journey home.

Wolfe wrote the first version of his novel in monthly installments for *Rolling Stone*. In the July 19–August 2, 1984, issue, a Puerto Rican woman named Julia Noganz looks across the aisle on the D train and is astonished at the man sitting opposite. He appears to be in disguise with a greasy poplin rain hat pulled down over his eyes and the *New York Post* held nervously in front of his face. What Julia Noganz especially notices is that he has a pair of long, thin, charcoal-gray socks rising about his cheap, purple-and-white-striped running sneakers. His incongruous clothes and his nervous glances about the train make him appear deranged. Julia Noganz easily decides that he is just another nut on the subway.

Then the train stops and three teenage boys get on. Julia knows their type. She knows them from their striped sneakers and their black thermo jackets. They are "the animals."

She sees that the man opposite has seen them as well and is clearly frightened. He pulls the newspaper around his face and shoulders, trying so conspicuously to disappear that he becomes an advertisement for disaster: "Either the animals will go to work on him or he'll just snap. Julia gets up and walks down to the other end of the car."[19]

This is Wolfe's first, magazine version of Assistant District Attorney Lawrence Kramer. He is a man so terrorized by an earlier brutal mugging that he rides the subway in fear, carrying his dress shoes in an A&P shopping bag and wearing Nike sneakers as a disguise.

The synopses in several succeeding issues of *Rolling Stone* mention Kramer's mugging. It was clearly preparation for a major plot development.

The parallels between this scene from the early, serialized version of *The Bonfire of the Vanities* and the Goetz case that broke four months later are astonishingly close: the white man traumatized by an earlier mugging, the teenagers, the passenger who avoids trouble by moving to the other end of the car. New York life was proving more sensational than anything a novelist could imagine and Wolfe at once saw that his fearful assistant D.A. with dreams of striking back would cut a pale figure next to the real Bernhard Goetz who was appearing in the daily headlines. In the book version of *The Bonfire of the Vanities* Kramer steps into the D train wearing a worn raincoat and Nike running shoes, with his own leather dress shoes concealed in an A&P shopping bag, but the subsequent flashback describing his mugging remained unwritten. This strand of the action was simply dropped.

A pity. Instead of a satire of the revenge fantasy, New Yorkers were treated to the real thing in its most blatant form. As soon as the news of the mysterious young man on the IRT reached them, the editors of the *New York Post* realized that they were confronting a story that was basically a repetition of one that had already seized the public imagination.

Death Wish was both a 1972 novel by Brian Garfield and a series of films starring Charles Bronson. The outlines of the plot were certainly familiar to all New Yorkers and had no doubt entered the fantasy lives of many. Four aspects of Garfield's novel are directly relevant to the *New York Post*'s coverage of the Goetz case:

1. The protagonist, Paul Benjamin, is a mild-mannered New York liberal who, driven mad by crimes against his wife and daughter, turns into a pitiless vigilante.

2. The subway is used to signify all that Benjamin hates in New York City.

3. Paul Benjamin arms himself, frequents high-crime areas, and then turns murderously on the punks and muggers who try to harm him. In the course of his progress from New York liberal to self-appointed executioner of punks, Garfield's protagonist finds himself aboard a lurching Broadway express: "He found he was looking from face to face along the rows of crowded passengers, resentfully scanning them for signs of redeeming worth: if you wanted to do something about overpopulation this was the place to start. He made a head-count and discovered that of the fifty-eight faces he could see, seven appeared to belong to people who had a right to survive. The rest were fodder."[20]

4. Though he realizes his murderousness, Paul Benjamin does not repent. On the last page of the novel he realizes that he has the barely concealed sympathy of the police. In the last scene of Michael Winner's extremely popular 1974 film version Charles Bronson, with a mischievous glint in his eye, transfers operations from New York to Chicago—thus making possible a series of popular sequels.

GOETZ STORIES AND COUNTERSTORIES

Though all New York newspapers put the Goetz case in their headlines, it was the *New York Post* that established the dominant interpretation. The *Post*'s strategy was simple. It simply slapped the *Death Wish* scenario on top of the few known facts about the incident in the

IRT. The still anonymous gunman, said its first front-page headline on December 24, 1984, was the "'DEATH WISH' SHOOTER."[21]

The *Post* had to work the *Death Wish* theme especially hard during the opening phase of the story because for the first week no one knew who the gunman was. Coverage on December 24 featured a photo of Charles Bronson firing his pistol directly at the reader and a Transit Authority police officer was quoted as conceding reluctantly that "the corollary between this and 'Death Wish' is there."[22]

The paper began identifying its Goetz stories with a small drawing showing a dark subway tunnel, a hand holding a pistol, and the words "Death Wish Vigilante." It published a psychological profile by Dr. Joyce Brothers who explained that "ectomorphs are very sensitive people" and concluded that the unknown gunman was imitating the *Death Wish* films.[23] On December 28 the paper interviewed Brian Garfield himself who explained that sometimes people feel they have no choice: "They are back up against a wall and feel a need to lash out. I don't blame them."[24]

Once Goetz's identity was revealed on January 1, 1985, the *Post* (as well as every other paper and TV station in town) was relentless in tracking down the smallest detail of its hero's life. It revealed that Goetz had a security clearance from the federal government and that he had once written to the city planning commission about a zoning matter. It published a photo of a toy fire engine which it claimed to be the same kind of toy fire engine that Goetz had purchased at a Toys 'R' Us store in Union, New Jersey.

Trivial as they are, these details serve a vital purpose. They present Goetz as an average man but a firm one. They put us in his shoes, and make it easier for us to act out our secret desires through daily retellings of his actions. When the *Post* finally tracked down Goetz in person, it reported:

> His voice was whisper-quiet and he seemed awed by the five people around him.
> Somehow he wished it would all go away.
> But the quiet-spoken Goetz was giving a signal: He had been bullied once too often.[25]

Like Paul Benjamin in Brian Garfield's novel, the *Post*'s Goetz is driven to act by the madness of the city, not by any demons within. He is simply a man who fights back, a hero for decent citizens.

In the year and a half that followed, as Goetz faced two grand juries and a criminal trial, the *Post* continued to present him as the subway rider who fought back. On March 4, 1985, it even interviewed him aboard a Seventh Avenue southbound train, quoting his conversations with fellow riders. When a transit police officer asked him to leave the train ("I don't want a riot on my hands") a black teenager quickly replied: "Come on, man, we dig the guy. Ain't nothing wrong with old Bernie. Nobody is gonna touch that guy. Wow." Two white women, on the other hand, were angered by the sight of him:

> They approached Goetz and one of them said: "We don't think you are a hero. We think you are a racist."
> Goetz looked at them and smiled: "Believe what you want. But I hope you never get raped. I hope you never get attacked. If you do I hope you have a weapon to protect yourself."

The other woman yelled back: "I have been raped."

Goetz told her: "I'm sorry to hear that. Then I can't understand why you attack me. Most victims of violence know what I'm talking about.

"I wish the whole thing didn't happen but I'm never going to be a victim again if I can help it. And I hope you won't ever be a victim again."[26]

The *Post* implied that Goetz had inspired the entire New York region to a frenzy of effective self-defense. The front page headline on January 22, 1985, for example, read "75-YR-OLD ROUTS TEEN MUGGERS." Below was a photo of plucky Nunzio Motola next to the subway headline: "SUBWAY DRAMA: 'I KICKED LIKE HELL.'" Inside was another story about a Long Island delicatessen owner who killed a bandit with a licensed pistol. At the top of page four was a ribbon containing the words "We're fighting back . . . we're fighting back . . . we're fighting back!"[27] A *Post* cartoon showed a subway stand selling Bernie Goetz face masks. None of the Goetz lookalikes are getting mugged.

Not surprisingly, a great many people were alarmed at this prospect of imitation vigilantes patrolling the city. Accordingly, they set out to construct counternarratives to the *Post* story.

The *Daily News*, the city's other tabloid, was much more critical of Goetz than the *Post*. Jimmy Breslin, its leading columnist, stressed Goetz's psychological quirks. He pointed out that, contrary to published reports, the four boys had not shown sharpened screwdrivers. He calculated that lifetime medical expenses for Daryll Cabey—half to be paid by the federal government, 25 percent each by the state and city—could come to well over two million dollars: "The medical care for Daryll Cabey comes out of the paychecks of the people who said 'At last!' when they heard of his shooting."[28]

An angrier counternarrative was presented by Harlem's *Amsterdam News*, which insisted Goetz represented not all New Yorkers against crime but only white New Yorkers determined to strike back violently at teenage blacks. The editors suggested a thought experiment: "Paint Goetz Black or Puerto Rican. Name him Jones or Suarez. Give him the college degrees and a similar life style. Let him shoot four whites, two of them in the back, for any reason. See what happens to him. You can be sure that it will not be applause."[29]

The *Post*, which had many African-American readers, anticipated this interpretation and worked hard to counter it. The editors made sure that Goetz stories appeared in close proximity to those of African Americans who had used similar violence to prevent crime.

In March 1985, for example, the IRT gunman shared the front pages with the IND candy man. This was Andy Frederick, a black ex-marine who attempted to prevent a theft from a subway candy vendor and stabbed the would-be thief to death in the ensuing struggle. On January 8, 1986, while the Goetz case was still before a grand jury, the paper highlighted James Grimes, a black token clerk who had shot a potential bandit with an unlicensed gun.

Another counternarrative was offered by the *New York Times* which was explicit in its distaste for the *Post*'s treatment. Columnist Sidney Schwanberg attacked it and several op-ed articles worried about the public's apparent support for vigilante justice.

Many of its readers feel that the *Times* does not tell stories as the tabloids do. It would be more accurate to say that it tells tales for the managerial class. It embodies the world view of a person constantly asking "What institution should deal with this social problem?" and "What procedures should be followed?"

Accordingly, its news stories gave us the problems and dilemmas that the Goetz case presented to the Governor, the Mayor, the Police Commissioner, and the District Attorney. Its reporters carefully described the processes of extradition, weighed the pros and cons of granting witnesses immunity, and went into great detail on the strategies of prosecution and defense lawyers.

The *Times's* editorials deplored the outpouring of enthusiasm for self-defense but at the same time exemplified to the point of parody the intelligent liberal's impotence in the face of rising crime rates. Conceding that dramatically increasing the number of transit policemen had not worked, the paper urged that the officers be better trained. A Police Corps would do the trick, offering young men college scholarships in exchange for three years of service.[30] The *Times* showed an invincible conviction that there was a bureaucratic solution to every social problem.

Two books, Lillian Rubin's *Quiet Rage: Bernie Goetz in a Time of Madness* and Alice R. Kaminsky's *The Victim's Song*, demonstrate polar responses to the Goetz shooting. Rubin's book is a psychotherapist's effort to explain the event by tracing its roots in the past. Bernhard Goetz, it appears, had a cold and demanding father. Worse, his father had been charged with sexually molesting young boys. Still worse and very significantly, he had attempted to buy a boy's silence with five dollars—the very same amount that Troy Canty had asked for on the subway.

Rubin makes a brave attempt to calm the passions that the Goetz shooting aroused but this explanation of Goetz's action reads like a parody of therapeutic liberalism. She does better with Darrell Cabey. His father had been a truck driver who bought his own truck and struck out on his own. He was murdered resisting a thief who was trying to steal his truck. His widow was left raising her children on her own, a task she performed with some success. Darrell was the son who was hard to control, the one who, without the guidance of his hardworking father, got into trouble. Rubin puts a face on Darrell Cabey and it turns out to be the face of a crime victim.

If Lillian Rubin wants to calm the violent passions that New York's crime wave aroused, Alice Kaminsky insists on shouting them out. Her son Eric had moved to New York where he was studying to be a concert pianist. One morning two young men, José Deltejo and Furman Urena, stopped him in the subway station at 181st Street. They first took his wallet, then stabbed him, cutting his aorta, and pushed him onto the subway tracks where he bled to death.

Alice Kaminsky wants to inundate the reader with anger and repugnance for the evil of her son's death. She rages against those who commit crimes and those who accept them. She denounces the token clerk who saw Deltejo and Urena enter the station without paying but did nothing. She condemns the witnesses who saw her son pushed onto the tracks and ran from the station but didn't bother to call a policeman. She assails the judge who reminded a slightly aggressive prosecutor that this was "only a murder case." Above all she denounces the indifference of the city which sees a crime wave and does nothing. Her longest chapter is titled "The Rotten Apple" and it contains a long list of crimes in the subway.

Alice Kaminsky reminds us that while one portion of the sympathy for Goetz was politically suspect and morally trashy, another very large portion was honestly motivated and rooted in bitter experience. She is all too typical of the contemporary climate of feeling, however, in her inability to move from a hatred of crime to a social program for resisting it. Describing a seventy-three-year-old subway rider who shot his would-be robber with a licensed .38 revolver, she asks: "If all the muggers knew that all the passengers on the subway carried guns, would the miserable, bullying thieves continue to do so?"[31] It is a heartfelt question. That Kaminsky does not find the spectacle of "all" the passengers on the subway carrying guns alarming shows how thoroughly passion was sweeping away prudence.

GOETZ'S OWN STORIES

In the days immediately after the shooting Bernhard Goetz became bitterly aware that others were manufacturing his story and he became eager to tell it himself. He did so three times. First he talked for an hour and twenty minutes to Officer Warren Foote of the Concord, New Hampshire, police department. Then he gave an hour-and-a-half audiotaped statement to Officer Foote and Detective Christopher Domian. Then he went over the ground again in a two-and-a-half-hour videotaped statement to Assistant District Attorney Susan Braver and two New York City detectives. Each version has essentially the same facts and the same confusions.

The audiotaped and videotaped confessions are among the most remarkable documents of America's urban crisis. An exhausted and emotionally drained Goetz alternates between precise, rational analysis and emotional tirades. At some points he is self-righteously confident that he has acted justly. By this time the press has reported that all four boys had been in trouble with the law before the shooting and were on their way to rob video parlors at Pace University when they approached him. He has no reason to think they weren't threatening violence.

Yet although he doesn't think the shooting was wrong, he thinks the entire experience was disgusting. He has trouble finishing sentences when he tries to describe it. He expresses dismay, regret, horror, and rage. He is trying to construct a story that will make sense of his own experience and he is succeeding only in part.

Goetz is sure that he is a crime victim who has turned on his victimizers. He had suffered an earlier mugging on Canal Street and that had prompted him to carry a weapon. Although the police refused him a permit, he bought several guns and a quick release holster. He refused to wear gloves in winter because they slowed his draw. When he boarded the downtown express on December 22 he was psychologically primed and physically ready.

Like Alice Kaminsky, Goetz assails an uncaring city that permits criminals to roam freely through its subway. His rage at the city on the audiotape is astonishing. "In the business world in New York," he says in attempting to explain how he could go about the city armed, "you have to hide—you know, to hide the person you are."[32] His failed attempt to get a gun permit had taught him that "the city doesn't care what happens to you." The city is lawless and its subway system is a disaster. Its bureaucracy is a sham, a disgrace, a joke. He admits that his shooting was cold-blooded, but says, "You have to think in a cold-blooded way in New York." "In New York," he says, "you have to have a gun." "In New York," he says later, "people do crimes all the time and get away with them."

He is even more furious with the city on the videotape. He explodes in anger at the mere sound of Susan Braver's New York accent: "Oh, God, you know, just when I hear New Yorkers speak, I don't even want to—." [33] Later he exclaims: "I can't stand it. Just the sound. It's—it's, uh—it's all, you know—" New York City, he is sure, "doesn't give a damn about violence."

It would be easy for Goetz to match his story to the Death Wish pattern but he refuses to do so. For all the justification he finds in his past mugging and the moral laxness of the city, Goetz is appalled at his own inner rage. He knows how the *Post* is portraying him and he explicitly repudiates their version of the story.

The Death Wish gunman is a fairly jaunty figure. Brian Garfield's hero grieves at the violence done to his wife and daughter but recovers his equilibrium once he becomes a vigilante. Charles Bronson is positively dapper by the end of the film version, even cracking one of his few cinematic smiles. Goetz, by contrast, expresses a sick, helpless anguish at what he has done even while he tries to justify it. He is at once dismayed and dismaying.

An explicit repudiation of the *Post* version of the story comes near the end of the video-tape when Goetz asks that his name and address be kept private. Told that this is impossible, he collapses with regret, grief, and exasperation.

In the *Post* version he says:

> "This means I'll never escape this. Some people are looking for a hero, some people are looking for a villain.
> "I'm not Clint Eastwood." [34]

What he actually said was this:

> People are looking for a hero, or they're looking for a villain, and neither is . . . nothing is the truth. What you have here, what you have here is nothing more, what you have here is nothing more than a vicious rat. That's *all* it is. It's not Clint Eastwood. It's not, uh, who's this guy . . . shooting around people, and uh, that one movie *Death Wish*, whatever it was, it's not what the cops said.

The *Post* would have tied Goetz's story into a tidy package. Goetz knows that he is not the *Death Wish* gunman and he wants to make sense of his experience. He fails in two respects and they dominated his two trials.

First, he seems puzzled throughout his statements by the question of whether he acted coldly or emotionally. He insists that you have to be cold-blooded in New York and he is sure that he was that day on the subway. He laid down his pattern of fire in advance. At the same time he is sure that he was swept up in the moment, that he was a vicious animal, a monster who wanted to murder those who were robbing him, hurt them, make them suffer as much as possible.

Second, he is unsure whether he paused before firing the fifth shot and said "You seem to be all right—here's another." Anyone who has any acquaintance at all with the Goetz story will seize on the delay and the fifth shot as its most damning details. But when Goetz comes to describe the fifth shot on both audiotape and videotape his account, chillingly precise until then, becomes halting and confused. He isn't sure that he said those words, though he insists that he thought them. He isn't sure that he wasn't fantasizing.

Barry Slotnick's successful defense of Goetz at the first trial rested on his ability, first, to invoke the subway as a place of menace; second, to argue that Goetz truly had been threatened; and, third, to persuade the jury that there had been no pause between the fourth and fifth shots.

Slotnick constantly used the subway as the symbol of a crime-ridden city. He insisted that the jury visit an actual subway car. He had four tough-looking black Guardian Angels appear in the courtroom to reenact the positions of the four youths. He kept slightly rewording the legal doctrine of self-defense so that instead of having his back "against the wall," Goetz had his back against the subway wall.

And he carefully led each witness in reenacting what he or she knew of the crime. The first witness, Christopher Boucher, seemed to support the prosecution's claim that Goetz had paused, then fired. But the other eight witness who testified heard the shots in rapid succession, with no pause. Once the jury concluded that Goetz had indeed felt threatened and that he had not paused before very deliberately firing the fifth shot, the road was open to acquittal on all but the gun possession charges.

The criminal trial took place in 1987. In 1996 Darrell Cabey, represented by lawyer Ron Kuby, sued Goetz in a civil procedure for $25 million in damages for pain and suffering and a further $25 million in punitive damages. Ron Kuby's version of the Goetz story differs from Barry Slotnick's in every conceivable way.

To begin with, the social context in which the story was told had changed. Shortly before the civil trial began a headline on the first page of the *New York Times* read: "NEW YORK'S VIOLENT CRIME RATE DROPS TO LOWS OF EARLY 70S."[35] During the first trial the headlines that surrounded the Goetz stories frequently dealt with urban crime and the menace of the subways. Now they were more likely to deal with O. J. Simpson, the bombing of the Oklahoma Federal Office Building, the Freemen standoff, and the Unabomber.

The audience had also changed. The newspapers were no longer much interested in Goetz. They treated him like some eccentric old relative who had unexpectedly come back to visit. The jury now consisted of six blacks and six Puerto Ricans, all from the Bronx. Both Cabey's and Goetz's lawyers acknowledged that a Bronx jury in 1996 would be very different from a Manhattan one in 1987.

And it was surely bad luck for Goetz that the storytellers had changed. Prosecutor Gregory Waples and Defense Attorney Barry Slotnick were evenly matched. At the second trial Ron Kuby was organized, forceful, and eloquent while Goetz's lawyer, Darnay Hoffman, was conducting only his second trial and doing so in a remarkably unassertive, confused manner.

Kuby had the advantage of focusing his case where Goetz was weakest. Slotnick had been able to start with Troy Canty, who approached Goetz, stood over him, and asked for money. He then persuaded the jury that the rest of the shootings took place on automatic pilot. But Kuby started with Darrell Cabey who was, by Goetz's own account, trying to pretend he was somewhere else when he was shot. The only important piece of evidence in Goetz's favor was columnist Jimmy Breslin's insistence that in the course of an interview after the shooting a lucid, coherent Cabey had said that his friends went after Goetz because he looked like "easy bait." That wasn't enough. The jury concluded, as one member told a television interviewer, "I mean Mr. Goetz came over to him again and he asked him, 'Oh, you look O.K.' So he shot it again . . . that was unfair."[36]

The jury awarded $18 million for past and future suffering and $25 million in punitive damages. That moves the case into a new phase. Goetz has declared bankruptcy and legal moves are underway to garnish 10 percent of his wages for the rest of his life. Like Tom Wolfe's Sherman McCoy, he has become a permanent defendant.

The first Goetz trial represents the nadir of the subway's evolution as an urban symbol. It was hard to believe, in 1987, that the subway had once represented a city's ability to rise to a great challenge and solve the fundamental contradictions of urban geography. In retrospect, however, we can see that the comparison of a subway to Hell had been implicit as soon as an underground transit system was first conceived. It was made explicit in the 1905 *World* cartoon that showed Dante gazing at the riders enduring summer but at that stage the comparison was still exaggerated and humorous. It had become much less so by the mid-twenties when Hart Crane wrote "The Tunnel." Here the journey underground had become a daily encounter with sexual sterility, professional failure, and despair. But although Crane finds the Hell metaphor profoundly meaningful, he still knows that it is only a figure of speech.

By 1987 it no longer seemed like a metaphor at all. The decline in the city was real, the graffiti on the cars was real, and Bernard Goetz in his statements to the police sounded like nothing so much as one of the damned.

But this perception of the subway carried too great a burden of hysteria to be permanently persuasive. Inevitably New York writers and artists would realize that the hellish subway was only a metaphor, that other metaphors were possible, and that by developing them artists and writers could participate in an urban rebirth. Even as the Goetz trial took place new and more positive readings of the city and its subway were beginning to appear.

CHAPTER TEN

REDEEMING THE CITY

T H E mundane reality of the New York City subway system is increasingly obscured by the mythology it generates. Semioticians tell us that a sign is never simply the transparent reflection of a thing—there is always some slippage between the two. This disparity has grown steadily in the past three decades as the subway's power to generate symbolic interpretations has gone into overdrive.

It is not possible, however, to go back to a time when the subway had a simple, direct signification. There never was such a time. From the beginning the subway was both a transportation conduit and a symbol of the city it helped bring into being. In the nineteenth century, when the subway was still a vision, it was an optimistic symbol. Later, when it was built but not extended rapidly enough, it became a focus of discontent but remained associated with dynamism and growth. Even those who used the subway to expose the pretensions of the skyscraper implicitly conceded that most people still considered New York a Wonder City. It was only in the mid-sixties that the subway became the symbol of a population divided against itself and a city in decline.

To judge the ordinary image of the New York City subway system today simply visit your local video store. Check out *The French Connection* (1971), *The Taking of Pelham 1-2-3* (1974), *Dressed to Kill* (1980), *Nighthawks* (1981), *Five Corners* (1986), *Blue Steel* (1990), *Carlito's Way* (1993), *Die Hard With a Vengeance* (1995), and *Money Train* (1995). The quality of these pictures varies widely but their subways merge into an unbroken sequence of noise and dirt, menace and mayhem.

Moreover, the violence accelerates. In 1974 the makers of *The Taking of Pelham 1-2-3* dramatized the hijacking of a subway train with minimal violence and careful attention to character. In 1995 the producers of *Money Train* relied on a realistically portrayed torching of a change booth and an absurd climax in which a careening train smashes through a long succession of steel pillars as if they were made of balsa wood. "There is a public perception out there that New York State is New York City," Governor Mario Cuomo once complained, "and New York City is Manhattan, and Manhattan is a subway that murders people every night."[1]

We seem to have arrived at Subway Hell. The platforms and tunnels have become the city's social underground and mental unconscious—the place where all its undesirables, all its hidden thoughts gather and fester. As we descend into it, however, an unexpected reversal takes place. We find ourselves in a place of unexpected enchantments and astonishing beauty. The subway no longer represents the average and the quotidien as it did for Reginald Marsh and Walker Evans. It now embraces extremes. It is both sordid and transcendent. Moreover, the sordidness and the transcendence are nearly indistinguishable.

All subway art since the 1970s has responded to the question of whether or not the city is livable. Many of New York's artists and writers have seized on the subway, which is clearly essential to the city and which clearly represents much that is wrong with it, as the key to its renewal. It represents everything that they find difficult and problematic in their city as well as much that they find challenging and rewarding. The subway emerges as a test case for urbanites, the most unlikely possible place for them to assert their faith in the city's present and its future.

REDEEMING THE CITY

We can see the transformation of Subway Hell into a subway wonderland by comparing first Paul Cadmus's painting *Subway Symphony* of 1976 with the thirty-seven-foot-long Subway Car that Red Grooms introduced that same year into his installation *Ruckus Manhattan* and then Sol Yurick's novel *The Warriors* (1965) with the film version that Walter Hill released in 1979.

The difference between Cadmus's view of the city and Grooms's is partly one of generations. Paul Cadmus was born in 1904, Red Grooms in 1937. Cadmus began his career with satirical paintings of the American scene. Grooms began his in the world of Assemblages, Environments, and Happenings. Where Cadmus demands a sense of critical distance, Grooms required participation. The New York that Grooms shows in *Ruckus Manhattan* uses the same raw data as Cadmus's *Subway Symphony* but what fills the older man with dismay strikes the younger one as a marvelous, fun-filled carnival.

Cadmus painted his *Subway Symphony* in 1975–76 (Ill. 78). "I know the subway well," Cadmus said. "I lived in Brooklyn and traveled to New York all the time. I was appalled by the ugliness, the dirt and the violence of the disgraceful system."[2] But he does not paint only the scene that assaulted his eyes each day. Instead, he uses the subway to show the personal exhibitionism and cultural posturing that has produced a larger urban breakdown.

The canvas is an anthology of all the distortions of the human ideal that might be encountered in modern New York. There are more than fifty figures. At the left a white construction worker, the word HATE written in graffiti over his head, stuffs a hero sandwich

78 ■ Paul Cadmus. *Subway Symphony.*
1975–1976. Acrylic on canvas, 46 × 92 in. Private Collection, Courtesy Midtown Payson Galleries, New York.

into his mouth and looks angrily at the couple making love (almost literally) on the plat-form. Next to them a woman in hair curlers blows bubble gum while her companion grins in idiotic delight at whatever is playing on his transistor radio. Next to them a balding, over-weight, overaged hippie, sporting a copy of *Everyman's Picasso* (Gold Edition), sprawls on the bench, his arm round his anorexic but pregnant girlfriend, while a middle-class woman with tinted hair arranged in an elaborately contrived beehive hairdo glares balefully at him. Just off the center of the composition we can see down the stairway to a lower level where a mugging victim lies unconscious on the platform.

This astonishing work produces a remarkable, but perhaps unintended, effect on spec-tators. They ought to be repelled by it, as they are, for example, by Cadmus's paintings of the *Seven Deadly Sins*. Instead, they crowd in close, clearly fascinated. They begin chuckling and pointing out details to their friends.

It is an old accusation against satire—that it exhibits a confusion of values by taking pleasure in what it condemns. Cadmus seeks to escape this dilemma by providing us with a standpoint from which to scrutinize and condemn the scene before us. He includes two artists in it. One is the young African-American girl leaning against a column, the other is Cadmus himself sitting on the back stairway with a sketchbook in hand and a disapproving look on his face. Both exhibit a balance that the other figures conspicuously lack. Cadmus's choice of two artists—one female and one male, one black and one white—is a calculated attempt to show that sanity and brotherhood are still possible even in this extravaganza of cultural dissonance.

Where Cadmus saw decline, Red Grooms saw carnival. *Ruckus Manhattan* is a re-creation of Manhattan in sticks and wire, plaster and foam rubber. Visitors become gawking tourists as they admire a fifteen-foot-high Statue of Liberty, stare up at a seventeen-foot Woolworth Building, and stroll down fifty feet of re-created Wall Street. All of Manhattan's energy is on

display and all of its aggravations—there is an urban terrorist, a pimpmobile, and a por-
nographic bookstore. We are in a world of grotesquely exaggerated people and buildings
that seem ready to topple over on us at any minute.

The visitor enters Grooms's subway car at the 14th Street IRT station, since remod-
eled but in 1976 the noisiest, most chaotic in the system, with the narrow passageways
blocked by intrusive record stores and tie shops (Ill. 79). Grooms portrays all of this
with loving devotion. The visitor pushes past three misshapen nude figures at the token
booth, walks through an actual turnstile, down a graffiti-stained platform, and enters the
train.

A sound system ensures that the noise of the No. 6 train will reach at least a hundred
decibels. The floor of the car consists of separate slabs mounted on coiled springs to keep
the imagined rider constantly off balance. The car walls feature graffiti and parodies of
subway ads. One reads: "9 Out of 10 Americans Are crazy—Give to Mental Health." Another commands: "Attention Birdbrains, the computer field is wide open to anybody with
half a brain. CALL 000-0000." The passengers are a cross section of New Yorkers from the
hippie by the door to the Wall Streeter reading his *Times* and the Hasidic Jew reading the
Yiddish newspaper *Forward*. A man squeezes his companions by holding his pooch carrier
on his lap. A drunk snoozes on the lap of a mortified lady. A repellent middle-aged male
harasses a howling Goldilocks.

79 ▪ Red Grooms. Detail of *Subway.*
1975–1976. Mixed Media, 9′ × 18′7″ × 37′2″. © 1995 Red Grooms/Artist Rights Society. Courtesy:
Marlborough Gallery.

If there is any single key to the significance of *Ruckus Manhattan* it is in the passage that Grooms's seated hippie is reading:

> Je suis un éphémère et point trop mécontent citoyen d'une métropole crue moderne parce que tout goût connu a été éludé dans les ameublements et l'extérieur des maisons aussi bien que dans le plan de la ville.[3]

This is the first sentence of Rimbaud's prose poem "Ville" which appears in his *Illuminations*. It was written about nineteenth-century London but it is as close as Grooms comes to offering a one-sentence summary of *Ruckus Manhattan*. The lines assert that the city is tasteless in its plan, its buildings, and its furnishings but the poet, while not entirely abandoning his discontent, is letting it dwindle into a weary acceptance.

But even this quotation does not fully describe Grooms's attitude, which is not weary like Rimbaud's but boyishly enthusiastic. He seems to be saying that Manhattan is so eye-poppingly awful, so extravagantly profuse in its energies, that it ought to be relished. He insists that awfulness and beauty not only can go together but very frequently do. Unlike Cadmus, he offers no viewpoint exterior to the scene he portrays. He places his spectator inside the subway car. There is even a single empty seat. The visitor is invited to sit down along with all the other grotesques who line the benches. Most do.

The comparison of Sol Yurick's novel *The Warriors* to Walter Hill's film similarly shows a subway that is losing its old status as underground ordeal and acquiring a new one as an adventure playground. Yurick's novel is a modern re-creation of Xenophon's *Anabasis*. In the Greek story a band of warriors, their leader killed in Persia, has to fight through hostile territory to reach the sea. In the novel an enigmatic prophet named Cyrus has summoned all the city's gangs to Van Cortlandt Park for the Fourth of July. They are sixty thousand strong, he tells them. They far outnumber the police. If they could cooperate, the city would belong to them.

But of course they do not cooperate. Someone slaps at a mosquito; another misinterprets the gesture; fights break out and soon the rally turns into a riot. The Dominators have to make their way back from the northern reaches of the Bronx to their native Coney Island. Both the subway and the city they travel through is intricately subdivided into separate turfs and they have to fight a new tribe at each step of their journey. They inhabit a kind of parallel subway which belongs not to the commuters but to the successive gangs they meet along the way.

Yurick's novel springs from a period in the city's life when youth gangs had grown powerful enough to alarm middle-class opinion but had not yet been dissolved by heroin. He tells his story in an impersonal, third-person style that captures both the tone of Greek narrative and the unsophisticated outlook of urban teenagers. On the surface the language seems restricted to an objective accounting of events but it actually expresses the boys' extremely subjective, anxiety-ridden view of the city. Though they would like to believe that they are as heroic as Xenophon's warriors (the original story reappears inside the novel as a comic book that one of the gang members is reading), they are shown to be insecure, endlessly concerned with their reputations, and constantly fearful that someone else will prove to be even tougher than they are.

The real city largely ignores them and they know little of it. They have never been so far from home. They do not know the subway system (one fails miserably in his effort to understand the subway map) and the streets fill them with fear. They are facing, as Cyrus told them, a city that constantly puts them down. In response they create a fantasy city of the mind where a warrior confronts fear in a rat-filled tunnel and temptation in a Times Square toilet. In their fantasy city they can prove that they are men, that they have reputation, that they command respect.

Hill's film surely diminishes the moral complexity of Yurick's novel. This is worth saying because the novel has been lost behind the popularity of the film and it deserves to be rediscovered. In the movie a searching presentation of gang mentality becomes an urban action drama. The random cruelty of Yurick's gang members becomes a chivalrous nobility. The Puerto Rican girl who is raped in Yurick's novel becomes a spunky sidekick who accompanies the gang to their Coney Island home. Yurick's episode in which Hinton the graffiti writer breaks down in terror inside a subway tunnel becomes a love scene between the gang leader and his girl, with an oncoming train symbolizing passion much as the Pacific Ocean did for Bert Lancaster and Deborah Kerr in *From Here to Eternity*. Where Yurick's gang members are most obviously threatened by their own insecurities, Hill's have a diabolical enemy named Luther with whom they have the obligatory final fight by the sea. Everything that was dark, gritty, and dead serious in Yurick's novel becomes bright, graceful, and oddly glamorous in the film.

But these substitutions have their rewards. Hill projects a teenage fantasy in which the manhood and family cohesion of the gang is first tested, then vindicated. His warriors are challenged by an astonishing range of wildly inventive fantasy figures: one gang attacks on roller skates, a second wears New York Yankees uniforms and wields baseball bats, a third, called the Lizzies, is composed entirely of lesbian warriors. There is more dayglo orange than blood red. The fights are no more real (and no less entertaining) than the production numbers in a Broadway show. Hill takes a subway system that many deplore and shows that it is really a wonderland, a dark background for sudden explosions of color and energy.

THE GOOD SIDE OF GRAFFITI

Where Paul Cadmus found evidence of social decline in the subway, Red Grooms and Walter Hill found unexpected entertainment. Both these points of view appeared in attitudes toward graffiti. It was, without doubt, a two-edged phenomenon. That is why it appears twice in this book—in Chapter Nine as a disaster for the city and here as a revelation of new artistic possibilities in the subway. At its worst, graffiti told New Yorkers that both they and their government were impotent to prevent a daily harassment. At its best, graffiti brought surprise to a ride that had seemed the foundation of the daily grind. The city offered few sights more remarkable that the view of the intersecting el tracks near East Tremont Avenue at West Farms Plaza where the Bronx River flowed in the foreground while two trains, their entire surfaces painted in bold forms and bright colors, passed overhead.

There had, of course, been graffiti since the system opened in 1904. Before the seventies it was drawn with pencil or pen on advertising posters or scratched on the walls. Sex was its most popular subject but not the only one. Politics and religion received almost as much attention. Folklorist Allen Walker Read notes that during the fifties and early sixties, when the subways were filled with posters on the theme of "Religion in American Life," graffiti writers quickly responded with their own sarcastic additions.[4] A New York Bible Society poster in the 50th Street IRT station reading I AM THY GOD . . . I WILL HELP THEE earned the addition "If You're White and Middle Class." The slogan "The Family That Prays Together Stays Together" was rewritten in the 116th Street IRT station as "The Family That Shoots Together Loots Together." It was presumably graffiti such as this that inspired Simon and Garfunkel's sardonic observation in "Mrs. Robinson" (1967) that the words of the prophets are written on the subway walls.

The new graffiti was larger and more colorful than the old and was almost entirely devoid of sexual innuendo, ethnic and racial insults, or religious references. It was born in Philadelphia.[5] In the mid-sixties teenage gang members there began staking out territory with markings made with felt-tipped pens. Before long, a few graffiti writers, more interested in self-display than territory, began marking their names on the city's subways and buses. In 1971 the *New York Times* published an article with the headline "PHILADELPHIA, GRAFFITI CAPITAL OF THE WORLD."[6] A year later that headline would have been impossible.

Graffiti, which hadn't changed dramatically since the Romans, suddenly began to show stylistic evolution. Graffiti writers compared notes, traded designs, and accumulated books of drawings, moving from simple outlines filled in with color to bubble letters, candy cane letters, letters filled with polka dots, and 3-D effects. "We picked up on each others' styles," FAB 5 FRED told art critic Suzi Gablik, "we taught each other different techniques. Many styles began to merge and out of that came 'Wild Style.' It's Brooklyn-style structured lettering with Upper Manhattan spray techniques. Wild Style is totally illegible unless you're initiated."[7]

The new graffiti was almost entirely concerned with publicizing the writer's name and thus inflating his (or, less frequently, her) reputation. As a young man who had spent long hours putting his tag in as many subway cars as possible explained: "I been the king. The whole school knows what I done, what I can do again. I got respect, I'm a writer."[8] As another such writer said: "We wanted to put a little fame in our lives. People in slum areas really want to make themselves known, but we don't know how to do it."[9]

Of course it was never the actual name that was used. The pleasure of the pseudonym was that it allowed the graffiti-writer to hear himself admired without having to reveal authorship outside a small group of admirers. Writers created an amazing collections of pseudonyms: AFRO 182, ATOM 138, BAM BAM, BAM BAM 2, COOL CLYDE 104, CORNBREAD, "*DAZE*," EVIL ERIC, FROG 152, IZ THE WIZ, KING KOOL, LOVE MAN 176, MR. BLADE, QUEEN EVA 62+, RASTA, SHERLOCK HOLMS, SHOT GUN, TEA MO 115, ULTRASLICK, WILDCAT 135, and ZIP 138 among many others.

City officials were totally frustrated. Graffiti is one of the few crimes where the perpetrator publicizes himself. Police quickly assembled mug books containing the work of each graffiti writer accompanied by name and address. It was relatively easy to arrest graffiti writers but very difficult to persuade judges to put them in jail with more dangerous criminals. The young men were often assigned to graffiti-cleaning work gangs, which more nearly resembled networking sessions than punishment.

The authorities gnashed their teeth, introduced attack dogs into the train yards, and even passed a law making it illegal to carry a can of spray paint in any public facility unless it was in a sealed container. Nothing worked until the Transit Authority cleaned each car in the system. Then, if graffiti reappeared, the car was taken off the rails at the end of its very next run and not returned until the offending markings were removed. By 1989 all the trains were graffiti free. The result was unexpected. Visiting out-of-towners wanted to see the graffiti.

As a sign of the creativity of inner-city teenagers, graffiti won quick acceptance in the world of popular culture. In 1972 a letter writer to the *New York Times* pointed out that he hadn't seen any racism or obscenity in the graffiti and declared that "as a social phenomenon, it is heartening to see individuals invent ways to humanize the brutally impersonal and mechanical environment of the trains and stations."[10] Richard Goldstein published one of the first defenses of graffiti in the March 26, 1973, issue of *New York*. The magazine featured a Graffiti Hit Parade and awarded the first TAKI Awards to STAY HIGH and HONDO 1. Graffiti began to decorate the covers of rock albums. P-NUT, JESTER, and DIABLO achieved glory among graffiti writers when a train featuring their masterpieces was used in prime time each week to open the popular TV comedy *Welcome Back Kotter*.

Graffiti also began to attract scholarly attention. In 1989 Martin Wong opened a Museum of American Graffiti. He had collected 150 paintings and 50 piece books—one from as early as 1957. Photographers began building up archives of graffiti. Mervin Kurlansky, a consultant with the British design firm Pentagram, encouraged photographer Jon Naar to systematically document works that the Transit Authority was trying hard to scrub out of existence. The result was *The Faith of Graffiti*, a book of extraordinarily vibrant photographs that recorded the work of writers from ABAD 144 to ZIP 138 in warm, saturated colors. Norman Mailer was asked to provide the text for the Naar photographs. The choice seemed obvious. Who better than the author of *Advertisements for Myself* to analyze calligraphic assertions of personal glory?

More straightforward works of photographic documentation and scholarly analysis soon followed. Craig Castleman's *Getting Up; Subway Graffiti in New York* (1982) brought an anthropologist's perspective to the subject and included fascinating interviews with several of the important writers. Martha Cooper and Henry Chalfant's *Subway Art* (1984) displayed 239 illustrations by two photographers who had worked closely with the teenage writers. Richard Lachmann discussed "Graffiti as Career and Ideology" in the *American Journal of Sociology* (1988). Jack Stewart's NYU Ph.D. dissertation, *Subway Graffiti: An Aesthetic Study of Graffiti on the Subway System of New York City, 1970–1978* (1989), provided a photographic record, interviews with many writers, and a thorough analysis of the stylistic evolution of graffiti.

A certain part of the art world was attracted by the color, energy, and, above all, by the outlaw aspect of graffiti. "It's a radical art with a radical ideology, because it's illegal," said Tim Rollins. "It's radical because, mostly, the artists are non-artists. Formally, it's not like anything else. It's art that falls out of a social condition."[11]

Twyla Tharp's ballet "Deuce Coupe," which opened at the New York City Center on April 1, 1973, featured six young graffiti writers who came onstage with spray cans to create three panels. The Sidney Janis and Tony Shafrazi Galleries exhibited graffiti. FUTURA

80 ▪ *We Are Not Afraid.*
A Mass Media Campaign by Les Levine, © Les Levine, 1981.

2000 dropped the 2000 from his tag, created an album cover and stage sets for the British rock group The Clash, and began exhibiting his paintings on glass. FAB 5 FRED, a black graffiti artist from Brooklyn who had painted a train with Warhol-like soup cans, collaborated with the rock group Blondie, and showed his paintings at the Fun Gallery. SAMO dropped his tag and became Jean-Michel Basquiat.

Until graffiti, the art of the subway consisted of portraying it in works which were scrutinized elsewhere. Now artists realized that the subway itself could be their medium. They seized on the system's advertising spaces in order to transform the underground environment. In 1982 Les Levine produced a poster of an Asian couple staring slightly nervously forward over the words "We Are Not Afraid" (Ill. 80). Levine is an artist fascinated by the repetition inherent in photographic processes and he clearly relished the prospect of seeing multiple copies of his image circulating simultaneously through the city. He returned to the subway later in the decade with 4,800 ads ironically juxtaposing images from Michelangelo with the sardonic slogans "Consume or Perish" and "Pray for More." [12]

Other artists soon followed with mock-advertisements but none was more ambitious than Alfredo Jaar. In 1986 he rented all the advertising spaces in the Spring Street IND station for the entire month of December in order to transform the subway world into an Environment. Instead of smiling models and consumer products, riders saw photographs of Serra Pelada, Brazil, where tens of thousands of poverty-stricken workers dig with their hands and crude tools in a frenzied effort to find a few ounces of gold. Interspersed with the photographs were signs announcing world oil prices in Frankfurt, Paris, London, and New York. "This installation is titled 'Rushes'," Jaar told Jim Dwyer. "It's not only a gold rush, but it's also the subway rush. The sound of the subway is very similar also to the sound that is in the gold mines. It's a game of survival, just like the people in the subway, surviving until they win the lottery."[13]

Of all the artists who were inspired by graffiti to use the subways as a medium for communication, none had more immediate impact than Keith Haring. Between 1981 and 1985, he turned the subways into his own underground art gallery.

Like the graffiti writers, he worked illegally; unlike them, he took pride in leaving no permanent damage. When workmen have no new advertisement to paste up in a station, they simply cover the previous poster with a large sheet of black paper. Haring realized that this provided a perfect background for chalk drawings.

The creation of each drawing became a kind of performance art (Ill. 81). Haring deliberately worked during the day when he could be observed—and arrested. The drawings convey a mythology that Haring seemed to be inventing on the spot. They allude to prehistoric cave drawings, oriental calligraphy, Renaissance iconography, modern TV shows, and favorite movies. They reach back into ancient myth and forward to nuclear energy, but their immediate world is that of cybernetic space. The drawings contain no depth perspective, no day or night. Instead, they reveal the nonspace of the computer screen and the dancing icons of the electronic age.

Like William Burroughs, whose work he greatly admired, Haring saw himself living at the end of the Christian millennium and the beginning of a new paganism. Haring's dancing cartoon figures seem to act out incidents from its mythology.

The major characters and situations of these drawings include a pregnant woman, a glowing child, a dancing man, and a barking dog. There are also frequent TV sets—sometimes

81 ▪ Keith Haring Drawing in the Subway.
© Estate of Keith Haring. Photograph © 1997. Estate of Tsong Kwong Chi–MTDP/Artists Rights Society (ARS), New York.

they appear with significant images on their screens, sometimes they sprout bodies and run. The serpent, a traditional symbol of cycle and renewal, appears in many of the drawings. Still others focus on a dancing pregnant woman and the baby whom poet Rene Ricard has named the radiant child.[14]

Although they contain images of crisis and alarm, the dominant mood of Haring's drawings is joyful. It comes as a slight shock to remember that they were drawn just as the tensions that would erupt in the Goetz shooting were building to a climax. They should be viewed as a deliberate challenge to the urban despair and self-destructive anger which the Goetz mythology expressed. Like Red Grooms, Haring rejects the intellectual's traditional postures of critical distance and social alienation. He made his art a casual part of the daily journey and helped reclaim a crucial urban space.

NEW UNDERGROUNDS

In the last two decades a large and varied group of writers and artists have engaged in a vigorous, constantly shifting debate over the imaginative significance of the subway. Their work is not easily reduced to orderly categories but it is at least possible to trace four tendencies.

First, there is a continuing fascination with subway mayhem. Abraham Rodriguez Jr. shows the day of a subway motorman in his story "Short Stop" as a succession of encounters with would-be suicides and crack addicts waving pistols.[15] Rodriguez presents his subject realistically but gleeful exaggeration is more common. Peter Saul's painting *Subway #1* (1979) shows cops and robbers literally exploding out of a sleek, metallic subway car on a canvas more than 14′ 8″ long. Luis Cruz Azeceta uses large canvases and a graffiti-like style to dramatize a subway of crime, dirt, and daily aggravation. All three use the subway to portray a culture of violence and a city that makes more demands on your sympathy than you can possibly respond to.

Second, many are struck by the changing composition of the subway crowd. The city now has as many immigrants as it did in the early years of the century. They now come not from eastern or southern Europe but from Asia, the Caribbean, and Central America. The conservative writer Peter Brimelow opened a polemic against immigration in the *National Review* by comparing the waiting rooms of the Immigration and Naturalization Service to the tenth circle of hell and then went on to explain that, like the subway, they were "an underworld that is almost entirely colored."[16]

Others view the situation with much more satisfaction. Harvey Dinerstein's oil paintings *Underground* (1986) and *D Train to Coney Island* (1988) celebrate a multiracial world. Sophie Rivera set out to photograph the minorities who ride peacefully in the subway but are unnoticed by the majority until a crime occurs. Xin Han, an immigrant from the People's Republic of China, found the subways an ideal place to analyze his new home. "On the subway," he has said, "we see the whole structure—happiness, hate, isolation, *and* the desire for the American ideal."[17] In 1990 Tom Finkelpearl and Bolex Greczynsky borrowed the spaces of the Transit Museum to create an installation titled *The D Train Project* which represented each neighborhood the train passed through from Coney Island to Woodlawn

Cemetery. At each "stop" the viewer found images that evoked the surrounding neighborhood—a newsstand stocked with foreign language papers at Newkirk Avenue, a Spanish language radio broadcast at 170th Street, a Cambodian Buddhist temple at Tremont Avenue. Jim Dwyer's *Subway Lives: 24 Hours in the Life of the New York City Subway* (1991) takes care to show how the city's newest ethnic groups add color to its transportation system.

A third tendency gives new emphasis to the physical shape of the subway. "No people," Serge Hambourg told his wife as he set out to photograph the system's stairways, ramps, and grills, "only the subway itself, only this extraordinary underground world."[18]

The spaces of the subway help form a city child's mind and persist in the memory with remarkable vigor. Long after he had left the city Richard Pantell's imagination was so saturated with his New York upbringing that, when he had trouble falling asleep, he recited the names of subway stops instead of counting sheep. When he painted the subway he deliberately kept his figures small so that he could show the intricate structure of tunnels and tracks, stairways and corridors.[19]

Working on special effects in Hollywood, former Brooklynite Alan Wolfson found that he could construct an entirely convincing diorama of a subway station entirely from memory. He has since produced a fascinating series of miniature subway stations, most of them about a foot and a half long, combining the color of Reginald Marsh with the menace of Mickey Spillane.[20]

This interest in the physical subway has also expressed itself in a new fascination with the system's long-neglected mosaics. If Red Grooms seems to continue the nineteenth-century fascination with the city as spectacle, Daniel Greene revives the interest in the picturesque effects of time. He shows the mosaics weathered by experience but still bright with life. "I decided at the beginning," Greene has said, "not to paint the tiles in an absolutely pristine, clear way but to replicate the soiled quality that has occurred over many, many years. . . . I find their patina particularly appealing. It gives you a sense of history, and it varies from wall to wall."[21]

This brings us to the fourth and most pervasive aspect of recent subway art. As the system nears its hundredth birthday, it increasingly provides the foundation for metaphors that use the tunnels beneath the city to explore the personal and social unconscious. Since World War II, as both Blanche Gelfant and William Sharpe demonstrate, the fictional protagonist has tended to turn inward or to burrow underground.[22] Influential texts by Sigmund Freud and Gaston Bachelard suggest that these two directions might really be the same. Freud points out in *Civilization and Its Discontents* that the unconscious is comparable to the ruins of a city. Gaston Bachelard argues in *The Poetics of Space* that physical environments have an "intimate depth" which is emotional as well as spatial. These insights help us understand why the subway should increasingly appear as a landscape that is at once real and dreamlike.

Elizabeth Bishop was one of the earliest writers to explore this theme. Her poem "The Man-Moth" (1946), inspired by a newspaper misprint for mammoth, is about a creature who, continually disappointed in his aspirations toward infinite light, constantly returns to his subway home where his rushing brain becomes a subway car roaring through artificial tunnels and recurring dreams. In the Beat writers the subway appears as an appropriate locale for divine madness. The protagonist of Jack Kerouac's first novel, *The Town and the*

Country (1950), is initiated into subterranean wisdom by a mad trio—a poet, an addict, and a hoodlum—whom he meets in the subway. In *Howl* (1956) Allen Ginsberg celebrated hipsters who "chained themselves to subways for the endless ride from Battery to Holy Bronx on benzedrine."[23] A few years later Benny Profane, the protagonist of Thomas Pynchon's *V* (1963), introduced himself to the mythology of the modern city by yo-yoing back and forth on the 42nd Street shuttle until three Puerto Rican teenagers taught him how to hunt alligators in the sewers.

The exploration of the subway through metaphor becomes steadily more complicated. In recent years we encounter it in a book of photographs, a series of sculptures, a comic book novel, and a journalist's account of the homeless.

At first glance the plates in Bruce Davidson's *Subway* (1986) seem examples of documentary photography exploring teenage violence and racial tension. They show a world where tough-looking adolescents swagger and edgy members of the middle class try to withdraw from the sordidness around them. In one a homeless woman piles junk on the floor in front of her for a bonfire and lifts her dress to expose her pubic hair—a strategy that she hopes will scare off muggers. In another we actually see a crime in progress—from the angle of vision of the intended victim.

But although everything that Davidson shows can actually be found somewhere in the system, his purposes go far beyond documentation. Where Walker Evans hoped to be an impersonal observer, Davidson, as his preface makes clear, constantly thinks of the subway in terms of something else. He describes it as a jungle in which the photographer stalks his prey. He compares the graffiti to ancient hieroglyphics with hidden messages. His New Yorkers are like "immigrants huddled in steerage." He himself is a "pervert, voyeur, and flasher all rolled into one photographic monster."[24] His subway trains are cattle cars carrying European Jews to the death camps. His subway is the home of the repressed, the dramatization of all his nightmares. And, like some nightmares, it has an uncanny beauty.

Like Davidson but in a very different medium, Donna Dennis combines surprising realism with challenging metaphor. She has explored this combination in a remarkable series of sculptures: *Subway Station with Lighted Interior* (1974), *Subway Station with Yellow and Blue* (1974–76), *Subway with Silver Girders* (1982–83), and *Deep Station* (1981–85).

The last is the most frequently exhibited of the series. *Deep Station* is twenty-four feet long and eleven feet, three inches high (Ill. 82). This is almost the scale of *Ruckus Manhattan* but where Red Grooms's subway car is colorful and amusing, this one is monochromatic and austere. A visitor's first impression is that this is almost an exact reproduction of the end of one of the old IRT stops where a traveler standing on the platform can look past the stationmaster's room and down the curving track. The work is conceived with realistic fidelity. The floor is as dirty as it would be in an actual station and the walls look covered with grime. A first response is to simply shrug and ask why something so drab has been reproduced with such fidelity.

But the longer the work is studied, the greater the unease it inspires. What seems at first so obvious reveals unexpected ambiguities. The scale, for instance, is disturbing—very large for a work of sculpture but definitely smaller than a real subway station. Dennis took the scale from her own body. The entrance lintel is placed at precisely her height—five feet, eight and one half inches from the floor. That makes the space large enough to stand

82 ▪ Donna Dennis. *Deep Station.*
1981–1985. Mixed Media, 135″ × 240″ × 288″ (detail view). Photograph: Peter Mauss/ESTO.

in but with no headroom whatever. We would know how to deal with a bigger space—it would be so realistic as to be pointless. We would also know how to deal with a significantly smaller one—it would be one of Alan Wolfson's dioramas. But this space is too large for a work of art, too small for real life.

These ambiguities, moreover, are supplemented by an unsettling conflict between openness and exclusion. We can see through the grille, down the platform, into the stationmaster's room but have no means of penetrating those spaces. The open grilles invite our eyes to catch glimpses of what lies beyond them but bar us from actual entry. This is one of those urban spaces which are so haunting when they are empty because the distant echoes of the crowd makes their desolation all the more uncanny.

The title *Deep Station* belongs to a family of phrases that includes not only the obvious deep throat but also deep seated, deep meaning, deep syntax, deep fear, and deep neurosis. For Dennis the subway is both vividly itself and a metaphorical space that suggests something forbidden and mysterious.

Treating the subway as the symbolic foundation of cultural superstructures, Dennis sees it in terms of an interplay of masculine and feminine. "I thought of the platform as being public and male," she wrote in her journal, "and the track as being private and female." Structures of patriarchal control, such as the control tower in *Subway with Silver Girders* and the station master's room in *Deep Station*, watch over this underground world but, as Dennis writes, "control doesn't seem to reach very far."

The track moves out from the platform without restraint, "representing infinitely expanding possibilities . . . as a rhythmically flowing river overhung by trees and vines, a 'jungle' full of life and unharnessed potential, unknown, underestimated, and possibly dangerous." In *Deep Station* one of the I-beams and a connecting girder shift, so that they are aligned not with the platform but with the diagonal of the tracks. Dennis associates this with a reorientation of masculine and feminine—with "things shifting at their very roots."[25]

If subway art can now be as large as *Deep Station*, so it can also be as compact as a page. Eric Drooker's *Flood! A Novel in Pictures* (1992) draws on both the comic book format and the woodblock novels of Franz Mazarel and Lynd Ward to present a devastated city of empty streets, barren tenements, and closed factories. *Flood!* refers to both the actual deluge that closes the novel and the flood of troubles which have come upon the citizens.

The middle section consists entirely of a subway ride on the L Line, still better known to most New Yorkers as the 14th Street–Canarsie crosstown. It is a ride that captures the full range of the actual subway experience, from menace to fantasy and back again.

The rider's descent down the station stairs is also a regression in time. The walls are covered with mysterious markings—graffiti tags, dollar signs, Keith Haring's radiant child, Chinese ideograms—which, while they can all be found in a New York station, also suggest a movement toward other, earlier cultures. By way of the suggestion offered by a travel poster and a Camel cigarette ad, the scene transforms itself into the deep chambers of an Egyptian pyramid—the graffiti become hieroglyphs, the wide-flange beams become lotus columns, the teenagers take on the flat outlines of ancient carvings.

Then as the rider enters the train, falls asleep on the bench, and sinks into his dreams, he moves still further back into a tunnel decorated by Lascaux cave paintings until he finds himself in a primitivist dreamland where naked African maidens run with gazelles. The drawings become larger, the dreams more erotic as our rider sinks deeper and deeper into a dream of sexual bliss until he is finally awakened by the loud barking and snarling teeth of a transit cop's German shepherd.

It is not dismaying that artists and writers should explore the subway in terms of its mythic resonances. It is disturbing, however, when myth overwhelms mundane reality. This is the situation in Jennifer Toth's journalistic account of *The Mole People* (1993).[26]

Every subway rider sees the homeless on the subway platforms and in the trains. No one should have been surprised to learn that they have also found shelter in the intricate network of tunnels beneath the city's streets. Yet there is something especially horrifying in this. It raises uncomfortable memories of Dante's *Inferno*, of the trolls in innumerable fairy tales, of the man-eating morlocks who dwell underground in H. G. Wells's *The Time Machine*, and of the ghastly figures who emerge from the subway tunnels in *Escape from New York*.

Toth found that city officials practiced a kind of anxious denial when she began inquiring about them. Track maintenance workers were more direct. They regarded those who lived in tunnels with fear and referred to them as the "CHUD people"—short for Cannibalistic Human Underground Dwellers. They are frightening, in spite of their pathetic condition, because they seem to have regressed to an imagined primitive state. They represent the unsettling phenomenon of human beings who have been completely subsumed within a mythic identity.

They know this and resent it. "The one thing I can't stand is labels," says a man in his early fifties frying a rat over a fire in a raised bunker that once served as a tool shack for subway workers; "I am simply a person."[27] It is a tragically futile declaration. Toth herself struggles valiantly against symbolic stereotyping. She even agonizes over her choice of title. But it is impossible to read her chapters without feeling that in the subway the mythic is overtaking the actual and concealing it.

SORDIDNESS AND TRANSCENDENCE

The subway is now ordinarily represented as a place where the sane encounter the mad. In retrospect, the riders who appeared in the work of Reginald Marsh and Walker Evans, Betty Smith and Isabel Bishop, Ann Petry and James Baldwin seem surprisingly ordinary. In recent portrayals, by contrast, every subway car contains at least one figure who violates decorum.

A mild form of this encounter with a deviant occurs in Molly Peacock's poem "Subway Vespers." Its speaker gives thanks that

> . . . the man with whiskey breath and
> bloodshot eyes, business suit, plus monogrammed
>
> cuffs (likely to behave) is significantly
> taller than I am, leaving me inches of free
> space between my place at the pole, his, and the lady
>
> weeping below me.[28]

We aren't told why the lady is weeping. She is simply there—wholly lost in a private world of grief, as much a natural element of the scene as the center pole she stands at.

Jay McInerny's *Bright Lights, Big City* (1984) presents the encounter of the sane and the mad in a more extreme form. The young protagonist finds his morning ride to work on the West Side IRT disrupted when a man, neatly dressed but with his eyes focused on some other place, taps him on the shoulder. "'My birthday,' he says, 'is January thirteenth. I will be twenty-nine years old.' Somehow he makes this sound like a threat to kill you with a blunt object."[29]

Such confrontations became so common in subway art that they began to produce ironic variations. In the film *Ghost* (1990) the recently murdered hero pursues his killer into the subway car and finds himself assaulted by an equally ghostly but far more dangerous spirit who, having been murdered in this very train, regards it as his personal space and violently refuses to share it.

But the madness need not be entirely external. Some writers present the subway as a place where the conscious mind confronts its hidden impulses. Liebowitz, the subway rider in Leonard Michaels's story "Getting Lucky," feels a hand—"a soft, inquisitive spider"—unzipping his fly and caressing his penis.[30] It is a liberation that he has subconsciously longed for. Rather than scream out, Liebowitz looks through the car at his fellow passengers, finally fixing his attention on a schoolgirl, her face thick with cheap cosmetics, who is staring up at an advertisement for suntan lotion as if it were a letter from God. They—the caressing hand, Liebowitz, the girl, and the radiant sun—form a kind of erotic union. Liebowitz awakens to life. "After so many years in the subway without feeling, or feeling he wasn't feeling, he felt."

But at some point—and Michaels may well have reached it—the subway of the imagination becomes so extreme as to be absurd. Many who care about the subway would like to see the system stripped of all the metaphoric accretions it has acquired over the years and judged simply as a means of transportation. But there is no possibility of going back to a period when the relation of the symbolic subway to the actual system was simple, straightforward, and untroubled. There never was such a period. The subway was mythic from the moment it was conceived. It has always generated meaning far in excess of its straightforward role as a means of rapid transit. The excess now proliferates out of control but that does not mean that we can go back to a time when there was a straightforward relation between signified and signifier.

Can we go forward? The film *Ghost* seems to hint that we can. The deranged spirit in the subway car appears in a later scene where he teaches the hero how, by focusing all his violent passions, he can move physical objects and so rescue his widow and punish his killers. The departed madman provides not only a moment of urban humor but also the crucial plot twist that leads to a happy ending.

Can subway craziness be a path to salvation? That seems to be implied at the end of Mary Gaitskill's novel *Two Girls, Fat and Thin* (1991). Here the lunatic is our protagonist herself, Dorothy Never, swearing, sputtering, and pouring out her grievances to all her fellow riders. Not surprisingly, they edge away. But they also fail to see what is happening: Dorothy's behavior is therapeutic. She is moving fast toward the psychological health that she reaches on the novel's last page.

Will the subway ride, so often a symbol of the city's pathology, be part of its cure? It is certain that the subway that most of America knows is the one it sees in *Nighthawks*, *Blue Steel*, *Die Hard With a Vengeance*, and *The Money Train*—a place of sneering villains, flying bullets, and fiery explosions. But in recent years New Yorkers have begun to encounter a rather different subway. In the early eighties the Transit Authority realized that it was not enough to make the trains cleaner and more efficient. It also had to enter the debate over the cultural meanings of the system.

ART FOR TRANSIT

Commissioning works of art is no longer an unusual thing for a transit system to do. Montreal, Brussels, London, Stockholm, Paris, and other foreign cities have introduced arts programs into their underground routes. In the U.S. there are programs in Los Angeles, Boston, Miami, Seattle, Atlanta, and Portland. New York, however, had particularly compelling reasons to embark on a program of art patronage. By the eighties even the most hardened bureaucrat realized that the semiotic environment of the subway was just as important as clean trains, efficient air conditioning, and convenient schedules. The Metropolitan Transportation Authority cannot stop anyone else from portraying the subway as a place of dirt and delay, murder and mayhem. It can, however, expose this standard portrayal as a cliché by entering what has in effect become a public debate over the symbolic significance of the subway.

The Arts for Transit program was set up in 1982 to commission works for both the city subway and the suburban commuter lines. It has commissioned over ninety works and about half of these have been completed. Inevitably the success of individual works varies. Some are lost in the busy, complicated spaces that contain them. Their general level, however, is extraordinarily high. Just as important, the range of meaning that they find in the subway is extremely varied.

Some works relate the subway to the city's natural setting. Harry Roseman's *Subway Wall* at the Wall Street station of the No. 2 and No. 3 lines explores this theme dramatically. A commuter walking up the stairs to the street sees the tile of the station wall dissolving into a series of great boulders. Within a few more steps he finds himself walking next to a forty-foot bronze landscape of hills, trees, and water. This is the vista that an early New Yorker could still have seen and one that should not be lost from the city's collective memory. Steve Woods's *Fossils*, farther north at 137th Street, consists of 180 bronze tiles showing the ancient life forms that can be found in nearby rock strata. Nancy Holt's *Astral Grating* at Fulton Street brings the night sky into the subway.

Another group of works relates directly to the theme of city transit. Rhoda Andors's *Kings Highway Hieroglyphs* in Brooklyn humorously orients travelers to their possible destinations. As they pass through the turnstiles riders see giant hieratic figures in profile, the kind you would normally expect to encounter in an ancient pyramid, some oriented toward Manhattan, others toward Coney Island. The Manhattan side is ornamented with such symbols as a newspaper, a briefcase, and the twin towers of the World Trade Center while the Coney Island side features a beach umbrella, a fishing rod, and the curving outline of the Cyclone roller coaster. The artist called her work an archeology for the future. "The subway, like the pyramids, is a great monument," she explained. "It is no accident that the style of these murals is hieroglyphs. I wanted all the cool dignity and symbolism full of messages, the cordial sense of humanity found in the Valley of Kings."[31]

In a similar spirit, Liliana Porter has designed *Alice: The Way Out* for the 50th Street West Side station in which the White Rabbit from Lewis Carroll's *Alice in Wonderland* appears as a rushing commuter. Across town, beneath Bloomingdale's, Elizabeth Murray's mural mosaic *Bloom* features richly colored shoes and coffee cups. "The shoes are an image of motion," she explained. "They take people through the subway and up to the street. Coffee cups are a symbol of the morning and evening."[32]

Other works lighten the mood of subway riders by introducing an element of lyricism and whimsy into their daily experience. Michele Oka Donner created a 165-foot wall of brick-shaped tiles coated in gold-lustre glaze for the Sixth Avenue and 34th Street IND station. "I don't believe in confrontational art," she explained. "The amount of aggression in the city is already overwhelming. I think of the project as a spiritual sculpture. . . . Each of the eighteen thousand people who walk along the wall each day becomes enveloped by this mysterious power."[33] Michelle Greene had a similar motive in creating *The Rail Riders' Throne* that sits without explanation on the downtown platform of the 116th Street and Broadway station. "I wanted to make something whimsical that would make people feel special, kind of less alienated," the artist explained.[34]

Finally, there are works which celebrate the connections between the subway and the neighborhoods above it. Vincent Smith, Faith Ringgold, and Willie Birch explore Harlem history at the 116th, 126th, and 135th Street stations. Bing Lee uses Asian themes and symbols derived from Zen Buddhism and Chinese calligraphy at Canal Street on the East Side. Nitza Tufino alludes to the heritage of Spanish Harlem with Aztec, Mayan, and Latin American motifs for the Lexington Avenue station at 103rd Street.

The Arts for Transit program is only one part of an ongoing rehabilitation of the underground environment. The Metropolitan Transportation Authority auditions and encourages musicians at the same time that it patronizes the visual arts. In 1992 it launched, in cooperation with the Poetry Society of America, its Poetry in Motion program by putting up placards in advertising spaces in subways and on buses featuring poems by writers as diverse as Emily Dickinson, Langston Hughes, Gregory Corso, and Amy Clampitt.

For nine decades New Yorkers have used the subway to register their discontent with the larger city. Its public image will not be transformed quickly. It will always figure, as it does in the long title poem of T. R. Hummer's *Walt Whitman in Hell* (1996), as the place where democratic hopes meet their severest trial. The special virtue of the Arts for Transit program is that it demonstrates that the subway is also a place to celebrate the urban experience. Its artists have shown that the symbolic meanings of the subway system are far richer than even the city's most enthusiastic booster could have believed. No doubt the subway will always be a problematic part of the city, part convenience, part ordeal, but it will remain an area of lively and contested debate. That has always been part of its fascination.

NOTES

INTRODUCTION

1. The comparison of the subway to Hell may be a western habit. Amarendranath Basu, discussing a proposed Bombay subway, used eastern mythology to argue that the urge to go underground expresses a wish for the safety of the womb. See "Metro-Rail and the Unconscious," *Samiska* 39 (1985), 16–27.

2. [William Sidney Porter], *The Complete Works of O. Henry* (New York: Doubleday, 1953), 1411–1414.

3. Alan Trachtenberg, "Experiments in Another Country; Stephen Crane's City Sketches," in *American Realism*, ed. Eric J. Sundquist (Baltimore: The Johns Hopkins University Press, 1982), 138.

4. James McCabe, *The Secrets of the Great City* (Philadelphia: Jones Brothers, 1868), 15.

5. James W. Shepp and Daniel B. Shepp, *Shepp's New York Clty Illustrated* (Chicago: Gebbe Bible Publishing company, 1894), 7.

6. Henry James, *The American Scene* (New York: St. Martin's, 1987), 59–60.

7. Steven Marcus, "Reading the Illegible: Some Modern Representations of Urban Experience," in *Visions of the Modern City*, ed. William Sharpe and Leonard Wallock (Baltimore: The Johns Hopkins University Press, 1987), 232–256.

8. Raymond Queneau, *Zazie dans le métro* (Paris: Gallimard, 1959), 12.

9. T. R. Ybarra, "In the Subway of Four World Cities," *New York Times*, November 30, 1930, sec. 5, 11.

10. William Barclay Parsons, "Rapid Transit in New York," *Scribner's Magazine* 27 (May 1900), 554.

CHAPTER ONE. IMAGINING A SUBWAY

Harry James Carman's *The Street Surface Railway Franchises of New York City* (New York: Columbia Studies in the Social Sciences, 1919) gives a dry but comprehensive history of the horsecars. Early attempts at subway design are discussed in James Blaine Walker's *Fifty Years of Rapid Transit, 1864–*

1917 (New York: Arno Press, 1970) and in Benson Bobrick's *Labyrinths of Iron* (New York: Newsweek Books, 1981). Plans for early elevateds are discussed in William F. Reeves's *The First Elevated Railroads in Manhattan and the Bronx* (New York: New York Historical Society, 1936).

1. *Arcade Underground Railroad. Evidence Before the New York State Senate Railroad Committee* (State of New York, 1868).

2. "How to Get Down Town," *New York Times*, May 9, 1860, 4.

3. "Relief of Broadway and the People of New-York—An Underground Railroad a Necessity," *New York Times*, December 22, 1865, 4.

4. "Metropolitan Conveyances—The Omnibus Situation," *New York Herald*, October 2, 1864, 4.

5. "City Railroads and City Travel," *New York Times*, January 6, 1860, 4.

6. "Metropolitan Conveyances—The Omnibus Nuisance," *New York Herald*, October 2, 1864, 4.

7. "The City Cars," *New York Times*, May 31, 1866, 4.

8. "Metropolitan Conveyances—The Omnibus Nuisance," 4.

9. "City Railroads and City Travel," *New York Times*, January 6, 1860, 4.

10. "Headway," *New York Herald*, May 6, 1871, 11.

11. *The New York Illustrated News* 9 (January 23, 1964), 205.

12. "Rapid Transit," *New York Times*, November 23, 1873, 4.

13. "Our City's Need," *New York Tribune*, February 2, 1866, 4.

14. "The Broadway Underground Railroad," *New York World*, March 20, 1871, 4.

15. Quoted in "Railways in New York City," *Scientific American* 30 (August 15, 1874), 100.

16. "Elevated Promenade and Railroad for Broadway," *Scientific American* 9 (January 21, 1854), 152.

17. Information on the variety of the early plans for elevateds can be found in William F. Reeves's *The First Elevated Railroads in Manhattan and the Bronx of the City of New York* (New York: New York Historical Society, 1936), 1–3.

18. Quoted in I. N. Phelps Stokes, *The Iconography of Manhattan Island* (New York: Robert H. Dodd, 1928).

19. "The Three-Tiered Railway," *New York Times*, March 25, 1867, 4.

20. John Randel Jr., *Explanatory Remarks and Estimates of the Cost and Income of the Elevated Railway* (New York: George F. Nesbitt, 1848), 7–8.

21. "Improved Elevated Atmospheric Railway," *Scientific American* 15 (August 18, 1866), 111.

22. Benson Bobrick, *Labyrinths of Iron* (New York: Newsweek Books, 1981), 204.

23. "An Underground Railroad," *New York Illustrated News*, April 6, 1864, 386.

24. Quoted in James Blaine Walker, *Fifty Years of Rapid Transit, 1864–1917* (New York: Arno Press, 1970), 28–29.

25. "From the State Capital," *New York Times*, February 3, 1866, 4.

26. *Illustrated Description of the Broadway Pneumatic Underground Railway* (New York: S. W. Green, 1870), 4.

27. Ibid.

28. *Illustration Description of the Broadway Underground Railway*, 9.

29. "Tunnel Versus Viaduct," *New York Tribune*, March 29, 1871, 8.

30. "Up-Town Transit," *New York World*, March 26, 1871, 5.

31. "Albany," *New York Times*, March 18, 1870, 1.

32. "The Viaduct Railway," *New York Tribune*, July 8, 1871, 1.

33. "Railway Transit for New York," *Scientific American* 24 (March 25, 1871), 199.

34. "Albany," *New York Times*, March 10, 1871, 5.

35. "The City's Great Want," *New York Tribune*, March 11, 1873, 8.

36. "The Future of New York," *Galaxy* 9 (April 1870), 550.

37. Ibid., 548.

38. Ibid., 553.

39. F.G.F, "New York A.D. 1900," *New York World*, March 27, 1870, 3.

40. "A Ride Under Broadway," *New York Times*, June 26, 1882, 8.

41. "The Underground Railroad," *New York Times*, August 17, 1884, 9.

42. "The Arcade Scheme Dead," *New York Times*, March 13, 1885, 2.

43. Ibid., 2.

44. "Rapid Transit," *New York Times*, November 23, 1873, 4.

45. "Rapid Transit," *New York Times*, November 1, 1873, 3.

46. "The Railroad in the Air," *St. Nicholas Magazine* 6 (October 1879), 801.

47. Ibid., 808.

CHAPTER TWO. AN UNHEAVENLY CITY

Robert C. Reed's *The New York Elevated* (New York: A. S. Barnes, 1978) gives a wide-ranging discussion of its subject. I have benefited from reading and partly disagreeing with the chapter on *A Hazard of New Fortunes* in Amy Kaplan's *The Social Construction of American Realism* (Chicago: University of Chicago Press, 1988). Howells's understanding of New York is also discussed in Morton and Lucia White's *The Intellectual Versus the City* (Cambridge: Harvard University Press and The M.I.T. Press, 1962). Important essays on the city of the els can be found in Rebecca Zurier, Robert W. Snyder, and Virginia M. Mecklenburg's *Metropolitan Lives: The Ashcan Artists and Their New York* (Washington, D.C.: National Museum of American Art, 1995).

1. "Evolution in Building," *New York Times*, April 29, 1888, 14.

2. "Apartment Houses," *Real Estate Record and Builder's Guide* 18 (April 1, 1876), 238.

3. Ibid., 17 (April 1, 1876), 238.

4. "Table-Talk," *Appleton's Journal*, December 2, 1871, 4.

5. "The Apartment House from a New Point of View," *Real Estate Record and Builder's Guide* 31 (April 7, 1883), 136.

6. "The Future of the Apartment House," *Real Estate Record and Builder's Guide* 33 (November 10, 1883), 881.

7. Ferdinand Fish, "Rufus Hatch Replied To By A Real Estate Broker," *Real Estate Record and Builder's Guide* 34 (October 25, 1884), 1074.

8. "Report of the Plans for New York Rapid Transit," *Scientific American* 65 (March 21, 1896), 178–179.

9. John P. McKay, *Tramways and Trolleys: The Rise of Urban Mass Transport in Europe* (Princeton: Princeton University Press, 1976), 197.

10. *Transactions of the American Society of Civil Engineers* IV (1870), 15.

11. "Rapid Transit in Earnest," *Frank Leslie's Illustrated Newspaper* 46 (April 27, 1878), 132.

12. "Elevated City Railways Cause Eye Troubles," *Scientific American* 50 (May 17, 1884), 304.

13. "Rapid Transit in Two Cities," *New York Tribune*, October 12, 1878, 12.

14. The evidence does not support the popular assumption that the els must have depressed the streets in which they appeared. Olivier Zunz shows that assessed property values on Third Avenue rose during the nineteenth century. He credits their subsequent fall to emigration and population shifts rather than the el. See Olivier Zunz, "Technology and Society in an Urban Environment: The Case of the Third Avenue Elevated Railway," *Journal of Interdisciplinary History* 3 (Summer 1972), 89–101.

15. "Rapid Transit in Earnest," 132.

16. "Extension of Rapid Transit Facilities in New York City," *Scientific American* 67 (December 3, 1892), 352.

17. Thomas Curtis Clarke, "Rapid Transit in Cities. II.—The Solution," *Scribner's Magazine* 11 (June 1892), 743.

18. "A Ride on the Elevated," *New York Times*, August 1, 1880, 5.

19. "Travelling Up in the Air," *New York Times*, October 13, 1878, 5.

20. "A Ride on the Elevated," 5.

21. "Fast Time up in the Air," *New York Times*, September 20, 1880, 2.

22. "Life on the Elevated Road," *New York Tribune*, July 4, 1882, 3.

23. "In a Commission Train," *New York Times*, December 10, 1882, 2.

24. "The Many Woes of the Guard," *New York Times*, May 10, 1885, 4.

25. "Rapid Transit," *Harper's Weekly* 22 (July 20, 1878), 578.

26. "East Side Rapid Transit," *New York Times*, August 27, 1878, 8.

27. "Fast Time Up In the Air," *New York Times*, September 20, 1880, 2.

28. "Rapid Transit Problems," *New York Tribune*, January 11, 1879, 5.

29. "Trying to Get Upstairs," *New York World*, February 15, 1892, 1.

30. "A Startling Revelation of Danger," *New York Tribune*, December 10, 1890, 6.

31. "Life on the Elevated Road," *New York Tribune*, July 4, 1882, 3.

32. M. G. Van Rensselaer, "Picturesque New York," *Century* 45 (December 1892), 168.

33. "Night Scene in the Bowery," *Harper's Weekly* 25 (February 26, 1881), 135.

34. "An Elevated Station in Winter," *Harper's Weekly* 31 (February 5, 1887), 99.

35. Mario Maffi, "Architecture in the City, Architecture in the Novel: William Dean Howells's *A Hazard of New Fortunes*," *Studies in the Literary Imagination* 16 (Fall 1983), 41.

36. William Dean Howells, *A Hazard of New Fortunes*, text established by David J. Nordloh (Bloomington: Indiana University Press, 1976), 28. Further citations are contained in the text.

37. Frederick Law Olmsted, "Preliminary Report of the Landscape Architect and the Civil and Topographical Engineer, upon the Laying Out of the Twenty-third and Twenty-fourth Wards," in *Landscape into Cityscape*, ed. Albert Fein (Ithaca: Cornell University Press, 1967), 356.

38. Frederick Law Olmsted, "The Future of New York," *New York Tribune*, December 28, 1879, 5.

39. Kenneth S. Lynn, *William Dean Howells: An American Life* (New York: Harcourt Brace Jovanovitch, 1971), 299.

40. "Protection and Immigration," *New York Times*, August 26, 1888, 4.

41. "Contract Immigration," *New York Times*, August 7, 1888, 4.

42. Wanda Corn, "The New New York," *Art in America* 61 (July–August, 1973), 59–64.

43. Maffi, "Architecture in the City," 42–43.

44. Hubert Beck, "Urban Iconography in Nineteenth-Century American Painting: From Impressionism to the Ash Can School," in *American Icons*, ed. Thomas W. Gaehtgens and Heinz Ickstadt (Santa Monica: Getty Center, 1992), 338.

45. Quoted in E. John Bullard and David W. Scott, *John Sloan* (Washington: National Gallery of Art, 1971), 170.

46. Aline B. Louchheim, "The Last of 'The Eight' Looks Back," *New York Times*, November 2, 1952, sec. 2, 9.

47. Quoted in Rowland Elzea and Elizabeth Hawkes, *John Sloan—Spectator of Life* (Wilmington: Delaware Art Museum, 1988), 133.

48. Paul V. Beckley, "Reginald Marsh Honored, Pines for City of Yesteryear," *New York Herald Tribune*, March 10, 1954, 7.

CHAPTER THREE. OPENING DAY—AND THE FOLLOWING YEAR

Clifton Hood's *722 Miles: The Building of the Subways and How They Transformed New York* (New York: Simon and Schuster, 1994) gives an important perspective on the building of the subway as well as on its subsequent history. The process by which New York's elites agreed on the need for a subway is described in David C. Hammack's *Power and Society: Greater New York at the Turn of the Century* (New York: Columbia University Press, 1987). Information on August Belmont and his business environment can be found in Cynthia Morse Latta's *The Return on the Investment in the Interborough Rapid Transit Company*, Ph.D. diss., Columbia University, 1975. Gregory F. Gilmartin's *Shaping the City* (New York: Clarkson Potter, 1995) is the definitive account of the Municipal Art Society. The report on the *Interborough Rapid Transit Subway (Original Line)* for the Historic American Engineering Record contains important chapters on the history, design, and engineering of the system. Philip Ashforth Coppola is publishing a remarkable station-by-station account of the New York subway system with many detailed drawings: *Silver Connections* (Maplewood, N.J.: The Four Oceans Press, 1988—). So far two volumes have appeared (really three bound volumes, since Volume I occupies two separate books). They cover the Contract 1 and Contract 2 stations in Manhattan and the early el stations in Brooklyn.

1. Alan Trachtenberg, *Brooklyn Bridge: Fact and Symbol* (Chicago: University of Chicago Press, 1979).

2. Clifton Hood, *722 Miles*, 26.

3. "The Underground Man," *New York World Magazine*, March 24, 1900, 2.

4. Quoted in Adna Ferrin Weber, *The Growth of Cities in the Nineteenth Century* (Ithaca: Cornell University Press, 1963), 474.

5. City of New York, City Commission on Congestion of Population, *Report*, in *City Record* 34 (March 7, 1911), 18. Cited in Peter Derrick, *The Dual System of Rapid Transit: The Role of Politics and City Planning in the Second Stage of Subway Construction in New York City*, Ph.D. diss., New York University, 1979, 216.

6. Edward E. Pratt, *Industrial Causes of Congestion of Population in New York* (New York: Columbia University Press, 1911), 13–14.

7. Quoted in *Shaping the City*, 5.

8. "The Rebuilding of New York," *Social Economist* 5 (December 1893), 330.

9. Peter Hall, *Cities of Tomorrow* (Oxford: Basil Blackwell, 1988), 202.

10. "The Architectural Problem in Great Cities," *Real Estate Record and Builders' Guide* 50 (September 24, 1892), 376.

11. Rem Koolhaas, *Delirious New York* (New York: Oxford University Press, 1978), 70.

12. Dr. Louis Bell, "Overcrowded Street Cars," *New York Times*, February 15, 1903, 33.

13. "Magnificent New York," *New York World*, Special Supplement, November 2, 1902, 1.

14. *New York World Magazine*, March 6, 1904, 8.

15. Charles Cheape, *Moving the Masses: Urban Public Transit in New York, Boston, and Philadelphia, 1880–1912* (Cambridge: Harvard University Press, 1980), 45.

16. Quoted in *Moving the Masses*, 51.

17. "The Underground Road," *Evening Post*, January 17, 1900, 1.

18. Mark David Hirsch, *William C. Whitney, Modern Warwick* (New York: Dodd, Mead, 1948), 522.

19. "Gave $1,500,000 For $40,000 Road," *New York Times*, February 11, 1916, 1.

20. "The Manhattan Lease," *New York Times*, November 27, 1902, 8.

21. "A Real Transit System," *New York Commercial Advertiser*, February 20, 1903, 8.

22. "How I Will Build the Transit Road," *New York World*, January 18, 1900, 3.

23. "John B. McDonald, Who Will Build the Rapid Transit Tunnel," *New York Journal*, January 18, 1900, 16.

24. "How I Will Build the Transit Road," 3.

25. *New York American*, October 22, 1905, editorial section, 1.

26. "Rapid Transit in Sight," *Evening Post*, January 17, 1900, 6.

27. "M'Donald Repulses Croker's Secretary," *New York World*, March 26, 1900, 1.

28. "What the Boys Say," *New York World*, January 17, 1900, 2.

29. "John B. McDonald, 'The Man That Built the Subway,' Interviewed by Kate Carew," *New York World*, October 23, 1904, metropolitan section, 1.

30. "Belmont Ignores M'Donald," *New York American*, October 23, 1904, 38.

31. Parsons, "Rapid Transit in New York," 545.

32. Ibid., 547.

33. "The Old Rapid Transit and The New," *Real Estate Record and Builder's Guide* 74 (October 29, 1904), 896.

34. "The Real Estate Boom in West End Avenue," *Real Estate Record and Builder's Guide* 89 (June 29, 1912), 1392.

35. "The Seventy-Second Street Station," *New York Times*, December 5, 1904, 6.

36. "Subway Pictured for the Biograph," *New York Times*, May 22, 1905, 14.

37. "Women Faint in Bad Subway Atmosphere," *New York Times*, November 6, 1904, 8.

38. "Subway Temperatures," *New York Times*, June 12, 1905, 8.

39. "Dante's Visit to New York's Inferno," *New York World*, June 26, 1905, 9.

40. "Six Months of Subway Operation," *New York Times*, April 29, 1905, 10.

41. Ray Stannard Baker, "The Subway 'Deal,'" *McClure's* 24 (March 1905), 468.

42. An account of the Metropolitan's financial maneuvering can be found in Latta's *The Return on the Investment*, 71ff.

43. John Hettrick interview, Columbia University Oral History Project, 9.

44. Quoted in Derrick, *The Dual System of Rapid Transit*, 109.

CHAPTER FOUR. WILLIAM RANDOLPH HEARST AND THE TRACTION TRUST

The standard biography of Hearst is W. A. Swanberg's *Citizen Hearst* (New York: Scribner's, 1961). Gaynor is discussed by William Russell Hochman, *William T. Gaynor: The Years of Fruition*, Ph.D. diss., Columbia University, 1955, and Lately Thomas [pseud. Robert Steele], *The Mayor Who Mastered New York* (New York: William Morrow, 1969). There is no biography of Hylan. Important insights and data are provided by Latta's *The Return on the Investment*, Derrick's *The Dual System of Rapid Transit*, and Joel Fischer's *Urban Transportation: Home Rule and the Independent Subway System in New York City, 1917–1925*, Ph.D. diss., St. John's University, 1978.

1. James Blaine Walker, *Fifty Years of Rapid Transit* (New York: The Law Printing Company, 1918), 236.

2. "Mr. Hearst's Diagnosis Confirmed by Autopsy," *New York American*, October 22, 1912, 20.

3. "August Belmont Now Owns ALL Your Streets," *New York Evening Journal*, December 23, 1905, 12.

4. "We Shall See A Subway City Within 20 Years," *New York American*, October 22, 1905, 5.

5. "New York City Twenty Years Hence," *New York Times Magazine*, February 6, 1910, 12.

6. August Belmont to T. P. Shonts, Belmont Family Papers, Box 9, Columbia University.

7. "No More Subways, Declares Belmont," *New York Times*, January 12, 1908, 2.

8. William J. Gaynor, "New York's Subway Policy," *Municipal Affairs* 6 (1901), 434.

9. Headline, *New York American*, October 7, 1909, 3.

10. "Mr. Hearst Will Not Run For Mayor," *New York American*, October 6, 1909, 2.

11. "Tammany Candidate Stands on His Record," *New York American*, October 12, 1909, 2.

12. Quoted in Hochman, *Gaynor*, 389.

13. "Gaynor Links Ivens with Metropolitan," *New York Times*, October 17, 1909, 1.

14. "Gaynor Warns Shonts to Rush His Subways," *Evening Journal*, January 26, 1910, 1.

15. "Shonts Plea Won Gaynor's Support," *New York Times*, February 18, 1916, 5.

16. "Gave A Principality, Gaynor Told Towns," *New York Times*, March 10, 1916, 20.

17. "To Force Action on Subway Plan Today," *New York Times*, January 5, 1911, 2.

18. "Mayor Attacks Hearst; Diners in an Uproar," *New York World*, April 29, 1910, 2.

19. George McAneny, Oral History Collection of Columbia University, 1949, 12.

20. "How Gaynor and His Followers Have Repudiated Their Pre-Election Pledges for a City Subway," *New York American*, January 6, 1911, 9.

21. "Gaynor Urged Prendergast to Forget Pledge to the People," *New York American*, January 14, 1911, 1.

22. "Prendergast and Mitchel Rally the Public to Their Support," *New York American*, January 6, 1911, 16.

23. [untitled], *Brooklyn Citizen*, May 3, 1911, 6.

24. "Merrill Describes Prendergast's Visit," *New York Times*, June 25, 1913, sec. 1, 13.

25. "Willcox's Record on Subway," *Evening Journal*, January 6, 1913, 1.

26. "Traffic Jam Relief," *New York Times*, November 18, 1921, 16.

27. Benjamin De Casseres, "Subways: The National Gym," *New York Times Book Review and Magazine*, February 13, 1921, 3.

28. "League Would Void Subway Contracts," *New York Times*, May 9, 1916, 18.

29. "Hylan Tells How He Lost B.R.T. Job," *New York Times*, December 31, 1924, 3.

30. "Subway System in Utter Collapse," *New York American*, August 3, 1918, 9.

31. "Mayor as Subway Rider Surveys Bewilderment Created by 'H' System," *New York American*, August 4, 1918, 6.

32. "Holds City Paid For Fare Rise Publicity," *New York Times*, June 28, 1927, 1, and "Wants $1,000,000 Spent by Interboro Restored to City," *New York Times*, June 3, 1927, 1.

33. "Address of Oswald Garrison Villard at the Thirty-Seventh Semi-Annual Dinner of the American Railway Guild, May 18, 1915" in Box 19 of the Ivy Lee Papers at Firestone Library, Princeton University.

34. "The Appeal by the Interborough for Help," *Electric Railway Journal* 49 (April 7, 1917), 629.

35. See Chapter 6, page 9 of the manuscript of Ivy Lee's *An Intelligent Citizen's Guide to Propaganda* in Box 2 of the Ivy Lee Papers at Princeton University.

36. A collection of *Subway Suns* and *Elevated Expresses* can be found in the Ivy Lee papers at Princeton University.

37. "Smith Opens Fire on Wm. R. Hearst," *New York Times*, October 19, 1919, 1.

38. "Smith, in Speech, Denounces Hearst," *New York Times*, October 30, 1919, 3.

39. *New York World*, September 30, 1921, 14.

40. "The Subway Son's First Name is Henry," *New York Evening Journal*, October 28, 1921, 36.

41. "Curran Pledges to Oust Hearst as City Hall Boss," *New York Times*, November 5, 1921, 1.

42. "Curran Dares Hylan to Deny He's a Tool in Hearst's Hands," *New York Times*, November 4, 1921, 1.

43. "Curran's Final Plea Made By Wireless," *New York Times*, November 8, 1921, 1.

44. "Hearst Links Smith With Conservatives," *New York Times*, August 18, 1922, 1.

45. "A Landslide," *New York World*, November 8, 1922, 10.

46. "Mr. Smith's Victory," *New York Tribune*, November 8, 1922, 12.

47. "Citizens Organize to Demand Subways, 'Do It Now' Their Plea," *New York World*, July 26, 1923, 1.

48. "Citizens To Enlist All Straphangers," *New York World*, July 31, 1923, 4.

49. "Mayor Scores Leading Foes of City-Owned Buses," *New York American*, July 31, 1923, 1.

50. "Hylan Uses Radio in Transit Attack," *New York Times*, October 1, 1924, 23.

51. "Gen. O'Ryan Balks at Hylan as Censor," *New York Times*, October 4, 1924, 15.

52. "'Hylanism' A Blight to City, Says O'Ryan," *New York Times*, October 31, 1924, 17.

53. "Mayor Broadcasts Answer to O'Ryan," *New York Times*, November 1, 1924, 5.

54. Alfred E. Smith, *Up to Now* (New York: Viking: 1929), 332.

55. "M'Voy Renders Judgement," *New York World*, February 9, 1925, 12.

CHAPTER FIVE. SKYSCRAPER AND SUBWAY

1. William Barclay Parsons, "Twenty-Five Years of the New York Subway," *New York Times*, October 24, 1929, sec. 10, 1.

2. Davis Edwards, "Our Transit Problem as New Commissioner Sees It," *New York Times*, February 9, 1913, sec. 6, 4.

3. R. L. Duffus, "Our Great Subway Network Spreads Wider," *New York Times*, September 22, 1929, sec. 10, 4.

4. Edwin H. Spengler, *Land Values in New York in Relation to Transit Facilities* (New York: Columbia University Press, 1930), 60.

5. Quoted in Spengler, *Land Values*, 61.

6. Deems Taylor, "The City That Died of Greatness," *Vanity Fair* 31 (November 1928), 74. Taylor's article was reprinted by the City Club as a pamphlet in 1929.

7. Davis Edwards, "Our Transit Problem as New Commissioner Sees It." *New York Times Magazine*, February 9, 1913, 4.

8. "New Transit Lines Helping the Bronx," *New York Times*, March 6, 1927, sec. 11, 2.

9. "East Bronx Needs Subways, Says Day," *New York Times*, March 2, 1930, sec. 12, 1.

10. "Our Changing Cities: Protean New York," *New York Times*, January 23, 1927, sec. 4, 4.

11. "Transit Volume shifts to Midtown," *New York Times*, March 2, 1925, 19.

12. "Times Square Most Important Centre," *New York Times*, January 6, 1924, sec. 10, 1.

13. "Times Square Becomes Biggest Tube Station," *New York Times*, March 13, 1927, sec. 7, 4.

14. "New York Unique in Realty Values," *New York Times*, May 20, 1928, sec. 11, 2.

15. "Subway Congestion a Business Menace," *New York Times*, August 17, 1930, secs. 11 & 12, 2.

16. "Stagger Plan Gains," *New York Times*, November 2, 1930, sec. 11, 2. The idea of staggered hours was revived in the sixties when Professor Lawrence B. Cohen of Columbia University's Industrial Engineering Department made a detailed study. The idea was dropped when it was discovered that business strongly preferred its nine-to-five pattern. See "City Drops A Plan To Stagger House," *New York Times*, July 19, 1967, 41.

17. "Ed. Note," Daniel L. Turner, "Is There a Vicious Circle of Transit Development and City Congestion?" *National Municipal Review* 15 (June 1929), 321.

18. Ibid., 322.

19. Rose C. Feld, "Now the Skyscraper is Sharply Attacked," *New York Times*, July 4, 1926, sec. 8, 36.

20. "Curran To Ask Ban Upon Skyscrapers," *New York Times*, June 17, 1926, 25.

21. Harvey Wiley Corbett, "New Stones for Old," *Saturday Evening Post* 198 (March 27, 1926), 150.

22. Ibid., May 8, 1926, 189.

23. Hugh Ferriss, "The New Architecture," *New York Times Magazine*, March 19, 1922, 8.

24. Henry Curran, "The Skyscraper Does Cause Congestion," *National Municipal Review*, April 1927, 230.

25. Lewis Mumford, "A New York Adolescence: Tennis, Quadratic Equations, and Love," *New Yorker*, December 4, 1937, 86–89.

26. Lewis Mumford, "The Metropolitan Milieu," in *American and Alfred Steiglitz: A Collective Portrait*, ed. Waldo Frank, Lewis Mumford, Dorothy Norman, Paul Rosenfeld, and Harold Rugg (Garden City: Doubleday, Doran, 1934), 40.

27. Lewis Mumford, "The City of Tomorrow," *The New Republic* 61 (February 12, 1930), 332.

28. Lewis Mumford, "The Fourth Migration," *Survey Graphic* 54 (May 1, 1925), 132.

29. Lewis Mumford, *The City in History* (New York: Harcourt Brace, 1961), 509.

30. Lewis Mumford, "The Intolerable City," *Harper's* 152 (February 1926), 283.

31. Ibid., 284.

32. Ibid., 285.

33. "The Culture-Cycle and City Planning," *Journal of the American Institute of Architects* 14 (June 1926), 293.

34. Thomas Adams, *The Building of the City* (New York: Regional Plan of New York and Its Environs, 1931), 108.

35. Lewis Mumford, "The Plan of New York: II. Our Stake in Congestion, *The New Republic*, June 22, 1932, 147.

36. See Cy Adler, "The Transformation of the Pacific Electric Railway; Bradford Snell, Roger Rabbit, and the Politics of Transportation in Los Angeles," *Urban Affairs Quarterly* 27 (September 1991), 51–86.

37. John Ihlder, "Coordination of Traffic Facilities," *Annals of the American Academy of Political and Social Science* 133 (September 1927), 1, 7.

38. Quoted in Mark S. Foster, *From Streetcar to Superhighway* (Philadelphia: Temple University Press, 1981), 143.

39. A valuable account of the General Motors pavilion can be found in Roland Marchand's "The Designers go to the Fair II: Norman Bel Geddes, The General Motors 'Futurama,' and the Visit to the Factory Transformed," *Design Issues* 8 (Spring 1992), 23–40.

40. Robert Moses, "Tammany Versus New York," *National Municipal Review* 10 (November 1921), 545–547.

41. Clarence Stein, "Dinosaur Cities," *Survey Graphic* 54 (May 1, 1925), 135.

42. Robert Moses, "'Practical' or 'Long-Haired' Planning?" *New York Times Magazine*, December 5, 1948, 13. Moses also assailed advocates of decentralization in "Mr. Moses Dissects the 'Long-Haired Planners,'" *New York Times Magazine* (June 25, 1944), 16–17.

43. Robert Moses, "It's Going To Be Quite a Town," *New York Times Magazine*, February 16, 1947, 58.

CHAPTER SIX. BENEATH THE WONDER CITY

William R. Taylor discusses the commercial culture of New York in the twenties in his book *In Pursuit of Gotham* (New York: Oxford University Press, 1992). Merrill Schleier discusses art dealing with skyscrapers in *The Skyscraper in American Art* (New York: Da Capo, 1986). Two articles which deal with the subway in literature should be mentioned here: Kristiaan Versluys's "Voyages in the Dark: The Subway Motif in Pound, Eliot, Tate, and Crane," *Thought* 62 (September 1987), 329–338 and Gianfranca Balestra's "Poetry of the Subway," *Rivista di Studi Anglo-Americani* 6 (1990), 89–100.

1. Elmer Rice, *The Subway* (New York: Samuel French, 1929), 94–95.

2. "Is New York American?" *Scribner's Magazine* 90 (August 1931), 165.

3. Booth Tarkington, "The World Does Move," *Saturday Evening Post* 200 (April 7, 1928), 3.

4. James, *The American Scene*, 55–56.

5. Paul Bourget, *Outre-Mer* (New York: Scribner's, 1895), 28.

6. W. Parker Chase, *New York—The Wonder City* (New York: Wonder City Publishing Company, 1932), 184.

7. Cited in "New York of the Future—If," *Literary Digest* 81 (June 14, 1924), 31.

8. Fiske Kimball, "The Family Tree of the Skyscraper," *Forum* 79 (March 1928), 391.

9. S. J. Vickers, "The Graybar Building," *Architectural Record* 42 (1927), 189.

10. "Painting of Subway Shown," *New York Times*, January 5, 1927, 10.

11. "Polish Savant Vividly Pictures New York," *New York Times*, September 8, 1936, 15.

12. Waldo Frank, *Our America* (New York: Boni and Liveright, 1919), 171–173.

13. Claude McKay, "Subway Wind," in *Harlem Shadows* (New York: Harcourt Brace, 1922), 54.

14. Maxwell Bodenheim, "Summer Evening: New York Subway Station," *Dial* 71 (August 1921), 170.

15. Ruth Comfort Mitchell, *The Night Court and Other Poems* (New York: The Century Company, 1916), 53–56.

16. Some of the situations and themes of Mamoulian's *Applause* are repeated in Vincente Minnelli's *The Clock* (1945). This time a young lady (Judy Garland) shows a soldier on leave (Robert Walker) the sights of the big city. Once again the subway separates the lovers as she boards the local at Grand Central and he, pushed by the crowd, blocked by the closing doors, and not understanding the system, tries to meet her at the next station by taking the express.

17. Fortunato Depero, *So I Think, So I Paint* (Milan-New York: n.p., 1947), 101.

18. Maurizio Scudiero and David Leiber, *Depero, Futurista & New York* (Rovereto: Longo Editore, 1986), 215.

19. Fortunato Depero, "ABC of Italian Futurism," in *Depero, Futurista & New York*, 246.

20. Elmer Rice, *Minority Report* (New York: Simon and Schuster, 1963), 45.

21. Rice was not the first or the only dramatist to be interested in the subway. Ossip Dymow's *Bronx Express* was produced by the Jewish Art Theater in 1920 and then on Broadway in 1922. It dealt with an elderly button maker whose dreams are suddenly invaded by figures from the subway's advertising placards—Miss Murad, Aunt Jemima, and the Smith Brothers. Abraham Schulman's updated version, *Bronx Express 1968*, opened at the Folksbiene Yiddish Theater on April 15, 1968.

A more popular work, Eva Day Flint and Martha Madison's *Subway Express*, opened on Broadway on September 24, 1929. The action involved a murder which was both committed and solved on a moving West Side IRT train while tunnel lights flitted by in the background, stations crawled into view, and newspapers flew down the aisle. Brooks Atkinson complained in the *New York Times* that long as a ride was from 242nd Street to Brooklyn, it was even longer in the theater. But the play caught on. It ran successfully on Broadway and then traveled to what was called the Subway Circuit—theaters such as Brandt's Flatbush in the outer boroughs which attracted local audiences. A touring company played Chicago and Detroit and *Subway Express* became a film.

William Saroyan's first play, written in 1935, was entitled *Subway Circus*. It treats the subway as a kind of dream place in which successive characters—an elderly Jew, two young Negroes, an Italian fruit peddler—reveal their inner natures in a short dramatic scene, a ballet, or a song. It was printed by Samuel French in 1940.

22. Information on the production history of *The Subway*, including a 1925 set proposal by Mordecai Gorelik and an English musical version entitled *Rush Hour* by Beatrix Thomson, can be found

in the Elmer Rice Collection of the Harry K. Ransom Humanities Center of the University of Texas in Austin.

23. *John Dos Passos: The Major Nonfictional Prose* (Detroit: Wayne Statue University Press, 1988), 36.

24. John Dos Passos, *The Fourteenth Chronicle*, ed. Townsend Ludington (Boston: Gambit, 1973), 314.

25. John Dos Passos, *Manhattan Transfer* (New York: Houghton Mifflin, 1925), 13. Further references to this edition are incorporated into the text.

26. *Letters of Hart Crane and His Family*, ed. John Unterecker (New York: Columbia University Press, 1974), 305–306.

27. John Unterecker, *Voyager: A Life of Hart Crane* (New York: Farrar, Straus, and Giroux, 1969), 181.

28. *The Literary Correspondence of Donald Davidson and Allen Tate*, ed. John Tyree Fair and Thomas Daniel Young (Athens: University of Georgia Press, 1974), 120.

29. Allen Tate, "The Subway," in *Mr. Pope and Other Poems* (New York: Minton, Balch, 1928), 10.

30. Gianfranca Balestra, "Poetry of the Subway," *Rivista di Studi Anglo-Americani* 6 (1990), 89–100.

31. "The City of Dreadful Height," *Literary Digest* 86 (September 26, 1925), 30.

32. Unterecker, *Letters of Hart Crane*, 451.

33. The electro-pneumatic doors had only recently replaced the old hand-operated doors when Crane wrote "The Tunnel" in the early part of 1926. See "Pneumatic Doors Make I.R.T. Safer," *New York Times*, December 8, 1924, 16.

34. Claude Bragdon, "Skyscrapers," *American Mercury* 22 (March 1931), 295.

35. Elie Faure, "America and Rome: A Study in Destiny," *New York Times Magazine*, July 17, 1927, 19.

CHAPTER SEVEN. ART, REVOLUTION, AND THE SUBWAY

Frederick A. Kramer's *Building the Independent Subway* (New York: Quadrant Press, 1990) describes the progress of construction. It is illustrated with period photos.

1. James (Slim) Martin, "Subway Construction," *New Masses* 2 (January 1927), 25.

2. Waldemar Kahmpffert, "Burrowing into the Roots of the City," *New York Times Magazine*, July 17, 1927, 21.

3. The statement was made in the course of an interview with Gerald M. Monroe. It is cited in Virginia Carol Marquardt, *Louis Lozowick: Development From Machine Aesthetic to Social Realism*, Ph.D. dissertation, University of Maryland, 1983, 13.

4. Genevieve Taggard, "The Ruskinian Boys See Red," *New Masses* 3 (July 1927), 18.

5. Lewis Mumford, "That Monster—The Machine," *New Masses* 3 (September 1927), 23.

6. Louis Lozowick papers, Archives of American Art, microfilm roll 1336, frame 295.

7. Louis Lozowick, "The Americanization of Art," *The Little Review* (1927), 18. This issue of the magazine, the only one which appeared that year, served as the catalogue for the Machine Age Exposition.

8. Quoted in Marquardt, *Louis Lozowick*, 128.

9. Arthur Warner, "The City's New Underground Province," *New York Times Magazine*, November 22, 1931, 9.

10. L. H. Robbins, "With the Subway Surgeons," *New York Times Magazine*, May 17, 1936, 6.

11. Information on Dan Rico can be found in *The Federal Art Project: American Prints from the 1930s in the Collection of the University of Michigan Museum of Art* (Ann Arbor: The University of Michigan Museum of Art, 1985), 158.

12. Quoted in James C. Moore, *Harry Sternberg: A Catalog Raisonné of his Graphic Work* (Wichita: Edwin A. Ulrich Museum of Art, 1975), plate 8.

13. Information on Keller can be found in Ellen G. Landau's *Artists for Victory* (Washington: Library of Congress, 1983) and in the Charles Keller papers at the Archives of American Art.

14. Lozowick papers, roll 1336, frame 295.

15. Harry Sternberg, "Etching," *Graphic Works of the American Thirties* (New York: American Artist's Congress, 1936), 9.

16. *Subway Art: Catalog of the Exhibition* (New York: Museum of Modern Art, 1938).

17. Helen A. Harrison, "Subway Art and the Public Use of Arts Committee," *Archives of American Art Journal* 21 (1984), 3–12.

18. "WPA Artists Plan Murals in City Subway," *New York Times*, November 23, 1936, 23.

19. Quoted in *Squire Vickers, 1872–1947: Designing Architect of the New York Subway System* (New York: Shepherd Gallery, 1992), 8. This exhibition catalogue gives a good account of Vickers's career and illustrates his oil paintings as well as his subway work.

20. "Opinions Under Postage," *New York Times*, May 16, 1937, sec. 10, 9.

21. Quoted in Harrison, "Subway Art," p. 6.

22. Information on Ida Abelman, Elizabeth Olds, and Ruth Chaney can be found in *The Federal Art Project: American Prints from the 1930s.*

23. "I.R.T. Subway Held 'Too Dirty' for Art," *New York Times*, August 11, 1938, 19.

24. Louise Mitchell, "Art to Go Underground in New York," *Daily Worker*, February 10, 1938, 7.

25. Quoted in Harrison, "Subway Art," p. 7.

26. "Architect's Work To Be Shown Here," *New York Times*, February 21, 1938, 16.

27. Anita Brenner, "And Now There's Talk of Murals for Straphangers," *New York Times*, February 26, 1939, sec. 7, 12–13.

28. Owen Vincent Dodson, "The Shining Town," in *The Roots of African American Drama*, ed. Leo Hamalian and James V. Hatch (Detroit: Wayne State University Press, 1991), 334.

29. "Art for the Subway; 1st in a Series of 4 Broadcasts," in Ralph Mayer papers, Archives of American Art, roll D212, frame 1508.

30. Ibid., frame 1510.

31. *New York Times*, April 13, 1939, 19.

32. Marcia Minor, "A Progressive Muralist at the Fair," *Daily Worker*, November 24, 1938, 7.

33. The cultural significance of *Underneath New York* is discussed in Lisa Gittelman's "Negotiating a Vocabulary for Urban Infrastructure, Or, The WPA Meets the Teenage Mutant Ninja Turtles," *Journal of American Studies* 26 (1992), 147–158. Much of the material gathered for it appeared after the war in Harry Granick's *Underneath New York* (New York: Rinehart, 1947).

34. *Underneath New York.* WPA Papers, New York City Municipal Archives, roll 100, "Transportation," article 7.

35. Lisa Gittelman identifies the unnamed witness as Ralph De Sola.

36. Jerre Mangione, *The Dream and the Deal* (Boston: Little Brown, 1972), 325.

CHAPTER EIGHT. THE SUBWAY CROWD

Nicolaus Mills says illuminating things about *The Crowd in American Literature* (Baton Rouge: Louisiana State University Press, 1986) without, in my opinion, giving enough attention to the crowd of office workers and mass culture consumers. Gregory W. Bush's "Like 'a Drop of Water in the Stream of Life': Moving Images of Mass Man from Griffith to Vidor," *Journal of American Studies* 25 (August 1991), 213–234, explores themes that are relevant to this chapter. Andrew Thacker discusses images of the Underground and attitudes toward the London crowd in "Imagist Travels in Modernist Space," *Textual Practice* 7 (Summer 1993), 224–246. Marilyn Cohen's book and subsequent dissertation on Marsh provides valuable perspectives on the urban crowd. See Marilyn Ann Cohen, *Reginald Marsh's New York* (New York: Dover Publications, 1983) and Marilyn Ann Cohen, *Reginald Marsh: An Interpretation of His Art*, Ph.D. diss., New York University, 1987. Ellen Wiley Todd's *The "New Woman" Revised: Painting and Gender Politics on Fourteenth Street* (Berkeley: University of California Press, 1993) provides useful background and critiques of Reginald Marsh and Isabel Bishop.

1. Thomas Wolfe, *Of Time and the River* (New York: Scribner's, 1935), 416

2. Georg Simmel, "Sociology of the Senses" in *Introduction to the Science of Sociology*, eds. Robert E. Park and Ernest W. Burgess (Chicago: University of Chicago Press, 1921), 360.

3. Quoted in Cohen, *Reginald Marsh*, 201.

4. Walker Evans, "People in the Subway: Unposed Portraits Recorded by Walker Evans," in Sarah Greenough, *Walker Evans: Subways and Streets* (Washington, D.C.: National Gallery of Art, 1991), 125.

5. Richard Aldington, *Collected Poems 1915–1923* (London: George Allen and Unwin, 1929), 33.

6. Albert Jay Nock, "The Quest of the Missing Link," *Atlantic Monthly* 155 (April 1935), 402.

7. Ernest Poole, *The Harbor* (New York: Macmillan, 1915), 311.

8. Daniel Fuchs, *The Williamsburg Trilogy* (New York: Equinox Books, 1972), 81.

9. "Radio as a Crowd-Cure," *Literary Digest* 82 (September 8, 1924), 80.

10. Abram Lipsky, *Man the Puppet* (New York: Frank-Maurice, 1925), 98–99.

11. "An Underground City in New York," *Literary Digest* 76 (March 31, 1923), 52.

12. Everett Dean Martin, *The Behavior of Crowds: A Psychological Study* (New York: Harper, 1920), 6.

13. Christopher Morley, "Thoughts in the Subway," *Christopher Morley's New York* (New York: Fordham University Press, 1988), 113.

14. Quoted Cohen, *Reginald Marsh*, 48.

15. Quoted in John D. Fairfield, "The Scientific Management of Urban Space: Professional City Planning and the Legacy of Progressive Reform," *Journal of Urban History* 20 (February 1994), 196.

16. George Elliott Howard, "Social Psychology of the Spectator," *American Journal of Sociology* 18 (July 1912), 38.

17. Aben Kandel, "A Tabloid a Day," *Forum* 77 (March 1927), 379.

18. James Lane, "Around the Galleries," *Creative Art* 10 (April 1932), 299.

19. Richard N. Masteller, "Caricatures in Crisis: The Satiric Vision of Reginald Marsh and John Dos Passos," *Smithsonian Studies in American Art* 3 (Spring 1989), 25.

20. Marsh's editorial page cartoons appeared in the *Daily News* on the following dates:
November 11, 20, 23, 29, 30, 1922; December 4, 12–16, 19–21, 22–24, 26, 27, 30, 31, 1922; January 1, 2, 4, 5, 11–13, 15, 18, 23–25, 28, 31, 1923; February 2, 3, 5, 6, 8, 10, 12, 14, 15, 17, 20–24, 26, 1923; March 2, 3, 5, 7, 9, 12, 14, 15, 20–23, 28, 30, 1923; April 3, 5, 6, 11, 12, 14, 17–20, 22, 24, 25, 27, 1923; May 2, 3, 8, 10–12, 15–17, 25, 26, 31, 1923; June 1, 6, 7, 13–15, 20, 21, 26, 1923; July 3, 5, 7, 19, 24, 31, 1923; August 15, 17, 1923; September 18, 28, 1923; October 23, 1923.

21. Benjamin De Casseres, "The Broadway Mind," *American Mercury* 12 (October 1927), 179.

22. Quoted in Martin W. Weyrauch, "The Why of the Tabloids," *Forum* 77 (April 1927), 496.

23. Agee's views are discussed in Carol Shloss's *In Visible Light; Photography and the American Writer, 1840–1940* (New York: Oxford University Press, 1987), 179–187.

24. Walker Evans, "Unposed Photographic Records of People," in Greenough, *Walker Evans*, 126

25. Jerry L. Thompson, *Walker Evans at Work* (New York: Harper and Row, 1982), 151.

26. Ayn Rand, *The Fountainhead* (New York: New American Library, 1971), 661.

27. Walker Evans, "Twenty Thousand Moments Under Lexington Avenue: A Superfluous Word," in Greenough, *Walker Evans*, 127.

28. Quoted in Thomas H. Garver, *George Tooker* (New York: Rizzoli, 1985), 30.

29. Saul Bellow, *Seize the Day* (New York: Viking, 1956), 127.

30. Ibid., 129.

31. Ibid., 130.

32. Saul Bellow, *The Victim* (New York: New American Library, 1965), 23.

33. Ibid., 171.

34. Ibid., 244.

35. *Seize the Day*, 84.

36. See Laura Mulvey, "Visual Pleasure and Narrative Cinema," *Screen* 16 (Autumn 1975), 6–18 and "Afterthoughts on Visual Pleasure and Narrative Cinema," *Frameworks* 15/17 (1981), 12–15. See also Mary Ann Doane, "Film and the Masquerade: Theorizing the Female Spectator," *Screen* 23 (September/October 1982), 74–87, and Teresa de Lauretis, *Alice Doesn't: Feminism, Semiotics, Cinema* (Bloomington: Indiana University Press, 1984).

37. Janet Wolff, "The Invisible *Flâneuse*; Women and the Literature of Modernity," *Theory, Culture and Society* 2 (1983), 37–48.

38. Griselda Pollock, "Modernity and the Spaces of Femininity," in *Vision and Difference* (London: Routledge, 1988), 50–90.

39. Ibid., 89.

40. Blanche Gelfant, "Sister to Faust: The City's 'Hungry' Woman as Heroine," in *Woman Writers and the City*, ed. Susan Merrill Squier (Knoxville: University of Tennessee Press, 1984), 265–87.

41. "Club Women Oppose Separate Car Plan," *New York Times*, March 19, 1909, 9.

42. "Will Oppose Women's Cars," *New York Times*, April 22, 1909, 3.

43. "Subway Cars for Women," *New York Times*, March 27, 1909, 16.

44. "Women like Railroading," *New York Times*, October 11, 1918, 13.

45. "B.R.T. Women Beg Smith for Aid," *New York Times*, May 25, 1919, 1.

46. "B.R.T. Women Take Step to Save Jobs," *New York Times*, May 20, 1919, 10.

47. Todd, *The "New Woman" Revised* , xxvii.

48. James Gibbons Huneker, *The New Cosmopolis* (New York: Scribner's, 1915), 57–58.

49. Morley, "Thoughts in the Subway," 115–116.

50. James Montgomery Flagg, "The Adventures of Kitty Cobb," *World*, March 24, 1912, Metropolitan section, 1.

51. These films are described in the *American Film Institute Catalogue of Motion Pictures Produced in the United States, 1921–1930* (New York: Bowker, 1971—).

52. Cohen, *Reginald Marsh*, See especially Chapter 4.

53. Anne Beller, Sanford Garelik, and Sydney Cooper, "Sex Crimes in the Subway," *Criminology* 18 (May 1980), 51.

54. Betty Smith, *A Tree Grows in Brooklyn* (New York: Harper Perennial, 1992), 328.

55. Ibid., 333–334.

56. Background on Citron can be found in Ellen G. Landau's *Artists for Victory* (Washington: Library of Congress, 1983), 28. The position of women artists in the thirties is discussed by Helen Lang in "Egalitarian Printmakers and the WPA/FAP Graphics Arts Project," in *The Expanding Discourse; Feminism and Art History*, ed. Norma Broude and Mary D. Garrard (New York: Harper, Icon Editions, 1992), 409–423.

57. Cindy Nemser, "A Conversation with Isabel Bishop," *Feminist Art Journal* 5 (Spring 1976), 15.

58. Quoted in Helen Yglesias, *Isabel Bishop* (New York: Rizzoli, 1989), 16.

59. Tape-recorded interview with Isabel Bishop, on April 15, 1959, Warren Chappel and Henrietta Moore, interviewers, Archives of American Art, roll 3196, frame 0753.

60. Quoted in Ellen Wiley Todd, *The "New Woman" Revised: Painting and Gender Politics on Fourteenth Street* (Berkeley: University of California Press, 1993), 293.

61. Interview with Isabel Bishop, roll 3196, frame 0742.

62. Quoted in John H. Hewitt's "The Search for Elizabeth Jennings, Heroine of a Sunday Afternoon in New York City," *New York History* 71 (October 1990), 391.

63. "City Railroads," *New York Tribune*, February 10, 1864, 4.

64. Rupert Hughes, *The Real New York* (New York: Smart Set Publishing Company, 1904), 43.

65. Langston Hughes, *The Big Sea* (New York: Thunder's Mouth Press, 1986), 81.

66. Rudolph Fisher, "The City of Refuge," in *Black Literature in America*, ed. Houston A. Baker Jr. (New York: McGraw Hill, 1971), 169.

67. Owen Vincent Dodson, "The Shining Town," in *The Roots of African American Drama*, ed. Leo Hamalian and James V. Hatch (Detroit: Wayne State University Press, 1991), 332–353.

68. Ralph Ellison, *The Invisible Man* (New York: Vintage, 1952), 158.

69. Edward T. Hall, *The Hidden Dimension* (New York: Anchor Books, 1969), 118.

70. Ann Petry, *The Street* (Boston: Houghton Mifflin, 1946), 27.

71. Ibid., 57.

72. James Baldwin, *Another Country* (New York: Dial Press, 1962), 85–86.

73. James Baldwin, *If Beale Street Could Talk* (New York: Laurel, 1988), 124.

74. Valuable information on the zoot-suit phenomenon can be found in Stuart Cosgrove, "The Zoot-Suit and Style Warfare," *History Workshop* 18 (Autumn 1984) and Bruce Tyler, "Zoot-Suit Culture and the Black Press," *Journal of American Culture* 17 (Summer 1994), 21–33.

75. Quoted in Larry Neal, "Ellison's Zoot Suit," in *Ralph Ellison: A Collection of Critical Essays*, ed. John Hersey (Englewood Cliffs, N.J.: Prentice Hall, 1974), 67.

76. Larry Rivers, "The Cedar Bar," *New York* 12 (November 5, 1979), 42.

77. LeRoi Jones, *Dutchman and The Slave* (New York: Morrow Quill, 1964), 3.

78. Howard Taubman, "The Theater: 'Dutchman,'" *New York Times*, March 26, 1964, 46.

79. Saul Bellow, *Herzog* (New York: Viking, 1964), 176.

80. Walker Evans, "Draft text for publication of subway photographs, 1956–1966," in Greenough, *Walker Evans*, 125.

81. John Russell, foreword in Yglesias, *Isabel Bishop*, 7.

CHAPTER NINE. A SHOOTING ON THE SUBWAY

My account of the Goetz case deals with the public drama enacted in the press. Readers interested in the legal complexities of the trial will find a brilliant account in George P. Fletcher's *A Crime of Self-Defense: Bernhard Goetz and the Law on Trial* (Chicago: University of Chicago Press, 1988).

1. Eleanor Wachs, *Crime-Victim Stories; New York Cities Urban Folklore* (Bloomington: Indiana University Press, 1988). See especially Chapter 5. Wachs notes that Goetz's refusal to submit to an offender's power distinguishes his story from most of those that she has collected. I suspect that her informants were too decent and civilized to express a desire for revenge but that it was festering unacknowledged in their minds. Otherwise, it is difficult to explain the Goetz's story's extraordinary burst of popularity.

2. Edward T. Hall, *The Silent Language* (New York: Doubleday, 1990), 6.

3. Richard Reeves, "New Master Plan Outlines Wide Social Changes Here," *New York Times*, February 3, 1969, 1.

4. Wallace Sayre and Herbert Kaufman analyze the city's population in terms of money-providers

and service-demanders in *Governing New York* (New York: W. W. Norton, 1965). Eric E. Lampard surveys the city's changing economy in "The New York Metropolis in Transformation: History and Prospect," *The Future of the Metropolis*, ed. Hans-Jurgen Ewers, John B. Goddard, Horst Matzerath (New York: Walter de Gruyter, 1986), 27–109.

5. Gus Tyler, "A Tale of Three Cities," *Dissent*, fall 1987, 466.

6. Community Service Society, *The Changing Face of Poverty* (1984).

7. Kitty Hanson, "In the Rumble of the Subways—High School Gangs Are Turning Trains into Hell on Wheels," *New York Daily News*, December 3, 1958, 48.

8. Joan Hanauer, "Terror Lurks in the Dark, Lonely Hours," *New York Journal-American*, October 23, 1963, 13.

9. Felix Kessler and Erwin Savelson, *New York World-Telegram and Sun*, January 27, 1964, 1.

10. Leonard Katz and John Cashman, "Terror in the Subways," *New York Post*, March 8–12, 1965.

11. Charles Grutzner, "Blinker to Fight Crime in Subways," *New York Times*, February 13, 1965, 23.

12. Grace Lichtenstein, "New Funds Unlikely to Alter New York's View on Subway," *New York Times*, May 8, 1978, sec. B, 12.

13. Jesus Rangel, "Statistically, At Least, It Is Rather Safe Down There," *New York Times*, February 10, 1985, sec. E, 7.

14. Richard Levine, "The Numbers Say Subways Are Safer Than They Seem," *New York Times*, June 28, 1987, sec. E, 6.

15. Wesley Brown, "Where Pluralism and Paranoia Meet," *Dissent*, fall 1987, 482.

16. *New York Times*, November 25–27, 29, 1992.

17. "The Urban Jungle," *New York Times*, October 16, 1971, 30.

18. Bradley J. Steiner, *Subway Survival!* (Mason, Michigan: Loompanics Unlimited, 1980), 5.

19. Tom Wolfe, "The Bonfire of the Vanities," *Rolling Stone*, July 19–August 2, 1984, 24.

20. Brian Garfield, *Death Wish* (New York: Mysterious Press, 1985), 86.

21. *New York Post*, December 24, 1984, 1.

22. Ibid., 2.

23. Ibid., December 27, 1984, 2.

24. Ibid., December 28, 1984, 2.

25. Ibid., January 10, 1985, 5.

26. Steve Dunleavy, "Goetz Rides Again," *New York Post*, March 4, 1985, 5.

27. "Deli Owner Guns Down Holdupman on L.I.," *New York Post*, January 25, 1985, 5.

28. Jimmy Breslin, "Bite the Bullet for Subway Gunner," *New York Daily News*, December 27, 1984, 6.

29. "The Vigilante," *New York Amsterdam News*, January 19, 1985, 12.

30. "Why Surrender on the Subway?" *New York Times*, January 4, 1985, sec. A, 26.

31. Alice R. Kaminsky, *The Victim's Song* (Buffalo: Prometheus Books, 1985), 163.

32. Quotations from the audiotape are my own transcriptions from videotapes of the civil trial provided by Court TV.

33. Quotations from the videotape are from *The Confessions of Bernhard Goetz* released in 1987 by MPI Home Video (MP 1379).

34. Mike Pearl, "Goetz: I Wanted to Kill," *New York Post*, April 29, 1987, 52.

35. *New York Times*, December 31, 1995, 1.

36. "Bronx Jury Orders Goetz to Pay $43 Million to Man Paralyzed on Train," *New York Times*, April 24, 1996, sec. B, 4.

CHAPTER TEN. REDEEMING THE CITY

1. Kevin Sack, "The State of the State, Proudly Restated," *New York Times*, April 9, 1994, 23.

2. Lincoln Kirstein, *Paul Cadmus* (New York: Rizzoli, 1984), 102.

3. Arthur Rimbaud, *Oeuvres Complètes* (Paris: Pléiade, 1963), 188.

4. Allen Walker Read, "Folk Criticism of Religiosity in the Graffiti of New York City," *Maledicta* 10 (1988–1989), 15–30.

5. My account of subway graffiti draws on Jack Stewart's *Subway Graffiti: An Aesthetic Study of Graffiti on the Subway System of New York City, 1970–1978,* Ph.D. dissertation, New York University, 1989 and on Craig Castleman, *Getting Up: Subway Graffiti in New York* (Cambridge: The MIT Press, 1982).

6. "Philadelphia, Graffiti Capital of the World," *New York Times*, July 25, 1971, 31.

7. Suzi Gablik, " Report From New York: The Graffiti Question," *Art in America* 70 (October 1982), 39.

8. Quoted by Richard Lachmann, "Graffiti as Career and Ideology," *American Journal of Sociology* 94 (September 1988), 238.

9. Quoted in Stewart, *Subway Graffiti*, 236.

10. Ronal Gross, "Our 'Beautiful' Graffiti," *New York Times*, March 28, 1972, 42.

11. Quoted in Gablik, "Report from New York," 35.

12. "You Decide," *New Yorker*, October 16, 1989, 6.

13. Jim Dwyer, "A Little Digging Yields Clues to the Revolution," *New York Newsday*, December 4, 1986, 46.

14. Rene Ricard, "The Radiant Child," *Artforum*, December 1981.

15. Abraham Rodriguez Jr., "Short Stop," *The Boy Without A Flag: Tales of the South Bronx* (Minneapolis: Milkweed Editions, 1992), 75–86.

16. Peter Brimelow, "Time to Rethink Immigration," *National Review* 44 (June 22, 1992), 30.

17. John H. Glassie, "Emerging Artist: Xin Han," *American Artist* 50 (August 1986), 36.

18. "Subways," *Popular Photography* 87 (October 1980), 131–133, 146.

19. Information on Pantell can be found in Fridolf Johnson, "Richard Pantell," *American Artist* 51 (February 1987), 64–67, 94–95.

20. For information on Alan Wolfson's subway images see Eunice Agar, "Deceptive Miniatures: Alan Wolfson," *American Artists* 49 (August 1985), 68–71, 91–92 and Donovan Moore, "Mean Streets in Alan Wolfson's Tiny New York," *Connoisseur* 217 (March 1987), 99–101.

21. Daniel Greene's methods of painting are explored in Bebe Raupe, "Mastering Urban Realism," *The Artist's Magazine* 9 (October 1992), 47–51.

22. Blanche Gelfant, "Residence Underground: Recent Fictions of the Subterranean City," *Sewanee Review* 83 (July–September), 406–438, and William Sharpe, "Living on the Edge: New York in Literature," in *New York: Culture Capital of the World, 1940–1965*, ed. Leonard Wallock (New York: Rizzoli, 1988), 72.

23. Allen Ginsberg, *Howl and Other Poems* (San Francisco: City Lights Books, 1956), 10.

24. Bruce Davidson, *Subway* (Weston, Mass.: Aperture, 1986), 10.

25. Dennis's journals are quoted by Cary Lovelace in "Donna Dennis: Intimate Immensity," *Arts Magazine* 62 (Summer 1988), 71–73.

26. Jennifer Toth, *The Mole People* (Chicago: Chicago Review Press, 1993).

27. Ibid., 31.

28. Molly Peacock, "Subway Vespers," *Original Love* (New York: Norton, 1995), 74.

29. Jay McInerny, *Bright Lights, Big City* (New York: Vintage, 1984).

30. Leonard Michaels, "Getting Lucky," *I Would Have Saved Them If I Could* (New York: Farrar, Straus, and Giroux, 1882), 41.

31. Quoted in a Metropolitan Transportation Authority press release dated September 14, 1987.

32. "Bright Murals for a Grim Subway Station," *New York Times*, November 25, 1993, sec. C, 3.

33. "Commuter Comfort," *New Yorker* 67 (June 10, 1991), 16.

34. Eleanor Blau, "Subterranean Throne: A Seat Worth Tussling For," *New York Times*, October 28, 1991, sec. B, 3.

INDEX

ABOUT THE AUTHOR

Michael Brooks has been fascinated by New York City since he arrived in Manhattan at age sixteen. He explored the city on foot and on bicycle and began leading tours of New York's SoHo when it was still a quiet backwater of cast-iron loft buildings. He is professor of English at West Chester University, whose academic work focuses on creative responses to the built environment. He has published a book on *John Ruskin and Victorian Architecture*.